LEGAL LIABILITIES
IN EMERGENCY
SERVICES

LEGAL LIABILITIES IN EMERGENCY SERVICES

Thomas D. Schneid

Department of Loss Prevention and Safety
Eastern Kentucky University

TAYLOR & FRANCIS
ALERE FLAMMAM
Founded 1798

Denise T. Schanck, *Vice President*
Robert H. Bedford, *Editor*
Catherine M. Caputo, *Assistant Editor*
James A. Wright, *Marketing Director*
Albert Ezratty, *Marketing Associate*

Published in 2001 by

Taylor & Francis
29 West 35th Street
New York, NY 10001

Published in Great Britain by

Taylor & Francis
11 New Fetter Lane
London EC4P 4EE

Library of Congress Cataloging-in-Publication Data
Schneid, Thomas D.
    Legal liabilities in emergency medical services / by Thomas D.
Schneid.
        p.   cm.
    Includes index.
    ISBN 1-56032-899-1 (alk. paper)
    1. Emergency medical personnel—Legal status, laws, etc.—United
States.   2. Emergency medical personnel—Malpractice—United
States.   3. Employer liability—United States. I. Title.
KF2915.E4 S36   2000
344.73'03218—dc21   00-033762

Contents

Preface

The aim and goal of this text are to open the eyes of many emergency medical professionals and organizations as to the myriad of legal issues that they face, often unknowingly, on a daily basis. Knowledge of the various legal issues and challenges can assist the emergency medical professional and organization in addressing the legal issue in a proactive manner and thus avoid or minimize the potential risk of costly legal entanglements and litigation.

Historically, emergency medical organizations, not unlike fire departments and police departments, were the groups providing emergency services in time of need and few ever envisioned suing the emergency medical organizations for the services they provided or failed to provide. However, in today's litigious society, virtually every call, every employee, and every decision possesses a potential risk of costly litigation. Prudent emergency medical professionals and organizations should become knowledgeable as to the potential legal risks and address these issues before the risk becomes a reality.

Lastly, I would hope that the emergency medical professionals reading this text realize that the law is a moving target. Every day in this country, court decisions are being made, legislatures are making new laws, and the interpretations of the law are being provided by agencies that possess the ability to impact your emergency medical organization. Emergency medical professionals are urged to continue your education and maintain your competency in the legal issues involving your profession just as you do with the technical components of your job.

Thomas D. Schneid
Professor/Attorney
Department of Loss Prevention and Safety
Eastern Kentucky University

July 2000

Foreword

Emergency Medical Personnel—consider the following scenario. Your are traveling down the interstate one weekend evening going to visit a relative in another state. You're a little tired because you have just finished a long shift. All of a sudden you come across a serious accident scene. You appear to be the first person on the scene. There are bodies and blood everywhere. You stop and take assessment of the most seriously injured. You begin to do what you know best. Stop the bleeding. One person has a arterial wound that is pumping blood, others are screaming. You wish you had an emergency kit and a radio. Another person stops to help. You ask them to hold a compress on the bleeder and show them the proper method. You then start to care for several other seriously injured victims. One has a blocked airway. You look back. Your helper is going through the pockets of the injured. You lose control. What is this world coming to? You scream and chase off this person. Back to work. You must save as many lives as you can. You're racing around but there are too many that are seriously injured. No emergency kit. You do the best you can.

Soon others passersby stop. Can they help? Its dark and you don't want another thief. Too many questions are being asked. One tries to do CPR but doesn't know what he's doing. He is twisting the victim's head in an awkward position. Don't any of these people have training? "Get back, I'll do it myself." Another couple of so-called helpers try to move a victim from next to a car. "Don't move that man, he may have a neck injury," you say. They want to argue with you. They state that the car may blow up. They saw it in a movie. You check on the bleeder, the thief released your compress; the victim is bleeding bad now and has lost a lot of blood. Where is the state patrol?

Finally, real help arrives. Many have died. You did the best you could. You saved some lives this night. Many people praise you. However, some passersby are upset with you. They wanted to help but you kept them back. They caused more harm than help. One trooper gets your name and address and thanks you. You finally head down the road.

A month later, you get a knock at the door. You are being served with a Complaint-At-Law. You are now named in a wrongful death lawsuit. It involves one of the victims who didn't make it. The next day, another Complaint arrives, then a third. What do you do?

Soon, the local newspaper calls. You find out that some of the passersby complained that you didn't let them help and that fact likely contributed to the deaths of these individuals. Your mind is spinning . Don't they know how hard you worked? How many lives you did save? One car had six children in it and several of them had serious wounds that you attended. Two people had blocked airways and you cleared them and saved their lives.

You go to work and your boss informs you that you are being placed on administrative leave with pay. He is sorry but there is a lot of heat on this one. You weren't on duty. You ask about the Good Samaritan Law. He responds that he can't talk to you. He suggests you hire an attorney. The city attorney has told them to put you on leave and not answer questions. You go home.

When you get home you begin to question your actions that night. What did I do wrong? Why can't I tell my story? Do I need a lawyer? What is this going to cost me? Will I lose my job?

This book by Thomas Schneid will help answer these questions. It does an excellent job of outlining the basics of the law and legal liabilities that emergency medical personnel face every day. Knowledge is power. It will also provide you with peace of mind to the extent that you will know what your rights are and what acts and/or actions you can and should take, whether on duty or off duty. Will it prevent the lawsuits in the above scenario? Not necessarily, because almost anyone can bring suit against you. But what it will do is give you information that will help you understand how the legal process works and what actions and situations lend themselves to placing you at risk for being charged with a negligent act. It will also explain how the Good Samaritan Act works and how and when you might lose protection under it. I recommend this book highly to anyone in the profession of emergency medical care.

—Michael S. Schumann, M.S., J.D.
Associate Professor—Loss Prevention and Safety
Eastern Kentucky University

EMERGENCY MEDICAL SERVICES; the law. They just do not seem to fit in the same sentence, or *do they*.

EMS has oftentimes been called the "third" public service. It is the newest profession in the response field. We only knew of its development when we saw the emergence of the Federal Department of Transportation (DOT) training curriculum in the late 1960s for training Emergency Medical Technicians and paramedics. The first television shows in the 1970s portrayed the skills embodied by this new field of life-saving responders.

The glow does seem to diminish a bit when we think of emergency operations being touched by litigation. In today's fast-paced society, lawsuits abound. No longer are we protected by the thought that EMS is "untouchable" by suits and actions. The public has come to expect and deserve a degree of professionalism from all of us.

The veil of insulation no longer exists in our growing society. We must take an important message from Tom's text, and that is: *We are responsible for our actions, and we are held accountable for what we do every day*.

Litigation is everywhere, and as my old criminal law professors once said, "It doesn't matter whether you are right or wrong I will defend you "til you run out of money, and then . . ." These are words to heed—we are in the public spotlight, each and every day, and our customers—and the public we serve—deserve and expect the very best from today's maturing EMS services. Taking the time to do the *Job* right and documentation of what was done or not done are both very important.

Tom has filled this text with some very important information on all phases of EMS operations, government standards, and regulations, and also contributed some very practical common sense that will benefit you, as the provider, and the public we choose to serve.

You have taken a very important step toward making this a reality for serving the public by reading and understanding the basic tenets of our service. *To do no harm*, and to be as professional about your training, education, and activities as possible. If in doubt, ask and learn the right practices and procedures. Do your best to benefit our ultimate customer—*the public that requires our professional services*.

There are many volumes written on case law that has evolved to deal with when things go wrong, but this text is the first step in trying to learn how to prevent loss. You may not realize how many laws, regulations, and agencies affect you in the performance of EMS activities. OSHA, DOT, and EPA, as well as civil and criminal statutes apply. This potpourri of rules and regulatory issues await you daily.

Your best defense is to make sure that your training and education are state of the art. Document your training activities from your first Emergency Service Training (EMT) course through your required in-service education seminars. Keep copies of *everything* that you do to enhance your skills. Remember, if it was not documented, it was *not* done. Document, Document, Document.

Education is the key to survival in the future. Your success depends on the lessons learned from this textbook. Safety is the responsibility of everyone involved. Education is also the responsibility of everyone in the EMS and responder fields.

Remember, any job worth doing is worth doing right the first time. Learn, train, and prepare yourself for a very rewarding career in the field of Emergency Medical Services.

Our name says it all. Service, to the people that need our assistance. Remember, we are here to deliver the best care and customer service we can; after all isn't that the care you would like to receive?

—Michael J. Fagel, Ph.D.
North Aurora, Illinois

Michael Fagel has been in safety, fire, and EMS work for over three decades, serving in various agencies throughout his career.

Acknowledgments

Special thanks to my wife, Jani, and my daughters, Shelby, Madison, and Kasi, for their time, consideration, and motivation in making this text possible.

Thanks to Ms. Verna Casey for all of her research efforts and ideas.

Thanks to Shiella for her tireless work in researching, assembling, and correcting all of my mistakes.

CHAPTER 1

Introduction and Overview

History is the study of other people's mistakes.
—Philip Guedalla

Excellence is an art won by training and habituation. We are what we repeatedly do. Excellence, then, is not an act but a habit.

—Aristotle

The legal issues involving the emergency medical services have greatly expanded to encompass a broad spectrum of potential liabilities in the past decade. In concept, the emergency medical service was developed to first and foremost assist injured individuals. However, in today's litigious society, potential legal liabilities that can have a devastating effect on the emergency medical organization and EMS personnel have become part and parcel of our everyday decision-making process.

One of the major considerations when dealing with legal issues in the emergency medical service is the fact that the law is constantly moving. The law is absolutely not a stagnate creature that can always provide absolute "black and white" answers to every situation. To this end, it is important that emergency medical service personnel, charged with the responsibility of managing potential risks and thus potential liabilities, be aware of not only the laws themselves but also the court interpretations and changes in the laws by the various legislative and executive bodies at the federal, state, and local levels.

Laws directly and indirectly affecting the emergency medical service usually are initiated at the federal or state levels. Remembering back to our grammar school civics classes, the federal level is a checks-and-balance system consisting of the legislative branch (i.e., Congress), the executive branch (i.e., the president), and the judicial branch (i.e., the Supreme Court). Most states possess a similar structure. Laws are usually initiated by either the executive branch or legislative branch and are interpreted after becoming law by the judicial branch (i.e., case law).

In this text, a number of the major laws that have a direct or indirect effect on the emergency medical service are identified and discussed. It should be noted that all of the potential legal liabilities for any given emergency medical service organization have not been addressed, given the voluminous nature of this endeavor. Emergency service personnel with responsibilities in this area are encouraged to identify the potential risks in their organization and the various laws that directly or indirectly affect their specific operations. In addition to the laws themselves, it is vitally important that emergency service personnel be able to locate and understand the court interpretations of the laws, also known as case law, in order to be able to ascertain the applicability of the law to the situation and circumstances at hand.

Case law is the accumulation of court decisions, which, in essence, shapes and develops new law and clarifies old law. In each chapter throughout this text, you will find cases that will exemplify the particular point of law addressed in the chapter, while other cases in the appendix address related issues. It is important that you read, evaluate, and brief each of these cases in order to acquire a complete understanding of the law in the particular area. As the basic rule of thumb, when analyzing and/or briefing a case you should read through the case in detail at least three times. On the first reading, identify the type of case and the court, and acquire a basic understanding of the case type. In the second reading, you should identify the basic issues, facts, and holding of the decision as well as any dissenting opinion. In the third reading of the case, you should take notes regarding the actual brief of the case, which you will be referring to at some later point. It is essential that you take good notes and brief your case extremely well so that you can refer to the brief and refresh your memory later in your studies.

FINDING THE CASE

Finding the case in the library is often one of the most difficult tasks of your total analysis. As illustrated by the various cases provided in this text, other cases are referenced and numerous "cites" are provided throughout this text. All reported decisions of cases in the United States judicial system are listed according to the publication in which the case appears (called a reporter), the volume in which the case is located, and the initial page number. An example of a cite is 36 S.E. 2d 924. If you were searching for this case, you would go to the South Eastern Reporter, second edition, look for volume number 36, and find the case at page 924. In the federal judicial system, the publications tend to be organized by region; in most state judicial systems the cites are located in a state reporter. It should be noted that not all cases are reported and published. Generally, trial court decisions are not published because these decisions do not serve as mandatory precedent for other courts to follow. Usually only decisions of federal and state appellate courts are published.

Statutes, regulations, and standards can be located in other publications such as the Code of Federal Regulations. This system is set up utilizing the same citation system of publication, volume, and page number as are the reporters of judicial court decisions. However, the series numbers may reflect the particular regulation or standard. For example, 29 C.F.R. 1910.120 is the

Occupational Safety and Health Administration's Standard regarding hazardous waste operation and emergency response. If you were searching for this particular standard, you would go to the Code of Federal Regulations, which is signified by the C.F.R. designation, volume 29 and section 1910.120.

In addition to the normal procedure for locating a case, some law offices and law libraries provide an electronic database for locating cases. The two major databases are Westlaw and Lexis. Each of these databases normally provides training and publications to assist you in locating the particular case. As a general rule, these databases provide a basic menu of the various areas where the law is located and numerous subdatabases that guide your search. For example, if you were searching for a federal decision, you may enter the federal database and then narrow your search to the particular area of law that you are seeking. If you should possess the case name, the case name can normally be utilized to pull up the case. If you are searching for a particular issue of the law, these databases will provide the case cites for your review and evaluation. It is highly recommended that you acquire the particular training or assistance from the librarian at the law library prior to conducting any search on Westlaw or Lexis.

It is highly recommended that you become familiar with the particular library that you will be using during this course. Please take a few minutes out of your busy schedule and walk through the library to locate the different publications that are available and note the location of each of these publications. Please thumb through a few of the publications and test your skill at locating particular cases so that you can locate cases in a timely manner in the future.

BRIEFING THE CASE

The basic purpose for briefing a case is to help you understand the particular legal issues of the case and their significance. There are various methods of briefing a case and the following format is meant to illustrate only one of the methods. Your instructor may suggest an additional format for you or you may devise your own system to help you analyze these cases. No matter what method you should adopt, be sure that you read the case thoroughly prior to beginning to take notes for your brief.

The basic framework in which we would recommend you brief a case includes the following:

1. Issues

2. Facts

3. Holding (Decision)

4. Dissent

5. Your Opinion

6. Underlying Policy Reason

ISSUES

Identify the basic issue or issues that are in question before the court. In order to find the basic issue or issues involved, you have to identify the rule of law that governs the dispute and ask how it applies to the particular facts of the case. In most circumstances, you will be writing the issue for your case brief in the form of a question that combines the rule of law with the material facts of the case. For example, does the arson statute in the state of Kentucky apply to a minor child?

FACTS

The facts of the particular case describe the events between the conflicting parties that led to this particular litigation and tell how the case came before the court that is now deciding it. Often included in the facts are the relevance to the issue the court must decide and the basic reasons for its decision. When you first read through the case, you will not know which facts are relevant until you know what the issue or issues are in the particular case. Thus, it is vitally important that you read the case thoroughly prior to beginning to summarize the facts of the particular case.

In addition to the specific facts of the situation, it is important to note what court decisions have preceded the case that you are currently reviewing. Often, the decisions that are published are appellate decisions and thus a district court or circuit court has decided the matter previously and now the matter is on appeal. If the particular facts of the situation in an appellate case are not provided in detail, you may want to research and review the district or circuit court decisions in order to learn the particular facts in your case.

In this section, you should also include the relevant background for the case. You should identify who the plaintiff and the defendant are, the basis of the plaintiff's suit, and the relief the plaintiff is seeking. You may also want to include the procedural history of the case; for example, other motions that are relevant to the case such as Motions to Dismiss. In an appeals case, the decisions of the lower courts, grounds for those decisions, and the parties who appealed should also be noted.

Within this facts section, you should be as brief as possible. However, all pertinent points should be noted. Although this is a judgment call, most statement of facts in a brief should not be more than two or three paragraphs in length. Given the fact that you will have read the case at least three times while briefing it, the facts provided in your brief should be the major points used to refresh your memory.

HOLDING

The holding is the courts' decision on the question that was actually brought before it by the parties. The court, in a split decision, may provide the minority's decision or dissent also. The holding can normally be identified as the statement of the court's decision or the majority decision. A holding, in essence, provides the answer to the question you were asking in your issue statement. If there is more than one issue involved in any given case, there may be more than one holding.

DISSENT

Often in U.S. Supreme Court cases and appellate cases, the majority decision is the decision of the court. However, the minority position is also provided an opportunity to give its reasoning as to its dissent in the decision-making process. Although the dissenting opinion is not law and has no bearing on the case, the dissent provides another point of view on the particular issue of the case and may also be referred to in some later case.

OPINION

After you have reviewed the case thoroughly and have analyzed the court decision and briefed your case, you should have a good idea whether you agree or disagree with the court's opinion. In this section, you should provide your personal opinion as to whether you agree or disagree with the decision and the reasons for your agreement or disagreement.

POLICY

In many cases, there is an underlying social policy or a particular social goal that the court wishes to further. When a court explicitly refers to those policies in a particular case, this information should be included in your brief since it will provide you with a better understanding of the court's decision. For example, in the historic case of *Brown v. Board of Education*, the decision of the court was formed through an underlying social policy to eliminate discrimination in our school system. This underlying social policy is often very important in appellate and Supreme Court decisions. Attached is a sample brief for your review and evaluation. It is highly recommended that you "test" your skills by briefing several of the cases within this text or other cases prior to your initial briefing of a case for a class. In addition to the information stated above, several other helpful hints that may assist you in briefing the case are listed below.

1. It is best to try to confine your brief to a maximum of one page. If your brief is over two pages long, you have probably provided too much information. Remember, the purpose of a brief is to refresh your memory when you need to recall this information for class or other purposes.
2. The cases that are printed in this textbook have been edited by the author for the purposes of this book. In many cases, the full court opinion may run twenty or more pages. If you find that you are having difficulty understanding the case in the edited format, you may want to go to the library and read the full text opinion.
3. During your first few attempts at briefing a case, it is often difficult to extract its important elements and issues. Please keep in mind that not all

judges are expert writers so the opinions may often be confusing or difficult to understand. Additionally, you should realize that all courts do not follow the same format in writing opinions, so you may find some decisions more difficult to understand than others. Also, you may find that judges sometimes go off on a tangent and discuss other rules and points of law that are not essential to the determination of the particular case. It is your job to be able to filter through the information provided to identify the particular issues and laws that are applicable to the case.

4. You may often run across latin or "legal" terms with which you are not familiar. Since you will need to have a clear understanding of the terminology utilized in the particular case, it is advisable to look up the term in a legal dictionary. A good idea is to have a *Black's Law Dictionary, Ballantine Law Dictionary, Gilmer's Law Dictionary*, or other law dictionary available while you are reading and briefing the case. Standard dictionaries often do not provide these terms or the explanation provided may be incomplete.

5. When reading the cases provided in this text, you may want to look at the particular chapter and section headings of the textbook in which the case appears. If you are having difficulty identifying the particular issue of the case, you will normally find that the issue is related to the topic discussed in the chapter or section heading. The cases in this text have been inserted to illustrate the subject matter being discussed in each of the chapters.

6. Remember, the issue or issues in the particular case should always be stated in the form of a question. You should never begin your issue with the words, "whether or not" because this will not frame the question properly. Also, the terminology, "should plaintiff win" or "is there a contract" are not correct forms to use in stating the particular issue.

7. In determining the particular rule of law, ask yourself, "If I had to tell someone who knew nothing about this case what this case is about or what it stands for in one sentence, what would I say?" Often, the rule of law can be determined by taking the issue and putting it in the form of a declaration. For example, in the case of *Miranda v. Arizona*, 384 U.S. 436 (1966), the issue and rule may be as follows:

Issue: When a person is taken into police custody, or otherwise deprived of his freedom of action in a significant way, must his constitutional rights to remain silent and to have an attorney present be explained to him prior to questioning?

Rule: When a person is taken into police custody, the following warnings must be given prior to questioning:

1. That he has the right to remain silent.

2. That any statement he makes may be used against him as evidence.

3. That he has the right to have an attorney present.

4. If he cannot afford an attorney, one will be appointed for him.

8. Finally, do not use other people's briefs. To acquire the knowledge you need, you must read a particular case and analyze the court decision

yourself—use of another individual's brief of a case is essentially worthless. A brief is simply the codification of your thoughts and work, which you will refer to in the future in order to refresh your memory.

Example Case Brief

Case Name: *Marshall v. Barlow's, Inc.*, 436 U.S. 307 (1978)

Issue: Is Section 8(a) of the Occupational Safety and Health Act unconstitutional in that it violates the Fourth Amendment?

Facts: Appellee (Barlow's, Inc.) initially brought this action to obtain injunctive relief against a warrantless inspection of its business premises by Appellant (Secretary of Labor Marshall). The inspection was permitted under Section 8(a) of the Occupational Safety and Health Act of 1970 which authorizes agents of the Secretary of Labor to search the work area of any employment facility within OSHA's jurisdiction for safety hazards and OSHA violations without obtaining a search warrant or other process. A three judge Idaho District Court ruled in favor of Barlow's and concluded that the Fourth Amendment required a warrant for this type of search and that the statutory authorization for warrantless inspections was unconstitutional. This appeal resulted.

Holding: Yes, Section 8(a) of the Occupational Safety and Health Act of 1970 was unconstitutional in that it violated the Fourth Amendment. The U.S. Supreme Court affirmed the decision of the Idaho District Court and granted Barlow's an injunction enjoining the enforcement of the act to that extent.
The court states that the rule against warrantless searches applies to commercial premises as well as private homes. Although an exception to this rule is applied to certain "carefully defined classes of cases" including closely regulated businesses such as the firearm and liquor industries, this exception does not automatically apply to all businesses engaged in interstate commerce, as the Secretary alleges.

Opinion: I agree with the court in this case. I feel that requiring search warrants ensures that the search is a reasonable one and that the particular business being inspected is not merely being singled out (for one reason or another). I agree with the court in that requiring search warrants will not make inspections less effective nor will it prevent necessary inspections, but rather it will serve to ensure fairness in inspections.

Policy: Although no specific public policy was mentioned in the case, the implied policy was that of probusiness, antiregulation.

ORGANIZATION OF THE JUDICIARY SYSTEM

The aim of law is the maximum gratification of the nervous system of man.
—Justice Learned Hand

The American judicial system is composed of numerous levels of courts encompassed within two broad categories, namely the federal judicial system and the individual state or territory's judicial system. Jurisdiction and the specific rules governing a particular court dictate which court possesses the authority to render an enforceable decision over the particular matter in dispute.

Jurisdiction by the courts over any given matter can be determined in two basic manners: (1) jurisdiction over the person; or (2) jurisdiction over the object. In essence, for a court to be able to hear and make an enforceable decision over a particular matter, the case must involve a resident of the state or the situation, e.g., the automobile accident, must have occurred within the state. Some courts, such as tax courts and traffic courts, have special jurisdiction over specific particular matters.

A particular court's jurisdiction over a matter can also be limited by the type of case, the dollar amount involved, and other factors. In most states, specific jurisdictional requirements are established by the courts or legislature. These jurisdictional requirements can usually be found in the state's court rules or in the state statutes.

In the federal court system, the offense must be within the jurisdiction of the federal courts or diversity must exist in order for the federal court to be able to hear the case. For example, if an individual committed arson involving a federal building, the matter is a federal offense and the case would be heard in the federal court system. Conversely, if a West Virginia resident committed arson to a building owned by a West Virginia resident and the building was located in West Virginia, the West Virginia state court system would possess jurisdiction. However, if the building was located in another state, or the parties were not residents of West Virginia, diversity may exist permitting the federal court system to acquire jurisdiction. It should be noted that federal courts can adjudge cases involving questions of state law and state courts can consider cases involving federal law.

Jurisdiction is also classified as original or appellate. The court that originally hears the case is considered to possess original jurisdiction. If the decision of the original court is appealed to a higher court, the higher court must possess appellate jurisdiction in order to hear the appeal. In courts possessing original jurisdiction, usually known as trial courts, district courts, or circuit courts, the *Perry Mason* or *L.A. Law* type of hearings are held. In the court of original jurisdiction, evidence is presented, witnesses are called, arguments are made, and the court determines the matter of a factual basis. In courts possessing appellate jurisdiction, the determination is usually made with limited, if any, oral arguments, and is based on the record provided by the court of original jurisdiction. The appellate court reviews the judgment of the court of original jurisdiction to ensure all appropriate rules and procedures were followed and that there was appropriate factual evidence to support the decision of the jury or judge in the case. If the rules were followed and the facts substantiated the decision, most appellate courts are required to sustain the decision of the court with original jurisdiction.

In determining which court is appropriate for hearing a particular case at the original jurisdictional level, the first determination is who are the parties involved and where was the "situs" or location of the incident or offense in dispute. The second determination is which court system, federal or state, possesses original jurisdiction over the matter. The third level of determination is which court possesses jurisdiction over the matter, based on the amount of money involved or other specific requirements. The determination of the appropriate court is vital in ensuring that the issue in dispute is properly adjudicated.

FEDERAL JUDICIARY SYSTEM

Article III, Section 1 of the U.S. Constitution provides:

> *The judicial power of the United States, shall be vested in one Supreme Court, and in such inferior courts as the Congress may from time to time ordain and establish.*

The federal judicial system is composed of the U.S. Supreme Court, twelve circuit courts of appeal, district courts, and various special courts such as territorial courts and the U.S. Tax Court. Additionally, there is a specialized circuit court system known as the U.S. Court of Appeals for the Federal Circuit, which possesses exclusive jurisdiction to hear all appeals from the U.S. Court of Claims, the Court of International Trade, and the International Trade Commission.

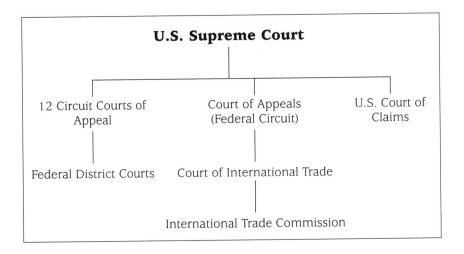

SUPREME COURT OF THE UNITED STATES

The United States Constitution designates the Supreme Court to be the highest court in the United States. The Supreme Court has original jurisdiction over multiple cases where one state is suing another, where courts of appeal have differences of opinions with regard to a federal issue, or in hearing appeals from the Circuit Courts of Appeal. The Constitution limits the jurisdiction of the Supreme Court to considering cases that involve international law, federal law, and federally protected rights. If none of the issues involves federal law or international law, the U.S. Supreme Court lacks authority to consider the case and must defer to the judgment of the state supreme courts. The Constitution does not expressly grant the Supreme Court the authority to declare a law that Congress or a state legislature has passed to be invalid. In the famous case of *Marbury v. Madison*, it was found that since the Constitution is the supreme law in the United States, a court may hold invalid any attempt to circumvent its provisions. John Marshall stated in *Marbury v. Madison* that the U.S. Supreme Court did not possess this authority and that it would nullify the values of the written Constitution and permit it to be altered by any statute that the current Congress or state legislature would happen to pass.

The U.S. Supreme Court is the highest appellate court in the United States. Some cases are required to be heard by the U.S. Supreme Court by writ. However, the vast majority of cases are brought up on certiorari. Writs of certiorari to the U.S. Supreme Court are basically requests for discretionary review of a lower court's ruling. The ruling of the U.S. Supreme Court is the final rule with most decisions in the United States; a U.S. Supreme Court decision can be modified or overturned only by an act of Congress (e.g., The Civil Rights Act of 1990).

CIRCUIT COURTS OF APPEAL

This judicial system is divided into 12 federal judicial circuits within the United States. Courts of Appeal consider all appeals from the District Courts within their jurisdiction or district unless the case is one in which the appeal could go directly to the U.S. Supreme Court. Each circuit encompasses between three and nine states and the U.S. Court of Appeals hears all appellate decisions from district courts within that region. The U.S. Courts of Appeal establish a legal precedent from which all United States District Courts within that particular circuit must follow. Law on a particular subject may vary among and between the circuits with resolution of any conflict coming only through appeal to and decision by the U.S. Supreme Court.

FEDERAL DISTRICT COURTS

District courts are the trial level courts of the federal judicial system. They are the courts in which witnesses will be heard, testimony will be taken, and an initial decision made. As noted in the diagram above, the Federal District

Court is the initial or entry level in most federal cases, and all levels of courts above the Federal District Court are considered appellate. District courts hear both criminal and civil actions.

SPECIAL COURTS

Federal District Courts normally have their own rules and procedures to be followed in five special courts. Within the federal judiciary system, special courts have been developed to address particular issues. At the circuit court level, there is a U.S. Court of Appeals for the Federal Circuit, which is based in Washington, D.C. and provides exclusive jurisdiction for appellate decisions from the U.S. Court of Claims, Court of International Trade, and International Trade Commission. In the area of tax, a special United States Tax Court has been developed for any appeals from decisions made by the Commissioner for the Internal Revenue Commission. The United States Tax Court does not handle claims for overpayment of taxes. These matters are normally handled by the U.S. Court of Claims or U.S. Federal District Court.

STATE COURT SYSTEMS

State Court systems are usually structured on the same basic arrangement as the federal court system. However, it should be noted that the names utilized for each of these courts may vary from state to state (for example, the New York Supreme Court is the trial level court). State Court systems are typically composed of a state appellate court, district courts of appeal or circuit courts of appeal, courts that may be called superior or supreme courts, and smaller specialized courts such as municipal courts, traffic courts, or justice courts.

The state supreme court is normally the highest appellate court within the state. Specifically, the state supreme court is made up of a chief justice and anywhere from four to eight associate justices. The state supreme court normally hears all appeal cases from the lower state courts or cases involving interpretation of state law from a federal court. Cases involving the death penalty, habeas corpus, or other criminal-related matters are heard by the state supreme court.

States have several courts of appeals, each responsible for a designated area within the particular state. These courts normally hear all of the appeal cases within that state. The court of appeals normally considers appeals from the trial court judgments and orders unless the state supreme court assumes jurisdiction over the matter. The entry level into most state court systems is the trial court or district court level. Courts can be called various names such as superior court, supreme court, or district court. District courts are the initial determining body in most civil and criminal matters. State district courts have jurisdiction to consider other cases involving such things as individual taxes, probate, domestic relations, and juvenile problems. District courts or trial courts are also the courts possessing jurisdiction over most criminal matters involving felonies and particular misdemeanors within the state.

MUNICIPAL COURTS AND OTHER COURTS

States with larger populations have established municipal courts, traffic courts, and other minor courts to handle particular matters. In some jurisdictions, municipal courts or small claims courts handle civil cases that do not involve a large amount of money. In other jurisdictions, municipal courts have been established to hear cases involving misdemeanors except those involving juveniles. In these states, special courts have been established to hear juvenile offenses.

In some states, courts have been established with special limited jurisdiction to hear particular matters. Such courts include city courts, city justice courts, and township courts. These courts are normally established to assist another court when there is a particular specialized problem, such as building and fire code violations, and specialized training is needed for the prescribing judge or court official.

In summation, the court systems in the United States are designed to act as referees between two or more adversarial parties in a dispute. Specialized roles and procedures have been established for both criminal and civil proceedings. The U.S. Constitution and other laws within our judicial court system guarantee citizens a means of redressing any injustice or wrong that has been done to them. Individuals must assert their rights in a civil action in order to be able to achieve justice.

Chapter 2

Personnel Issues in Emergency Services

You can employ men and hire hands to work *for* you, but you must win their hearts to have them work *with* you.

—Tiorio

Nine-tenths of the serious controversies which arise in life result from misunderstandings; results from one man not knowing the facts which to the other man seem important, or otherwise failing to appreciate his point of view.

—Louis D. Brandeis

One of the major areas of litigation for emergency service organizations involves human resource or personnel issues. Human resource issues in an emergency service organization can run the spectrum from uniform issues through harassment on the job. The management of the personnel function in an emergency service organization appears simple in concept but is, however, an extremely broad area encompassing a wide variety of activities and legal requirements. When an emergency service organization effectively and appropriately manages its human assets, there usually are no complaints and the emergency service organization functions smoothly. However, if even one minor mistake is made in this area, the situation can turn into an instant crisis.

CONFLICT SITUATIONS

Given the close quarters, intense situations, and number of highly qualified and skilled emergency service personnel involved in any organization, conflicts are inevitable. Substantial time and effort may be required within any emergency service organization to simply resolve conflicts. Whether the "problem" is a misunderstanding regarding the payment of workers' compensation benefits to an employee or a supervisor who wants to issue discipline to an employee, one or more members of the management of an emergency service organization usually is involved as the mediator, referee, or final judge.

Conflicts between employees can often escalate if not addressed or addressed improperly. Additionally, even the best efforts of the human resource manager or other designated emergency service management members can ultimately result in an escalation of the conflict. As emergency service personnel, you should attempt to resolve the conflict in the best way possible while safeguarding the conflicting parties, your company or organization, and yourself.

Below are several general rules for your consideration in resolving a conflict situation:

- Never permit the conflict to escalate to physical confrontation.

- Remove the conflicting parties from the general work population. Use your office, conference room, or other appropriate facility.

- Permit the conflicting parties to tell their side of the story uninterrupted by the other party.

- Provide both sides with the opportunity to tell their side of the story.

- Lower the level of aggression—keep the parties calm.

- If tensions and voice volume rise, ask the parties to lower their voice.

- If the party's voice rises, soften your voice. Don't get pulled into the conflict—it's not personal.

- Permit time for the parties to "cool off."

- Never make a "snap judgment." Permit yourself time to investigate the situation fully prior to making a decision.

- If physical violence is possible, take appropriate precautions.

- Physically separate the parties across a table or room.

- Don't permit the parties to leave the meeting together.

- Always follow company policies and procedures.

- Bring the issues to a final resolution.

- Take appropriate safeguards following resolution of issues.

- Document everything!

In many circumstances, if a conflict within the emergency service organization can be resolved internally, there is no need to pursue costly legal action. However, if the emergency service organization permits the situation to escalate, many of these conflicts can result in legal action by one or more of the parties resulting in an expenditure of time, monies, and effort to resolve the situation in a court of law.

POLICIES AND PROCEDURES

The life blood of most human resource programs within emergency service organizations is the written policies and procedures that provide guidance and direction in the decision-making process of the emergency service organization and provide perimeters of acceptable and unacceptable behavior for EMS personnel. In many emergency service organizations, extensive written policies and procedures governing virtually every aspect of the personnel and human resource functions have been formulated and reduced to written form.

In developing a written personnel and human resource policy, emergency service organizations should consider the following:

- What is the purpose of the policy?
- Who is going to be directly and indirectly affected by the policy?
- Do you possess upper management approval for the policy?
- Is the policy clearly written and understandable at all educational levels?
- Does the policy possess legal implications? Legal requirements?
- What, if any, will be the reaction to the policy?
- Has the policy been reviewed by appropriate individuals?
- Is there an enforcement provision in the policy?
- Has an appropriate period of time been allotted prior to enforcement?
- Will the policy be published through posting, handbook, or other methods?
- Will the policy be reviewed and revised on a periodic basis?

Emergency service organizations should be aware that policies and procedures are often subject to challenge by employees through internal or external tribunals. Policies and procedures should be written utilizing clear, unambiguous language at an educational level appropriate to the work force. Additionally, policies and procedures should be written in a defensive manner in anticipation of challenge and should be carefully reviewed by all levels of the management team and legal advisors prior to implementation.

Sample Policy

Bereavement Leave

Bereavement Leave will be granted to a full- or part-time employee who experiences a death in their family. If it is a loss of an immediate family member (spouse, child), the employee will be granted up to three (3) days of time off with pay. For parent, sibling, grandparents, only one (1) day off with pay will be granted. If additional time off is requested, it will be unpaid and the employee must receive written permission from the EMS Operations Manager.

Personnel and human resource policies and procedures should be evaluated and revised, as necessary, on a planned periodic basis. Personnel and human resource policies, not unlike other areas like safety and health, often require modification to the policies to adhere to changes in the laws, or court decisions, or even changes in the work force status. In many emergency medical service organizations, a planned "audit" of all policies and procedures is conducted on an annual basis and appropriate revisions are identified and initiated to ensure compliance with the current requirements.

Some emergency medial service organizations utilize personnel handbooks as a single source for all personnel and human resources, as well as other important areas, policies, and procedures. Emergency medical service organizations should exercise extreme caution when developing handbooks to ensure the handbook cannot be construed as a formal contract between the company or organization and the employee.

Emergency medical service organizations should also be aware that specific language utilized in handbooks and policies possess specific legal meanings. Some of the terms to be aware of include the following:

- Just Cause

- Good Cause

- Good Faith

- Guaranteed

- Secured

- Permanent

- Job Tenured

- Due Process

- Annual Review

- Permanent Job

- Guaranteed Employment

RECORD MAINTENANCE

One of the main responsibilities of the human resource area of any emergency service organization is the maintenance of important records and documents for future reference and use. Many documents must be maintained by law, while other documents are maintained for legal purposes or company requirements. The basic rule of thumb is to maintain employee documents for the life of the employee plus 20 years because most legal actions in which the document may be important usually will occur, if at all, during this period. However, some specialized documents, such as some environmental records, may need to be maintained beyond this period of time.

MEDICAL AND INSURANCE RECORDS

Two categories of records that often possess an extremely "long tail" are employee medical records and insurance records. The primary reason for the maintenance of these documents for an extended period of time beyond the employee's departure from the workplace is the potential exposures during their employment at your operation. In many circumstances, medical and insurance records are maintained for the period of the statute of limitations following an employee's death due primarily to the legal actions that can be brought following an individual's death under the wrongful death statutes of many states. As with any important document, medical and insurance records must be accurate and maintained in an appropriate environment so that they can be referred to many years in the future. Additionally, medical and insurance records can be viewed by the individual employee under many laws and such records are often the basis for future litigation.

PERSONAL ATTENDANCE RECORD MAINTENANCE

The Personnel Attendance Records are among the most important documents maintained by emergency medical service organizations. These records identify the days in which an individual has missed worked, the reason for missing work, the number of times an individual is late for work, and other pertinent information. This is often the base level document through which disciplinary action is taken against an employee under the prescribed disciplinary procedures. Personnel attendance records are normally maintained in a secure location with minimal access by employees. Employee attendance records are normally maintained for a specified period of time beyond their employment period with the company or organization in case of disputes involving the initiated disciplinary action or other applicable reasons.

RECORD ACCESS

Emergency medical service organizations should be aware that the OSHA standards permit employees access to their medical records and, in some circumstances, other laws permit employees access to other records within the facility. Emergency medical service organizations should prescribe a procedure through which employees would have access to the applicable records and establish procedures for the photocopying of records, access to other employees records, and so on.

In virtually every emergency medical service organization, personnel will leave the organization. The human resource department or other identified function within the emergency medical service organization is usually responsible for the documentation of any type of disciplinary action and/or termination records. These records are normally confidential in nature, however they may be subject to a Court Order or Arbitration Order. Employee records as to attendance, disciplinary action, and other personnel and human resource issues should be maintained separately from any medical-related records.

Who has access to your records? Who inputs the employees' attendance record data? Do supervisors have access to individual employee medical records? The issue of confidentiality and access to sensitive records is an important issue for emergency medical service organizations. Specific policies and procedures should be established to identify the procedures through which confidentiality is maintained, identifying who has access to each type of record, and additional issues in order to maintain confidentiality of appropriate records.

TAX REPORTS

An emergency medical service organization, like any company or organization, is normally responsible for the completion of appropriate federal, state, and often local tax reports that need to be generated on behalf of the company as well as for certain employees. Additionally, when employees are hired, specific tax forms (such as a Form W-4) must be completed and appropriately filed. In the area of current employees, records as to Federal Insurance Contribution Act (FICA) taxes, income tax withholding, social security, and unemployment tax as well as other taxes are often required. Additionally, many employers utilize the targeted job tax credits (TJTC) and other programs that require extensive tax records.

As with other tax withholdings identified above, the emergency medical service organization as well as the employee (i.e., payroll deduction), the equivalent shares of social security tax are often required to be forwarded to the appropriate government agency by the employer. There are many specific rules regarding the payroll deduction of such taxes and regarding the acquisition of social security benefits with which the emergency medical service organization should know. Emergency medical service organizations should also note that an employer identification number is required for the reporting of employment taxes or for providing employees with tax statements. There are specific forms utilized by the Internal Revenue Service as well as the Social Security Administration Office for these requests.

GOVERNMENT AGENCY REPORTS

Emergency medical service organizations should be aware that there are numerous reports that should be made available and/or are required to be forwarded to the Occupational Safety and Health Administration or Environmental Protection Agency regarding specific situations or incidents. Additionally, in some circumstances, the governmental agency will forward a request for additional information, which is required to be sent to the agency in a requisite period of time.

Although discussed in detail in later chapters, emergency medical service organizations should pay special attention to the potential legal liabilities involved in the hiring process, as discussed below.

AMERICANS WITH DISABILITY ACT (ADA) CONSIDERATIONS

The human resource manager or other member of the emergency medical service organization management team is often the individual "making the call" when hiring or promoting individuals, or in job changes, and so on. Individuals within the organization with this specific responsibility should possess a firm grasp of the ADA and be able to provide consideration and education in this area to other team members in order to ensure appropriate decision making.

REFERENCE INFORMATION AND EMPLOYING TESTING

Emergency medical service organizations should exercise extreme caution when providing information to other employers regarding references or past employment history. There has been a substantial amount of litigation regarding the provision of improper information about a terminated employee. Emergency medical service organizations may wish to establish procedures and policies about the type and nature of information provided to a request for references.

Effective communications between the emergency medical service organization management team and EMS personnel can minimize potential conflicts and thus costly legal actions. Effective communication includes not only oral communication but written communication. Communication with personnel is essential and must be clear and concise so that employees do not "assume" any facet of it. Some key points in the area of communications with personnel to keep in mind include:

Oral Communications—

- Clear and concise

- Never assume anything

- Use paraphrasing and other techniques

- Watch body language

Written Communications—

- Clear and concise

- Appropriate sentence structure

• No misspellings

• Appropriate format

One of the areas of potential risk and thus legal liability for many emergency service organizations is in employee testing programs. There are a wide variety of testing programs including, but not limited to, testing for controlled substances, truth testing, and recently, more sophisticated testing such as DNA testing. Emergency service organizations should be extremely cautious in the area of employee testing, given the recent laws regarding employee testing and privacy right issues.

Approximately 50 percent of the employers in the United States now perform some type of alcohol and controlled substances testing and most emergency service organizations are performing some level of testing. The testing for alcohol and controlled substances procedures normally involves some type of invasive procedures such as acquisition of blood, urine, and most recently hair. Due to the privacy rights issues arising because of the invasive nature of this type of testing, emergency service organizations should exercise extreme caution in the development of these programs as well as ensuring compliance as to the chain of custody, acquisition of samples, testing procedures, and so on.

Emergency medical service organizations should be aware that there is substantial risk of litigation regarding controlled substance and alcohol testing programs. Given the invasive nature of such testing as well as the possible repercussions from a positive test, it is imperative that emergency medical service organizations ensure that their testing procedures are absolutely in compliance and be prepared for challenges on every aspect of their testing program.

Potential Federal Laws That May Impact Testing Programs

1. Americans with Disabilities Act (42 U.S.C. § 12101)

   • Applied to EMS organizations with 15 or more employees

   • Prohibits discrimination in all employment areas (Title I) against qualified individuals with disabilities

   • Requires reasonable accommodation

   • Acquire information from the Equal Employment Opportunity Commission (EEOC).

2. Civil Rights Act of 1866 (42 U.S.C. § 1981)

   • Applies to public and private sector

   • Applies to "all persons" under recent U.S. Supreme Court decisions

- Religious bias not covered
- See *Patterson v. McLean Credit Union*, 109 S. Ct. 2263 (1989) but note that the Civil Rights Act of 1991 restored much of the protection restricted by this case.

3. Civil Rights Act of 1964 (42 U.S.C. § 2000e)
   - 15 or more employees
   - Bars discrimination based on race, sex, color, religion, or national origin
   - Sex discrimination includes sexual harassment in employment.

4. Civil Rights Act of 1991
   - Negates several Supreme Court decisions regarding the Civil Rights Act of 1964 and expanded remedies in sex discrimination and sexual harassment cases
   - Amended Civil Rights Act of 1866 to include prohibitions of race discrimination in the contract area
   - Permits injunctive relief, declaratory relief, and attorney fees in mixed motive cases
   - Applies to private and public sector
   - Cap on damages depending on the size of the employer.

5. Age Discrimination in Employment Act (29 U.S.C. § 621)
   - 20 or more employees
   - Applies to public and private sector
   - Prohibits discrimination based on age. Protects individuals over the age of 40
   - Age cap of 70 years of age removed.

6. Drug Free Workplace Act of 1988 (41 U.S.C. § 701, § 5151-5160)
   - Applies to federal contractors and grantees
   - Employers must certify a drug-free workplace
   - Employees must report drug convictions.

7. Employee Polygraph Protection Act of 1988 (29 U.S.C. § 2001)
   - Applies to public and private sector
   - Prohibits most employers from using polygraph examinations in most preemployment situations except for security or related businesses. Current employees can be tested only during on-going investigation
   - Numerous restrictions and prohibitions.

8. Family and Medical Leave Act of 1993 (29 U.S.C. § 2601)

   - 50 or more employees

   - Eligible to up to 12 weeks unpaid leave for serious health condition of the employee or family member or birth or adoption of child.

9. Labor-Management Relations Act of 1947 (29 U.S.C. § 141)

   - Allows employees to file a court action against the employer for breach of contract or against a union for breach of duty of fair representation.

10. Occupational Safety and Health Act of 1970 (29 U.S.C. § 651)

    - Private sector—1 or more employees; Public sector usually by state law

    - Requires maintenance of a safe and healthful work environment

    - Civil penalties up to $70,000 per violation

    - Criminal penalties.

11. Veterans Reemployment Rights Act of 1974 (38 U.S.C. § 2021)

    - Applies to public and private sector

    - Active military and guard training entitled to guaranteed job security

    - Other protections.

12. Vietnam Era Veterans Readjustment Assistance Act of 1974 (38 U.S.C. § 2012) and Employment and Training of Veterans Act (39 U.S.C. § 4211)

    - Federal projects over $10,000.00

    - Requires written affirmative action plans.

13. Vocational Rehabilitation Act of 1973 (29 U.S.C. § 701)

    - Federal contracts over $10,000.00

    - Affirmative action plan required for hiring and advancing qualified individuals with disabilities.

    NOTE: Civil actions based upon defamation (i.e., libel and slander) as well as wrongful discharge may also impact the testing area.

Potential State Laws Which May Impact Testing Program

For the purposes of this text, the laws of the Commonwealth of Kentucky were utilized as an example. Each state should be examined for applicable laws and regulations.

State Example Specific Law (Kentucky used for this example.)

(Kentucky Revised Statutes hereinafter referred to as "KRS").

- KRS 334.040 forbids discrimination in employment on the basis of race, color, religion, national origin, sex, or age.

- KRS 207.130 prohibits discrimination in employment because of handicap.

- KRS 121.310 forbids employers from interfering with the voting rights of their employees.

- Kentucky Public Acts, H.B. 100 (1978) and KRS 335(B)(2)(1) provide that no person shall be disqualified from public employment, nor shall a person be disqualified from pursuing, practicing, or engaging in any occupation solely because of a prior conviction of a crime, unless the crime is one limited to convictions for felonies, high misdemeanors, or crimes involving moral turpitude.

- KRS 338.011 addresses occupational safety and health for public and private sector employers.

- KRS 342.0011 establishes and regulates workers compensation. (In Kentucky, volunteer firefighters are specifically included in coverage under the Act.)

APPLICATION PROCESS

Emergency medical service organizations usually place substantial emphasis on the application process, application forms, interview process, and the checking of references and the gathering of other information to ensure compliance with the Americans With Disabilities Act (ADA), Title VII, and other applicable federal and state laws. Emergency medical service organizations should be aware that this has become a "hot" area for litigation and thus careful scrutiny should be provided in each of the information-gathering process steps.

Emergency medical service organizations should exercise extreme caution when evaluating the possible use of polygraphs or psychological or personality testing within their operation. It should be noted that there are a number of laws governing this area and this type of testing potentially possesses numerous inaccuracies. Such tests include, but are not limited to, the Minnesota Multiphasic Personality Inventory (MMPI) and the Rorschach Test. Although in some employment settings, employees such as police officers, airline pilots, and others may require some type of psychological or personality testing, these types of tests are not normally utilized in the private sector due to their high cost and invasive nature.

Emergency medical service organizations should exercise extreme caution any time that they are testing for HIV or AIDS or performing any type of genetic testing. Additionally, emergency medical service organizations should be aware of the implications of the Americans with Disabilities Act and of any recently enacted federal laws regarding this type of testing. HIV and AIDS testing can have other legal implications besides the individual issues involved in such testing. Genetic testing, although in its infancy stage, is extremely intrusive and emergency medical service organizations should exercise extreme caution in this area.

As discussed in detail in Chapter 3, emergency medical service organizations should possess a management team member who is completely versed in the methods and procedures that are permissible in the area of medical screening. The use of a "preemployment" physical or screening is prohibited by the Americans with Disabilities Act. Given the intrusive nature of this type of testing as well as the confidentiality issues involved, emergency medical service organizations should scrutinize current procedures and ensure that all future procedures adhere to all federal, state, and local laws.

UNION VS. NONUNION CONSIDERATIONS

Under Section 7 of the National Labor Relations Act (known as the NLRA), employees possess the right to form and join unions. The governing agency for any type of organizational campaign or representation is the National Labor Relations Board (known as the NLRB). Emergency medical service organizations must be fully knowledgeable regarding the rules and requirements in this area.

In a nonunion workplace, the organization normally has the ability to establish policies and programs through the company's management prerogative. However, in a workplace in which the employees are represented by a collective bargaining agent (i.e., union), most personnel and human resource issues are addressed in the collective bargaining agreement (i.e., union contract) or are negotiable issues concerning wages, hours, or conditions of employment.

In unionized workplaces, the employees are usually represented in any type of personnel action by the union business agent or union representative. The union agent possesses a right to be at any type of disciplinary action or other situation involving the EMS organization and the employee. (Emergency medical service organizations should be aware that this right to representation has been extended to nonunion employees.)

The union, through its election by the employees, possesses the right to collectively bargain with the employer on virtually every aspect of the employment relationship including wage issues, hours worked, safety issues, and any other term or condition concerning employment.

Under many union contracts, internal "hearing" or judicial proceedings are established through which any or all disputes are decided. The first step in many procedures is the filing of a "grievance" by the employee with the EMS organization representative and union representative. This is normally followed by a "grievance hearing" if the matter cannot be amicably resolved.

Many union contracts possess "arbitration clauses" through which disputes that cannot be resolved at grievance hearings are transferred to a panel of arbitrators providing either a final determination (i.e., "binding arbitration) or another level of determination that can be appealed (i.e., nonbinding arbitration).

Unionized EMS organizations should possess one or more management team members who possess the requisite level of knowledge regarding the collective bargaining agreement and the grievance/arbitration process. Proper documentation and preparation are essential throughout this type of dispute resolution process.

LEGAL CATEGORIES OF EMPLOYEES

It is essential that the emergency medical service organization be absolutely confident as to the status of its employees. There are various types of legal employment status and each category possesses specialized laws and rules. These categories include:

- At-will employee
- Union contract employee
- Independent contractor
- Probationary employee
- Full-time employee
- Nonunion employee with handbook
- Part-time employee

The EMS organization should be familiar with the various employment statuses within their facilities and the rules and regulations that apply to each category. Normally, the EMS organization will have specific company policies and procedures governing each employment category as well as specific legal considerations and tax considerations for each category. Two of the most often utilized categories by EMS organizations include the following:

"AT-WILL" EMPLOYEES

"At-will" employees can be terminated for good cause, bad cause, or no cause at all. However, if employees are governed by a collective bargaining agreement, employment contract, or other contracts, the at-will employment status is no longer valid. Additionally, courts have created substantial exceptions to the at-will employment doctrine that EMS organization must know:

- Handbook exception
- Public policy exceptions

- Oral contract exceptions
- Statutory duty exception
- Term of years

INDEPENDENT CONTRACTOR

There is a substantial difference between the classification of an employee and that of an "independent contractor." The independent contractor status possesses far-reaching consequences in terms of the law, specifically under the Fair Labor Standards Act (FLSA), Federal Insurance Contribution Act (FICA), Federal Unemployment Tax Act (FUTA), and Internal Revenue Code.

The U.S. Supreme Court has determined that there is no rule or test that can determine the status of an individual as an independent contractor under the FLSA. The Internal Revenue Service has provided some guidance as to its method of determining the independent contractor's status; however, in virtually all circumstances the totality of the circumstances is evaluated and significant weight is provided to the following categories:

- The nature of the relationship of the services provided to the principal's business.
- The permanency of the relationship.
- The amount of individual investment in facilities and equipment.
- The opportunities for profit and loss.
- The degree of independent business organization and operations.
- The degree of independent initiative or judgment.

Although this area can be a "gray" area for many EMS organizations, a simple test can assist in making this determination. If the answer is "yes" to any of the following, the individual is most probably an employee rather than an independent contractor:

- Does your company set the individual's work hours?
- Does your company mandate the ways of doing the job or methods by which the task is to be implemented?
- Does your company pay the individual by the hour?
- Does your company supply the tools, materials, and work area?
- Does your company supply the telephone, secretarial services, and work space?
- Does your company establish set geographical limits on the individual?

EMS organizations are advised to exercise extreme caution in the area of independent contractors. If the individual's status is in question, assistance should be sought from your legal counsel. Additionally, there are governmental publications available from the U.S. Department of Labor and the Internal Revenue Service, which can provide additional guidance at no cost.

EMPLOYEES' CONSTITUTIONAL RIGHTS AND OTHER LEGAL CONCERNS

EMS organizations should be aware of the growing trend in the laws and the court decisions governing the area of privacy rights for employees. EMS organizations should exercise extreme caution in the development of policies and procedures that may affect an employee's constitutional rights and/or rights guaranteed under federal, state, or local laws.

GROOMING AND DRESS

Many EMS organizations possess dress requirements for safety purposes and/or image purposes that are specified to employees and normally are a condition of employment. For example, many organizations require a suit and tie and some may require safety shoes. If the company policy requires specific items of clothing for safety reasons, the company is normally responsible for the cost of acquiring and providing for it.

The areas of hair length and the wearing of jewelry are often controversial. EMS organizations often establish policies for safety reasons to minimize the exposure of longer hair to machinery and to minimize exposure of jewelry, which could be caught in machinery or affect products. However, EMS organizations should be extremely cautious in this area given the potential religious significance, ethnic considerations, or other significance of the hair length or jewelry.

OFF DUTY ACTIVITIES

Although many EMS organizations do not directly address off-duty activities in policies and procedures, EMS organizations should be aware that policies may indirectly affect an individual's rights in this area. An example is company policies addressing an employee's right to assess a political party or run for political office. Additionally, many organizational policies address the issue of felony or misdemeanor arrests by employees. For example, many companies will terminate an employee who is arrested and convicted of a felony offense. Again, EMS organizations should exercise extreme caution and ensure compliance with all federal, state, and local laws.

SENIORITY AND PROMOTION

EMS organizations must be extremely sensitive to the numerous laws, including but not limited to Americans with Disabilities Act (ADA), Age

Discrimination in Employment Act (ADEA), and Title VII of the Civil Rights Act, which may directly or indirectly affect the issues of seniority and promotion within the organization. Careful evaluation and analysis of all seniority and promotion systems are advisable to ensure that the policy does not overtly or covertly discriminate against potential candidates.

DISABILITY

EMS organizations are advised to ensure compliance with the Americans with Disabilities Act, the Rehabilitation Act, and possible state disability or handicap laws. (Please refer to Chapter 3—Americans with Disabilities Act).

FREEDOM OF EXPRESSION

Can an EMS organization prohibit an employee from discussing or speaking on a particular topic? EMS organizations should be extremely sensitive as to any policies or procedures that may limit or prohibit any type of expression by employees especially outside of the workplace. The freedom of expression is a constitutionally guaranteed right that has been the subject of a number of lawsuits by employees who have been prohibited and/or disciplined by organizations for expressing this freedom.

HARASSMENT

EMS organizations should be knowledgeable as to the various requirements of Title VII of the Civil Rights Act, the Americans with Disabilities Act, and the Age Discrimination in Employment Act as well as the applicable correlating state and local laws.

GARNISHMENTS/BANKRUPTCIES

Although the private financial situation of employees is normally an individual issue, EMS organizations should be aware that they can easily be drawn into this kind of legal situation through a court-ordered garnishment and/or bankruptcy by the employee. EMS organizations should be extremely cautious and acquire the necessary legal guidance in these unique areas.

EMPLOYEE CREDIT REPORTS

As with the garnishment and bankruptcy issue noted above, some EMS organizations evaluate employees personal financial history through the acquisition of credit reports and other personal financial information. EMS organizations should be extremely cautious in this area and be aware that there have been a number of laws enacted as well as currently being proposed to protect employee credit reports.

FAIR LABOR STANDARDS ACT (FLSA)

EMS organizations should be aware of the documents that may be required to ensure compliance with the Fair Labor Standards Act in correlating state requirements. These may include, but are not limited to, the required wage and hour posting, information requested by the Department of Labor, and other documents.

FAMILY MEDICAL LEAVE ACT (FMLA)

EMS organizations should be aware that specific company documentation may be required about any request for such unpaid leave (see Chapter 4 for additional details).

PRODUCT SAFETY

Although normally not a direct responsibility of the EMS organization, product safety has become a major issue and EMS organizations can be drawn into expensive litigation as the result of using a product. EMS organizations should be aware of the governmental regulations governing this area and of the necessary documentation to be provided for governmental agencies such as the Food and Drug Administration, United States Department of Agricultural, federal and state consumer protection divisions, and other agencies.

CULTURAL DIVERSITY

Many EMS organizations have now established cultural diversity training programs and other programs to sensitize the employees to various cultural and ethnic differences. EMS organizations should tailor any type of cultural diversity training programs to their work force and ensure that the training itself is not discriminatory. Cultural diversity training can include, but is not limited to, the following:

- Gender

- Racial stereotypes

- Intercultural conceptions

- Attitudes toward differences

- Impacts of bias

IMMIGRATION

EMS organizations should be aware of the new laws recently enacted in the area of immigration. EMS organizations are now required to sign immigration and naturalization service Form I-9 certifying that they have examined the required documents and that the individual is either a citizen of the United States or an alien authorized to work in the United States. EMS organizations are now required to retain the I-9 Forms for a period of at least 3 years and may not dispose of the forms until a minimum of 1 year after the individual's termination of employment.

EMS organizations should be aware that they are now responsible for asking every job applicant for documents verifying that they are either a U.S. citizen or an alien authorized to work in this country. The EMS organization fulfills its responsibilities if the documents are examined and each document "reasonably appears, on its face, to be genuine." The new law does not require the EMS organization to verify the authenticity of these documents.

EMS organizations should be aware that the employer may be subject to civil penalties of $100 to $1,000 each time the employer fails to verify the status of a job applicant. Additionally, EMS organizations may not simply refuse to hire individuals who appear to be foreigners and may be subject to discrimination on the basis of national origin under the Civil Rights Act of 1964.

In summary, the management of the human assets within the EMS organization possesses the greatest potential risk of litigation. The EMS organization must take care to ensure compliance with all applicable laws and maintenance of the necessary documentation to provide "proof" of compliance in any inspection or litigation.

In the not so distant past, litigation against an EMS organization was virtually unheard of within our system. Today, EMS organizations, like fire and police departments, are another "deep pocket" subject to potential legal risk on many fronts. Preparation and anticipation, as well as compliance, are vital in protecting the assets of the EMS organization.

CHAPTER 3

Disabled Employees and the ADA

Ideas won't keep: something must be done about them.
—Alfred North Whitehead

Hands have not tears to flow.
—Dylan Thomas

The Americans with Disabilities Act of 1990 (known as the "ADA") has opened a huge new area of regulatory compliance that will directly or indirectly affect most emergency medical service organizations. In a nutshell, the ADA prohibits discrimination against qualified individuals with physical or mental disabilities in all employment settings. Given the impact of the ADA on the job functions of employees, especially in the areas of workers' compensation, restricted duty programs, facility modifications, and other areas, it is critical for EMS managers to possess a firm grasp of the scope and requirements of this new law.

From most estimates, the Americans with Disabilities Act has afforded protection to approximately 43 to 45 million individuals or, in other terms, approximately one in five Americans. In terms of the effect on the American workplace, the estimates of protected individuals when compared to the number of individuals currently employed in the American workplace (approximately 200 million) provides that employers can expect that approximately one in four individuals currently employed or potential employees could be afforded protection under the ADA.

SUMMARY OF ADA PROVISIONS

Structurally, the ADA is divided into five titles, and all titles possess the potential of substantially impacting EMS professionals in covered public or private sector organizations. Title I contains the employment provisions that protect all individuals with disabilities who are in the United States, regardless of national origin and immigration status. Title II prohibits discrimination against qualified individuals with disabilities and prohibits the excludon of qualified individuals with disabilities from the services, programs,

31

or activities provided by public entities. Title II contains the transportation provisions of the Act. Title III, entitled "Public Accommodations," requires that goods, services, privileges, advantages, and facilities of any public place be offered "in the most integrated setting appropriate to the needs of the individual."[1]

Title III additionally covers transportation offered by private entities. It addresses telecommunications. Title IV requires that telephone companies provide telecommunication relay services and that television public service announcements produced or funded with federal money include closed captions. Title V includes the miscellaneous provisions. This title noted that the ADA does not limit or invalidate other federal and state laws providing equal or greater protection for the rights of individuals with disabilities and it addresses related insurance, alternate dispute, and congressional coverage issues.

Title I of the ADA went into effect for all employers and industries engaged in interstate commerce with 25 or more employees on July 26, 1992. On July 26, 1994, the ADA became effective for all employers with 15 or more employees.[2] *Title II*, applies to public services such as emergency services and fire departments,[3] and *Title III*, requiring public accommodations and services operated by private entities, became effective on January 26, 1992,[4] except for specific subsections of *Title II* that went into effect immediately on July 26, 1990.[5] A telecommunication relay service required by *Title IV* was required to be available by July 26, 1993.[6]

TITLE I

Title I prohibits covered employers from discriminating against a "qualified individual with a disability" with regard to job applications, hiring, advancement, discharge, compensation, training, and other terms, conditions, and privileges of employment.[7]

> Section 101(8) defines a "qualified individual with a disability" as any person who, with or without reasonable accommodation, can perform the essential functions of the employment position that such individual holds or desires . . . consideration shall be given to the employer's judgement as to what functions of a job are essential, and if an employer has prepared a written description before advertising or interviewing applicants for the job, this description shall be considered evidence of the essential function of the job.[8]

The Equal Employment Opportunity Commission (EEOC) provides additional clarification as to this definition in stating "an individual with a disability who satisfies the requisite skill, experience and educational requirements of the employment position such individual holds or desires, and who, with or without reasonable accommodation, can perform the essential functions of such position."[9]

Congress did not provide a specific list of disabilities covered under the ADA because "of the difficulty of ensuring the comprehensiveness of such a list."[10] Under the ADA, an individual has a disability if he/she possesses:

A. a physical or mental impairment that substantially limits one or more of the major life activities of such individual,

B. a record of such an impairment, or

C. is regarded as having such an impairment.[11]

For an individual to be considered "disabled" under the ADA, the physical or mental impairment must limit one or more "major life activities." Under the U.S. Justice Department's regulations issued for Section 504 of the Rehabilitation Act, "major life activities" is defined as "functions such as caring for one's self, performing manual tasks, walking, seeing, hearing, speaking, breathing, learning and working."[12] Congress clearly intended to have the term "disability" construed broadly. However, this definition includes neither simple physical characteristics, nor limitations based on environmental, cultural, or economic disadvantages.[13]

Prudent EMS organizations should also be aware that at this writing, the United States Supreme Court is reviewing several cases that may change the definition of the disabled under the ADA. When the United States Supreme Court renders its decision, it is highly recommended that EMS organizations acquire and review the decision closely.

The second prong of this definition is "a record of such an impairment disability." The Senate Report and the House Judiciary Committee Report each stated:

> This provision is included in the definition in part to protect individuals who have recovered from a physical or mental impairment which previously limited them in a major life activity. Discrimination on the basis of such a past impairment would be prohibited under this legislation. Frequently occurring examples of the first group (i.e., those who have a history of an impairment) are people with histories of mental or emotional illness, heart disease or cancer; examples of the second group (i.e., those who have been misclassified as having an impairment) are people who have been misclassified as mentally retarded.[14]

The third prong of the statutory definition of a disability extends coverage to individuals who are "being regarded as having a disability." The ADA has adopted the same "regarded as" test used for Section 504 of the Rehabilitation Act:

> "Is regarded as having an impairment" means (A) has a physical or mental impairment that does not substantially limit major life activities but is treated . . . as constituting such a limitation; (B) has a physical or mental impairment that substantially limits major life

activities only as a result of the attitudes of others toward such impairment; (C) has none of the impairments defined (in the impairment
paragraph of the Department of Justice regulations) but is treated . . .
as having such an impairment.[15]

Under the EEOC's regulations, this third prong covers three classes of
individuals:

• Persons who have physical or mental impairments that do not limit
a major life activity but who are nevertheless perceived by covered entities
(employers, places of public accommodation) as having such limitations (for
example, an employee with controlled high blood pressure who is not, in
fact, substantially limited, is reassigned to less strenuous work because of
his employer's unsubstantiated fear that the individual will suffer a heart
attack if he continues to perform strenuous work. Such a person would be
"regarded" as disabled).[16]
• Persons who have physical or mental impairments that substantially
limit a major life activity only because of a perception that the impairment
causes such a limitation (for example, an employee has a condition that
periodically causes an involuntary jerk of the head, but no limitations on his
major life activities. If his employer discriminates against him because of
the negative reaction of customers, the employer would be regarding him as
disabled and acting on the basis of that perceived disability).[17]
• Persons who do not have a physical or mental impairment but are
treated as having a substantially limiting impairment (for example, a company discharges an employee based on a rumor that the employee is HIV
positive. Even though the rumor is totally false and the employee has no
impairment, the company would nevertheless be in violation of the ADA).[18]

Thus, a "qualified individual with a disability" under the ADA is any
individual who can perform the essential or vital functions of a particular job
with or without the employer accommodating the particular disability. The
employer is provided the opportunity to determine the "essential functions"
of the particular job before offering the position through the development
of a written job description. This written job description will be considered
evidence to which functions of the particular job are essential and which
are peripheral. In deciding the "essential functions" of a particular position,
the EEOC will consider the employer's judgment, whether the written job
description was developed prior to advertising or beginning the interview
process, the amount of time spent on performing the job, the past and
current experience of the individual to be hired, relevant collective bargaining
agreements, and other factors.[19]
The EEOC defines the term "essential function" of a job as meaning "primary job duties that are intrinsic to the employment position the individual holds or desires" and precludes any marginal or peripheral functions
that may be incidental to the primary job function."[20] The factors provided by the EEOC in evaluating the "essential functions" of a particular job

include the reason the position exists, the number of employees available, and the degree of specialization required to perform the job.[21] This determination is especially important to managers who may be required to develop the written job descriptions or may be required to determine the "essential functions" of a given position.

Of particular concern to EMS personnel is the treatment of the disabled individual, who, as a matter of fact or due to prejudice, is believed to be a direct threat to the safety and health of others in the workplace. To address this issue, the ADA provides that any individual who poses a *direct threat* to the health and safety of others that cannot be eliminated by reasonable accommodation may be disqualified from the particular job.[22] The term "direct threat" to others is defined by the EEOC as meaning "a significant risk of substantial harm to the health and safety of the individual or others that cannot be eliminated by reasonable accommodation."[23] The determining factors that managers should consider in making this determination include the duration of the risk, the nature and severity of the potential harm, and the likelihood the potential harm will occur.[24]

> Additionally, managers should consider the EEOC's Interpretive Guidelines which state: "[If] an individual poses a direct threat as a result of a disability, the employer must determine whether a reasonable accommodation would either eliminate the risk or reduce it to an acceptable level. If no accommodation exists that would either eliminate the risk or reduce the risk, the employer may refuse to hire an applicant or may discharge an employee who poses a direct threat."[25]

EMS organizations should note that Title I additionally provides that if an employer does not make reasonable accommodation for the *known* limitations of a qualified individual with disabilities, it is considered to be discrimination. Only if the employer can prove that providing the accommodation would place an undue hardship on the operation of the employer's business can discrimination be disproved.

Section 101 (9) defines a "reasonable accommodation" as:

a. "making existing facilities used by employees readily accessible to and usable by the qualified individual with a disability" and includes:

b. job restriction, part-time or modified work schedules, reassignment to a vacant position, acquisition or modification of equipment or devices, appropriate adjustments or modification of examinations, training materials, or policies, the provisions of qualified readers or interpreters and other similar accommodations for . . . the qualified individual with a disability (QID).[26]

The EEOC further defines "reasonable accommodation" as:

1. "Any modification or adjustment to a job application process that enables a qualified individual with a disability to be considered for the position such

qualified individual with a disability desires, and which will not impose an undue hardship on the . . . business; or

2. Any modification or adjustment to the work environment, or to the manner or circumstances which the position held or desired is customarily performed, that enables the qualified individual with a disability to perform the essential functions of that position and which will not impose an undue hardship on the . . . business; or

3. Any modification or adjustment that enables the qualified individual with a disability to enjoy the same benefits and privileges of employment that other employees enjoy and does not impose an undue hardship on the . . . business.[27]"

In essence, the covered employer is required to make "reasonable accommodations" for any and all known physical or mental limitations of the qualified individual with a disability unless the employer can demonstrate that the accommodations would impose an "undue hardship" on the business or the particular disability directly affects the safety and health of the qualified individual with a disability or others. Included under this section is the prohibition against the use of qualification standards, employment tests, and other selection criteria that tend to screen out individuals with disabilities, unless the employer can demonstrate the procedure is directly related to the job function. In addition to the modifications to facilities, work schedules, equipment, and training programs, employers are instructed to initiate an "informal interactive (communication) process" with the qualified individual to promote voluntary disclosure of specific limitations and restrictions by the qualified individual to enable the employer to make appropriate accommodations to compensate for the limitation.[28]

Job restructuring within the meaning of Section 101(9)(B) means modifying a job such that a disabled individual can perform its essential functions. This does not mean, however, that the essential functions themselves must be modified.[29] Examples of job restructuring may include:

• eliminating nonessential elements of the job,

• redelegating assignments,

• exchanging assignments with another employee,

• redesigning procedures for task accomplishment, and

• modifying the means of communication that are used on the job.[30]

Section 101 (10)(a) defines "undue hardship" as "an action requiring significant difficulty or expense," when considered in light of the following factors:

1. nature and cost of the accommodation,

2. the overall financial resources and work force of the facility involved,

3. the overall financial resources, number of employees, and structure of the parent entity, and

4. the type of operation including the composition and function of the work force, the administration and fiscal relationship between the entity and the parent.[31]

Section 102 (c)(1) of the ADA provides for prohibition against discrimination through medical screening, employment inquiries, and similar scrutiny. EMS professionals should be aware that underlying this section was Congress's conclusion that information obtained from employment applications and interviews "was often used to exclude individuals with disabilities—particularly those with so-called hidden disabilities such as epilepsy, diabetes, emotional illness, heart disease, and cancer—before their ability to perform the job was even evaluated."[32]

Under Section 102(c)(2), EMS professionals should be aware that conducting preemployment physical examinations of applicants and asking prospective employees if they are qualified individuals with disabilities are prohibited. Employers are further prohibited from inquiring as to the nature or severity of the disability, even if the disability is visible or obvious. Managers should be aware that an EMS Organizational Representative may ask any candidates for transfer or promotion who have a known disability whether he or she can perform the required tasks of the new position, if the tasks are job related and consistent with business necessity. An employer is also permitted to inquire as to the applicant's ability to perform the essential job functions prior to employment. The employer should use the written job descriptions as evidence of the essential functions of the position.[33]

EMS personnel may require medical examinations only if the medical examination is specifically job related and is consistent with business necessity. Medical examinations are permitted only after the applicant with a disability has been offered the job position. The medical examination may be given before the applicant starts the particular job and the job offer may be conditioned on the results of the medical examination if all employees are subject to the medical examinations and information obtained from the medical examination is maintained in separate confidential medical files. Employers are permitted to conduct voluntary medical examinations for current employees as part on an on-going medical health program but again the medical files must be maintained separately and in a confidential manner.[34]

The ADA does not prohibit EMS personnel from making inquiries or requiring medical examinations or "fit for duty" examinations when there is a need to determine whether an employee is still able to perform the essential functions of the job or where periodic physical examinations are required by medical standards or federal, state, or local law.[35]

Of particular importance to most public and private sector professionals is the area of controlled substance testing. Under the ADA, the employer is permitted to test job applicants for alcohol and controlled substances prior to an offer of employment under Section 104 (d). The testing procedure for alcohol and illegal drug use is not considered a medical examination as defined under the ADA. Employers may additionally prohibit the use of alcohol and illegal drugs in the workplace and may require that employees not be under the influence while on the job. Employers are permitted to test for alcohol and controlled substance use by current employees in their workplace to the limits permitted by current federal and state law. The ADA requires all employers to conform to the requirements of the Drug-Free Workplace Act of 1988. Thus, EMS professionals should be aware that most existing preemployment and postemployment alcohol and controlled substance programs that are not part of the preemployment medical examination or on-going medical screening program will be permitted in their current form.[36]

Individual employees who choose to use alcohol and illegal drugs are afforded no protection under the ADA, however, employees who have successfully completed a supervised rehabilitation program and are no longer using or addicted are offered the protection of a qualified individual with a disability under the ADA.[37]

TITLE II

Title II of the ADA is designed to prohibit discrimination against disabled individuals by public entities. This title covers the provision of services, programs, activities, and employment by public entities. A public entity under Title II includes:

- a state or local government,

- any department, agency, special purpose district, or other instrumentality of a state or local government, and

- the National Railroad Passenger Corporation (Amtrak), and any commuter authority as this term is defined in Section 103(8) of the Rail Passenger Service Act.[38]

Title II of the ADA prohibits discrimination in the area of ground transportation including buses, taxis, trains, and limousines. Air transportation is excluded from the ADA but is covered under the Air Carriers Access Act.[39] Covered organizations may be affected in the purchasing or leasing of new vehicles and in other areas such as the transfer of disabled individuals to the hospital or other facilities. Title II requires covered public entities to ensure that new vehicles are accessible to and usable by the qualified individual including individuals in wheelchairs. Thus, vehicles must be equipped with lifts, ramps, wheelchair space, and other modifications unless the covered public entity can justify that such necessary equipment is unavailable despite a good faith effort to purchase or acquire this equipment. Covered organizations may want to consider alternative methods to accommodate the qualified individual such as use of an ambulance service or other alternatives.

TITLE III

Title III of the ADA builds upon the foundation established by the Architectural Barriers Act and the Rehabilitation Act. This title basically extends the prohibitions that currently exist against discrimination in a facility constructed or financed by the federal government to apply to all privately operated public accommodations. *Title III* is focused on the accommodations in public facilities including such covered entities as retail stores, law offices, medical facilities, and other public areas. This section requires that goods, services, and facilities of any public place be provided "in the most integrated setting appropriate to the needs of the (qualified individual with a disability)," except where the qualified individual with a disability may pose a direct threat to the safety and health of others that cannot be eliminated through modification of company procedures, practices, or policies. Prohibited discrimination under this section includes prejudice or bias against the qualified individual with a disability in the "full and equal enjoyment" of these services and facilities.[40]

The ADA makes it unlawful for public accommodations not to remove architectural and communication barriers from existing facilities and transportation barriers from vehicles "where such removal is readily achievable.[41] This statutory language is new and is defined as "easily accomplished and able to be carried out without much difficulty or expense,"[42] for example, moving shelves to widen an aisle, lowering shelves to permit access, etc. The ADA also requires that when a commercial facility or other public accommodation is undergoing a modification that affects the access to a primary function area, specific alterations must be made to afford accessibility to the qualified individual with a disability.

Title III also requires that "auxiliary aids and services" be provided for the qualified individual with a disability including, but not limited to, interpreters, readers, amplifiers, and other devices (not limited or specified under the ADA) to provide the qualified individual with a disability with an equal opportunity for employment, promotion, and the like.[43] Congress did, however, provide that auxiliary aids and services need not be offered to customers, clients, and other members of the public if the auxiliary aid or service creates an undue hardship on the business. Managers may want to consider alternative methods of accommodating the qualified individual with a disability. This section also addresses modification of existing facilities to provide access to the qualified individual with a disability and requires that all new facilities be readily accessible and usable by the qualified individual with a disability.

TITLE IV

Title IV requires all telephone companies to provide "telecommunications relay service" to aid the hearing- and speech-impaired qualified individual with a disability. The Federal Communication Commission issued a regulation requiring implementation of this requirement by July 26, 1992, and has established guidelines for compliance. This section also requires that all public service programming and announcements funded with Federal monies be equipped with closed caption for the hearing impaired.[44]

TITLE V

Title V ensures that the ADA does not limit or invalidate other federal or state laws that provide equal or greater protection for the rights of individuals with disabilities. A unique feature of *Title V* is the miscellaneous provisions and the requirement of compliance to the ADA by all members of Congress and all federal agencies. Additionally, Congress required all state and local governments to comply with the ADA and permitted the same remedies against the state and local governments as apply to any other organizations.[45]

Congress expressed its concern that sexual preferences could be perceived as a protected characteristic under the ADA or the courts could expand ADA's coverage beyond Congress's intent. Accordingly, Congress included Section 511(b), which contains an expansive list of conditions that are not to be considered within the ADA's definition of disability. This list includes transvestites, homosexuals, and bisexuals. Additionally, the conditions of transsexualism, pedophilia, exhibitionism, voyeurism, gender identity disorders not resulting from physical impairment, and other sexual behavior disorders are not considered as a qualified disability under the ADA. Compulsive gambling, kleptomania, pyromania, and psychoactive substance use disorders due to current illegal drug use are also not afforded protection under the ADA.[46]

EMS professionals should be aware that individuals extended protection under this section of the ADA include all individuals associated with or having a relationship to the qualified individual with a disability. This inclusion is unlimited in nature, including family members, individuals living together, and an unspecified number of others.[47] The ADA extends coverage to all "individuals"; thus the protection is provided to all individuals, legal or illegal, documented or undocumented, living within the boundaries of the United States regardless of their status.[48] Under Section 102(b)(4), unlawful discrimination includes "excluding or otherwise denying equal jobs or benefits to a qualified individual because of the known disability of the individual with whom the qualified individual is known to have a relationship or association."[49] Thus, the protection afforded under this section is not limited to family relationships; there appear to be no limits on the kinds of relationships or association afforded protection. Of particular note is the inclusion of unmarried partners of persons with AIDS or other qualified disabilities under this section.[50]

As with the OSH Act, the ADA requires that employers post notices of the pertinent provisions of the ADA in an accessible format in a conspicuous location within the employer's facilities. Prudent EMS professionals may wish to provide additional notification on their job applications and other pertinent documents.[51]

Under the ADA, it is unlawful for an employer to "discriminate on the basis of disability against a qualified individual with a disability" in all areas including:

1. recruitment, advertising, and job application procedures;

2. hiring, upgrading, promotion, award of tenure, demotion, transfer, layoff, termination, right to return from layoff, and rehiring;

3. rate of pay or other forms of compensation and changes in compensation;

4. job assignments, job classifications, organization structures, position descriptions, lines of progression, and seniority lists;

5. leaves of absence, sick leave, or other leaves;

6. fringe benefits available by virtue of employment, whether or not administered by the employer;

7. selection and financial support for training including apprenticeships, professional meetings, conferences, and other related activities, and selection for leave of absence to pursue training;

8. activities sponsored by the employer including social and recreational programs; and

9. any other term, condition, or privilege of employment.[52]

The EEOC has also noted that it is "unlawful . . . to participate in a contractual or other arrangement or relationship that has the effect of subjecting the covered entity's own qualified applicant or employee with a disability to discrimination." This prohibition includes referral agencies, labor unions (including collective bargaining agreements), insurance companies and others providing fringe benefits, and organizations providing training and apprenticeships.[53]

EMS professionals should note that the ADA possesses no recordkeeping requirements, has no affirmative action requirements, and does not preclude or restrict antismoking policies. Additionally, the ADA possesses no retroactivity provisions.

The ADA has the same enforcement and remedy scheme as Title VII of the Civil Rights Act of 1964 as amended by the Civil Rights Act of 1991. Compensatory and punitive damages (with upper limits) have been added as remedies in cases of intentional discrimination, and there is a correlative right to a jury trial. Unlike Title VII, there is an exception where there exists good faith effort at reasonable accommodation.[54]

The enforcement procedures adopted by the ADA mirror those of Title VII of the Civil Rights Act. A claimant under the ADA must file a claim with the EEOC within 180 days from the alleged discriminatory event or within 300 days in states with approved enforcement agencies such as the Human Rights Commission. These are commonly called dual agency states or Section 706 agencies. The EEOC has 180 days to investigate the allegation and to sue the employer or issue a right-to-sue notice to the employee. The employee will have 90 days to file a civil action from the date of this notice.[55]

The original remedies provided under the ADA included reinstatement, with or without back pay, and reasonable attorney fees and costs. The ADA also provides for protection against retaliation against the employee for filing the complaint and for others who may assist the employee in the investigation of the complaint. The ADA remedies are designed, as with the Civil Rights Act, to make the employee "whole" and to prevent future discrimination by the employer. All rights, remedies, and procedures of Section 505 of the Rehabilitation Act of 1973 are also incorporated into the ADA. Enforcement of the ADA is also permitted by the Attorney General or by private lawsuit. Remedies under these titles include ordered modification of a facility, and civil penalties up to $50,000 for the first violation and $100,000 for any subsequent violations. Section 505 permits reasonable attorney fees and litigation costs for the prevailing party in an ADA action but, under Section 513, Congress encourages the use of arbitration to resolve disputes arising under the ADA.[56]

With the passage of the Civil Rights Act of 1991, the remedies provided under the ADA were modified. Damages for employment discrimination, whether intentional or by a practice that has a discriminatory effect, may include hiring, reinstatement, promotion, back pay, front pay, reasonable accommodation, or other action that will make an individual "whole." Payment of attorneys' fees, expert witness fees, and court courts were still permitted and jury trials were allowed.

Compensatory and punitive damages were also made available where intentional discrimination is found. Damages may be available to compensate for actual monetary losses, for future monetary losses, and for mental anguish and inconvenience. Punitive damages are also available if an employer acted with malice or reckless indifference. The total amount of punitive damages and compensatory damages for future monetary loss and emotional injury for each individual is limited, based upon the size of the employer.

Number of Employees	Damages Will Not Exceed
15–100	$50,000
101–200	100,000
201–500	200,000
500 or more	300,000

Punitive damages are *NOT* available against state or local governments.

In situations involving reasonable accommodation, compensatory or punitive damages may not be awarded if the employer can demonstrate that "good faith" efforts were made to accommodate the individual with a disability.

EMS professionals should be aware that the Internal Revenue Code may provide tax credits and/or tax deductions for expenditures incurred in achieving compliance with the ADA. Programs like the Small Business Tax Credit and Targeted Job Tax Credit may be available upon request by the qualified employers. Additionally, expenses incurred in achieving compliance may be considered a deductible expense or capital expenditure permitting depreciation over a number of years under the Internal Revenue Code.

TITLE I—EMPLOYMENT PROVISIONS

The two threshold questions often asked by EMS professionals are whether my organizations must comply with the ADA and who is a protected individual under the ADA. These are vitally important questions that must be addressed by managers in order to ascertain whether compliance is mandated and, if so, whether current employees, job applicants, and others who may directly affect the operation are within the protective scope of the ADA.

QUESTIONS ABOUT ADA—TITLE I

QUESTION 1: WHO MUST COMPLY WITH TITLE I OF THE ADA?

Title I covers all private sector employers that affect commerce; state, local, and territorial governments; employment agencies; labor unions; and joint labor-management committees that fall within the scope of a "covered entity" under the ADA.[57] Additionally, Congress and its agencies are covered but they are permitted to enforce the ADA through internal administrative procedures.[58] The Federal government, government-owned corporations, Indian tribes, and tax-exempt private membership clubs (other than labor organizations who are exempt under Section 501(c) of the Internal Revenue Code) are excluded from coverage under the ADA.[59]

Covered employers cannot discriminate against qualified applicants and employees on the basis of disability. Congress provided a time period to enable employers to achieve compliance with Title I. Coverage for Title I is phased in two steps according to the number of employees in order to allow additional time for smaller employers.

Number of Employees	Effective Date
25 or more employees	July 26, 1992
15 or more employees	July 26, 1994

State and local governments, regardless of size, are covered by employment nondiscrimination requirements under Title II of the ADA and must have complied by January 26, 1992. Certain individuals appointed by elected officials of state and local governments are covered by the same special enforcement procedures as were established for Congress.

Similar to the coverage requirements under Title VII of the Civil Rights Act of 1964, an "employer" is defined to include persons who are agents of the employer such as safety and health managers, supervisors, personnel managers, and others who act for the employer. Thus, the corporation or legal entity that is the employer is responsible for the acts and omissions of their managerial employees and other agents who may violate the provisions of the ADA.

In calculating the number of employees for compliance purposes, employers should include part-time employees who have worked for them for 20 or more calendar weeks in the current or preceding calendar year. The definition of "employees" also includes U.S. citizens working outside of the United States for U.S.-based corporations. However, the ADA provides an exemption from coverage for any compliance action that would violate the law of a foreign country in which the actual workplace is located.

Employers should be aware that the ADA is worded to afford protection against discrimination to "individuals" rather than "citizens" or "Americans." There is no distinction made under the ADA between individuals with disabilities who are illegal or undocumented versus U.S. citizens. ADA protection does not require an individual to possess a permanent resident alien card (known as a "green card"). According to the Judiciary Committee "[a]s in other civil rights laws . . . the ADA should not be interpreted to mean that only American citizens are entitled to the protection afforded by the Act."[60]

It should be noted that religious organizations are covered by the ADA but such religious organizations may provide employment preference to individuals of their own religion or religious organizations.

The second threshold question after an employer has ascertained that his or her organization or company is a "covered" entity required to comply with the ADA is which individuals are qualified for protection under Title I and how do you identify these protected individuals? This question can be answered by asking the following questions:

- Who is protected by Title I?

- What constitutes a disability?

- Is the individual specifically excluded from protection under the ADA?

QUESTION 2: WHO IS PROTECTED BY TITLE I?

The ADA prohibits employment discrimination against "qualified individuals with disabilities" in such areas as job applications, hiring, testing, job assignments, evaluations, disciplinary actions, medical examinations, layoff/recall, discharge, compensation, leave, promotion, advancement, compensation, benefits, training, social activities, and other terms, conditions, and privileges of employment. A qualified individual with a disability is defined as:

> an individual with a disability who meets the skill, experience, education, and other job-related requirements of a position held or desired, and who, with or without reasonable accommodation, can

perform the essential functions of a job.[61] Additionally, unlawful discriminationm under the ADA includes: "excluding or otherwise denying equal jobs or benefits to a qualified individual because of the known disability of an individual with whom the qualified individual is known to have a relationship or association."

This clause is designed to protect individuals who possess no disability themselves but who may be discriminated against because of their association or relationship to a disabled person. The protection afforded under this clause is not limited to family members or relatives but extends in an apparently unlimited fashion to all associations and relationships. However, in an employment setting, if an employee is hired and then violates the employer's attendance policy, the ADA will not protect the individual from appropriate disciplinary action. The employer owes no accommodation duty to a individual who is not disabled.

QUESTION 3: WHAT CONSTITUTES A DISABILITY?

Section 3(2) of the ADA provides a three-prong definition to ascertain who is and is not afforded protection. A person with a disability is an individuals who:

Test 1—has a physical or mental impairment that substantially limits one or more of his or her major life activities,

Test 2—has a record of such an impairment, or

Test 3—is regarded as having such an impairment.

This definition is comparable to the definition of "handicap" under the Rehabilitation Act of 1973. Congress adopted this terminology in an attempt to use the most current acceptable terminology but intended that the relevant case law developed under the Rehabilitation Act be applicable to the definition of "disability" under the ADA.[62] It should be noted, however, that the definition and regulations applying to "disability" under the ADA are more favorable to the disabled individual than the "handicap" regulations under the Rehabilitation Act.

The first prong of this definition includes three major subparts that further define who is a protected individual under the ADA. These subparts, namely (1) a physical or mental impairment; (2) that substantially limits; (3) one or more of his or her major life activities, provide additional clarification as to the definition of a "disability" under the ADA.

A Physical or Mental Impairment

The ADA does not specifically list all covered entities. Congress noted that:

it is not possible to include in the legislation a list of all the specific conditions, diseases or infections that would constitute physical or mental impairments because of the difficulty in ensuring the comprehensiveness of such a list, particularly in light of the fact that new disorders may develop in the future.[63]

A "physical impairment" is defined by the ADA as:

[a]ny physiological disorder, or condition, cosmetic disfigurement, or anatomical loss affecting one or more of the following body systems: neurological, musculoskeletal, special sense organs, respiratory (including speech organs), cardiovascular, reproductive, digestive, genital-urinary, hemic and lymphatic, skin, and endocrine.[64]

A "mental impairment" is defined by the ADA as:

[a]ny mental or psychological disorder, such as mental retardation, organic brain syndrome, emotional or mental illness, and specific learning disabilities.[65]

A person's impairment is determined without regard to any medication or assisting devices that the individual may use. For example, an individual with epilepsy who uses medication to control the seizures or a person with an artificial leg would be considered to have an impairment even if the medicine or prosthesis reduced the impact of the impairment.

The legislative history is clear that an individual with AIDS or HIV is protected by the ADA.[66] A contagious disease such as tuberculosis would also constitute an impairment; however, the employer would not have to hire or retain a person with a contagious disease that poses a direct threat to the health and safety of others, if reasonable accommodation could reduce or eliminate this threat. This is discussed in detail later in this section.

The physiological or mental impairment must be permanent in nature. Pregnancy is considered temporary and thus is not afforded protection under the ADA, but is protected under other federal laws. Simple physical characteristics, such as hair color, left-handedness, height, or weight within the normal range, are not considered impairments. Predisposition to a certain disease is not an impairment within this definition. Environmental, cultural, or economic disadvantages, such as lack of education or prison records, are not impairments. Similarly, personality traits such as poor judgment, quick temper, or irresponsible behavior are not impairments. Conditions such as stress and depression may or may not be considered an impairment depending on whether the condition results from a documented physiological or mental disorder.[67]

Case law under the Rehabilitation Act, applying similar language as in the ADA, has identified the following as some of the protected conditions: blindness, diabetes, cerebral palsy, learning disabilities, epilepsy, deafness, cancer, multiple sclerosis, allergies, heart conditions, high blood pressure, loss of leg, cystic fibrosis, hepatitis B, osteoarthritis, and numerous other conditions.

Substantially Limits

Congress clearly intended to have the term "disability" construed broadly but merely possessing a impairment is not sufficient for protection under the ADA. An impairment is only a "disability" under the ADA if it *substantially limits* one or more major life functions. An individual must be unable to perform or be significantly limited in performance of a basic activity that can be performed by an average person in America.

To assist in this evaluation, a three-factor test was provided to determine whether an individual's impairment substantially limits a major life activity. The test's parameters are:

• the nature and severity of the impairment,

• how long the impairment will last or is expected to last, and

• the permanent and long-term impact, or expected impact of the impairment.

The determination of whether an individual is substantially limited in a major life activity must be made on a case-by-case basis. The three-factor test should be considered because it is not the name of the impairment or condition that determines whether an individual is protected, but rather the effect of the impairment or condition on the life of the person. Some impairments such as blindness, AIDS, and deafness are by their nature substantially limiting but other impairments may be disabling for some individuals and not for others, depending on the nature of the impairment and the particular activity involved.[68]

For individuals with two or more impairments, neither of which by itself substantially limits a major life activity, the impairments may be combined together to impair one or more major life activities. Temporary conditions such as a broken leg, common cold, sprains, or strains are generally not protected because of the extent, duration, and impact of the impairment. However, such temporary conditions may evolve into a permanent condition which substantially limits a major life function if complications arise.

In general, it is not necessary to determine if an individual is substantially limited in a work activity if the individual is limited in one or more major life activities. An individual is not considered to be substantially limited in working if she or he is substantially limited in performing only a particular job or unable to perform a specialized job in a particular area. An individual may be considered substantially limited in working if the individual is restricted in his or her ability to perform either a class of jobs or a broad range of jobs in various classes when compared to an average person of similar training, skills, and abilities. Factors to be considered include:

• the type of job from which the individual has been disqualified because of the impairment;

• the geographical area in which the person may reasonably expect to find a job;

- the number and types of jobs using similar training, knowledge, skill, or abilities from which the individual is disqualified within the geographical area; and/or

- the number and types of other jobs in the area that do not involve similar training, knowledge, skill, or abilities from which the individual also is disqualified because of the impairment.[69]

In evaluating the number of jobs from which an individual might be excluded, the EEOC regulations note that it is necessary to show only the approximate number of jobs from which the individual would be excluded.

Major Life Activities

First, an impairment must substantially limit one or more major life activities to be considered a "disability" under the ADA. A major life activity is an activity that an average person can perform with little or no difficulty. Examples include:

- walking
- speaking
- breathing
- performing manual tasks
- standing
- lifting
- sitting[70]

- seeing
- hearing
- learning
- caring for oneself
- working
- reading

This list of examples is not all-inclusive. All situations should be evaluated on a case-by-case basis.

The second test of this definition of disability requires that an individual possess a record of having an impairment as specified in Test 1. Under this test, the ADA protects individuals who possess a history of, or who have been misclassified as possessing, a mental or physical impairment that substantially limits one or more major life functions. A record of impairment would include such documented items as educational, medical, or employment records. Safety and loss prevention professionals should note that merely possessing a record of being a "disabled veteran" or record of disability under another federal or state program dues not automatically qualify the individual for protection under the ADA. The individual must meet the definition under "disability" under Test 1 and possess a record of such disability under Test 2.

The third test of the definition of "disability" includes an individual who is regarded or treated as having a covered disability even though the individual does not possess a disability as defined under Tests 1 and 2. This part of the definition protects individuals who do not possess a disability that substantially limits a major life activity from the discriminatory actions of others because of their perceived disability. This protection is necessary because "society's myths and fears about disability and disease are as handicapping as are the physical limitations that flow from actual impairment."[71]

Three circumstances in which protection would be provided to the individual include:

1. when the individual possesses an impairment that is not substantially limiting but the individual is treated by the employer as having such an impairment;

2. when an individual has an impairment that is substantially limiting because of the attitude of others toward the condition; and

3. when the individual possesses no impairment but is regarded by the employer as having a substantially limiting impairment.[72]

To acquire the protection afforded under the ADA, an individual must not only have a disability but also must qualify under the above-noted tests. A "qualified individual with a disability" is defined as a person with a disability who:

> satisfies the requisite skills, experience, education and other job-related requirements of the employment position such individual holds or desires, and who, with or without reasonable accommodation, can perform the essential functions of such position.[73]

Managers should be aware that the employer is not required to hire or retain an individual who is not qualified to perform a particular job.

QUESTION 4: IS THE INDIVIDUAL SPECIFICALLY EXCLUDED FROM PROTECTION UNDER THE ADA?

The ADA specifically provides a provision that excluded certain individuals from protection. As set forth under Sections 510 and 511(a), (b), the individuals listed below are not protected.

- Individuals currently engaged in the use of illegal drugs are not protected when an employer takes action due directly to their continued use of illegal drugs. This includes use of prescription drugs illegally as well as illegal drugs. However, individuals who have undergone a qualified rehabilitation program and are not currently using drugs illegally are afforded protection under the ADA.

- Homosexuality and bisexuality are not impairments and therefore are not considered disabilities under the ADA.

- The ADA does not consider transvestism, transsexualism, pedophilia, exhibitionism, voyeurism, gender identity disorders not resulting from physical impairment, and other sexual behavior disorders as disabilities and thus these are not afforded protection.

- Other areas not afforded protection include compulsive gambling, klep-tomania, pyromania, and psychoactive substance use disorders resulting from illegal use of drugs.

A major component of Title I is the "reasonable accommodation" mandate, which requires employers to provide a disabled employee or applicant with the necessary "reasonable accommodations" that would allow the disabled individual to perform the essential functions of a particular job. EMS professionals should note that "reasonable accommodation" is a key nondiscrimination requirement in order to permit individuals with disabilities to overcome unnecessary barriers that could prevent or restrict employment opportunities.

The EEOC regulations define "reasonable accommodation" as meaning:

1. any modification or adjustment to a job application process that enables a qualified individual with a disability to be considered for the position such qualified individual with a disability desires, and which will not impose an undue hardship on the . . . business; or

2. any modification or adjustment to the work environment, or to the manner or circumstances which the position held or desired is customarily performed, that enables the qualified individual with a disability to perform the essential functions of that position and which will not impose an undue hardship on the . . . business; or

3. any modification or adjustment that enables the qualified individual with a disability to enjoy the same benefits and privileges of employment that other employees enjoy and does not impose an undue hardship on the . . . business.[74]

Section 101(9) of the ADA states that reasonable accommodation includes two components. First, there is the accessibility component, which sets forth an affirmative duty for the employer to make physical changes in the workplace so that the facility is readily accessible and usable by individuals with disabilities. This component "includes both those areas that must be accessible for the employee to perform the essential job functions, as well as nonwork areas used by the employer's employees for other purposes."[75]

The second component is modification of other related areas. The EEOC regulations set forth a number of examples of modifications that an employer must consider:

- Job restructuring

- Part-time or modified work schedules

- Reassignment to vacant position

- Appropriate adjustment or modification of examinations training materials

- Acquisition or modification of equipment or devices

- Providing qualified readers or interpreters[76]

Managers should note that the employer possesses no duty to make an accommodation for an individual who is not otherwise qualified for a position. In most circumstances, it is the obligation of the individual with a disability to request a reasonable accommodation from the employer. The individual with a disability possesses the right to refuse an accommodation, but if the individual with a disability cannot perform the essential functions of the job without the accommodation, the individual with a disability may not be qualified for the job.

An employer is not required to make a reasonable accommodation that would impose an undue hardship on the business.[77] An undue hardship is defined as an action that would require "significant difficulty or expense" in relation to the size of the employer, the employer's resources, and the nature of the operation. Although the undue hardship limitations will be analyzed on a case-by-case basis, several factors have been set forth to determine whether an accommodation would impose an undue hardship. First, if the undue hardship limitation would be unduly costly, extensive, or substantial in nature or disruptive to the operation or if the accommodation would fundamentally alter the nature or operation of the business.[78] Additionally, the ADA provides four factors to be considered in determining whether an accommodation would impose an undue hardship on a particular operation.

1. The nature and the cost of the accommodation needed

2. The overall financial resources of the facility or facilities making the accommodation, the number of employees in the facility, and the effect on expenses and resources of the facility

3. The overall financial resources, size, number of employees, and type and location of facilities of the entity covered by the ADA

4. The type of operation of the covered entity, including the structure and functions of the work force, the geographic separateness, and the administrative or fiscal relationship of the facility involved in making the accommodation to the larger entity.[79]

Other factors such as the availability of tax credits and tax deductions, the type of enterprise, and the like can also be considered when evaluating an accommodation situation for the undue hardship limitation. Managers should note that the requirements to prove undue hardship are substantial in nature and cannot easily be utilized to circumvent the purposes of the ADA.

The ADA prohibits the use of preemployment medical examinations, medical inquiries, and requests for information regarding workers' compensation claims prior to an offer of employment.[80] An employer, however, may condition a job offer (i.e., a conditional or contingent job offer) on the satisfactory results of a postoffer medical examination if the medical examination is required of all applicants or employees in the same job classification. Questions regarding other injuries and workers' compensation claims may also be asked following the offer of employment. A postoffer medical examination cannot be used to disqualify an individual with a disability who is currently able to perform the essential functions of a particular job because of speculation that the disability may cause future injury or workers' compensation claims.

Managers should note that if an individual is not employed because the medical examination revealed a disability, the reason for not hiring the qualified individual with a disability must be business related and necessary for the particular business. The burden of proving that a reasonable accommodation would not have enabled the individual with a disability to perform the essential functions of the particular job or the accommodation was unduly burdensome falls squarely on the employer.

As often revealed in the postoffer medical examination, the physician should be informed that the employer possesses the burden of proving that a qualified individual with a disability should be excluded because of the risk to the health and safety of other employees or individuals. To address this issue, Congress specifically noted that the employer may possess a job requirement that specifies "an individual not impose a direct threat to the health and safety of other individuals in the workplace."[81] A "direct threat" has been defined as meaning "a significant risk to the health and safety of others that cannot be eliminated or reduced by reasonable accommodation."[82]

Managers should be aware that the direct threat evaluation is vitally important in evaluating disabilities involving contagious diseases. The leading case in this area is *School Board of Nassau County v. Arline*.[83] This case sets forth the test to be used in evaluating a direct threat to others:

- the nature of the risk,

- the duration of the risk,

- the severity of the risk, and

- the probability the disease will be transmitted and will cause varying degrees of harm.[84]

The ADA imposes a very strict limitation on the use of information acquired through postoffer medical examination or inquiry. All medical-related information must be collected and maintained on separate forms and kept in separate files. These files must be maintained in a confidential manner with appropriate security and only designated individuals provided access. Medical-related information may be shared with appropriate first aid and safety personnel when applicable in an emergency situation. Supervisors and other managerial personnel may be informed about necessary job restrictions or job accommodations. Appropriate insurance organizations may acquire access to medical records when required for health or life insurance. State and federal officials may acquire access to medical records for compliance and other purposes.

In the area of insurance, the ADA specifies that nothing within the Act is to be construed to prohibit or restrict "an insurer, hospital, or medical service company, health maintenance organization, or any agent, or entity that administers benefit plans, or similar organization from underwriting risks, or administering such risks that are based on or not inconsistent with State laws."[85] However, an employer may not classify or segregate an individual with a disability in a manner that adversely affects not only the individual's employment but any provisions or administration of health insurance, life insurance, pension plans, or other benefits. In essence, this means that if an employer provides insurance or benefits to all employees, the employer must also provide this coverage to the individual with a disability. An employer cannot deny insurance to, or subject the individual with a disability to, different terms or conditions of insurance based upon the disability alone if the disability does not pose an increased insurance risk. An employer cannot terminate or refuse to hire an individual with a disability because the individual's disability or a family member's or dependent's disability is not covered under their current policy, or because the individual poses a future risk of increased health costs. The ADA does not, however, prohibit the use of preexisting condition clauses in insurance policies.

An employer is prohibited from shifting away the responsibilities and potential liabilities under the ADA through contractual or other arrangements. An employer may not do anything through a contractual relationship that it cannot do directly.[86] This provision applies to all contractual relationships that include insurance companies, employment and referral agencies, training organizations, agencies used for background checks, and labor unions.

Labor unions are covered by the ADA and have the same responsibilities as any other covered employer. Employers are prohibited from taking any action through a collective bargaining agreement (i.e., union contract) that it may not take directly by itself. A collective bargaining agreement may be used as evidence in a decision regarding undue hardship and in identifying the essential elements in a job description.

Although not required under the ADA, a written job description describing the "essential elements" of a particular job is the first line of defense for most ADA-related claims. A written job description that is prepared before advertising or interviewing applicants for a job will be considered as evidence of the essential elements of the job along with other relevant factors.

In order to identify the "essential elements" of a particular job and thus whether an individual with a disability is qualified to perform the job, the EEOC regulations set forth three key factors, among others, that must be considered:

- the reason the position exists to perform the function,

- the limited number of employees available to perform the function, or among whom the function can be distributed, and

- the task function is highly specialized, and the person in the position is hired for special expertise or the ability to perform the job.

TITLE II—PUBLIC SERVICES

Title II is designed to prohibit discrimination against disabled individuals by public entities. Title II covers all services, programs, activities, and employment by government or governmental units. Title II adopted all of the rights, remedies, and procedures provided under Section 505 of the Rehabilitation Act of 1973, and the undue financial burden exception is applicable.[87] The effective date for Title II was January 26, 1992.

The public entities to which Title II applies includes state or local government, any department, agency, special purpose district, or other instrumentality of a state or local government, and the National Railroad Passenger corporation (Amtrak) and any commuter authority as defined in the Rail Passenger Service Act.[88]

Title II possesses two basic purposes, namely to extend the prohibition against discrimination under the Rehabilitation Act of 1973 to state and local governments, and to clarify Section 504 of the Rehabilitation Act for public transportation entities that receive federal assistance.[89] Given these purposes, the main emphasis of Title II is directed at the public sector organizations and possesses minimal impact on the private sector organizations.

The vast majority of Title II's provisions cover transportation that is provided by public entities to the general public such as buses and trains. The major requirement under Title II mandates that public entities that purchase or lease new buses, rail cars, taxis, or other vehicles must ensure that these vehicles are accessible to and usable by qualified individuals with disabilities. This accessibility requirement includes disabled individuals who may be wheelchair-bound and requires that all vehicles be equipped with lifts, ramps, wheelchair spaces, or other special accommodations unless the public entity can prove such equipment is unavailable despite a good faith effort to locate the equipment.

Many public entities purchase used vehicles or lease vehicles due to the substantial cost of such vehicles. The public entity must make a good-faith effort to obtain vehicles that are readily accessible and usable by individuals with disabilities. As provided under the ADA, it is considered discrimination to remanufacture vehicles to extend their useful life for five years or more without making the vehicle accessible and usable by individuals with disabilities. Historical vehicles, such as the trolley cars, may be excluded if the modification to make the vehicle readily accessible and usable by individuals with disabilities alters the historical character of the vehicle.

Of particular importance to police, fire, and other emergency organizations is Title II's impact on 911 systems. Congress observed that many 911 telephone numbering systems were not directly accessible to hearing-impaired and speech-impaired individuals.[90] Congress cited as an example a deaf woman who died of a heart attack because the police organization did not respond when her husband tried to use his telephone communication device for the deaf (TDD) to call 911.[91] In response to such examples, Congress stated, "As part of its prohibition against discrimination in local and state programs and services, Title II will require local governments to ensure that these telephone emergency number systems (911) are equipped with technology that will give hearing-impaired and speech-impaired individuals a direct line to these emergency services."[92] Thus, public safety organizations must ensure compliance with this requirement no later than January 26, 1992.

Of importance for state governments and its instrumentality is the fact that Section 502 eliminates immunity of a state in state or federal court under the Eleventh Amendment for violations of the ADA. A state can be found liable in the same manner and is subject to the same remedies, including attorney fees, as a private sector covered organization.

Additionally, the claims procedures for instituting a complaint against a state or local government is significantly different than against a private covered entity. The ADA provides that a claim can be filed with any of seven federal government agencies including the EEOC and the Justice Department or EEOC may assist in such litigation. A procedure for instituting complaints against a public organization without going to court is provided in the Justice Department's regulations. The statute of limitations on filing such a claim with the designated Federal agency is 180 days from the date of the act of discrimination, unless the agency extends the time limitation for good cause. If the responsible agency finds a violation, the violation will be corrected through voluntary compliance, negotiations, or intervention by the Attorney General.

This procedure is totally voluntary. An individual may file suit in court without filing an administrative complaint, or an individual may file suit at any time while an administrative complaint is pending. No exhaustion of remedies is required.[93]

Under the Department of Justice's regulations, public entities with 50 or more employees are required to designate at least one employee to coordinate efforts to comply with Title II.[94] The public entity must also adopt grievance procedures and designate at least one employee who will be responsible for investigating any complaint filed under this grievance procedure.

TITLE III—PUBLIC ACCOMMODATIONS

Title III builds upon the foundation established by Congress under the Architectural Barriers Act and the Rehabilitation Act. Title III basically extends the prohibition against discrimination that existed for facilities constructed by or financed by the federal government to all private sector public facilities. Title III requires all goods, services, privileges, advantages, or facilities of any public place to be offered "in the most integrated setting appropriate to the needs of the [disabled] individual," except when the individual poses a direct threat the safety or health of others. Title III additionally prohibits discrimination against individuals with disabilities in the "full and equal enjoyment" of all goods, services, facilities, and the like.

Title III covers public transportation offered by private sector entities in addition to all places of public accommodation without regard to size. Congress wanted small businesses to have time to comply with this mandatory change without fear of civil action. To achieve this, Congress provided that no civil action could be brought against businesses that employ 25 or fewer employees and have annual gross receipts of $1 million or less between January 26, 1992, and July 26, 1992. Additionally, businesses with fewer than 10 employees and having gross annual receipts of $500,000 or less were provided a grace period from January 26, 1992 to January 26, 1993 to achieve compliance. Residential accommodations, religious organizations, and private clubs were made exempt from these requirements.

Title III provides twelve categories and examples of places requiring public accommodations.

- Places of lodging, such as inns, hotels, and motels, except for those establishments located in the proprietor's residence and not more than 5 rooms are for rent

- Restaurants, bars, or other establishments serving food or drink

- Motion picture houses, theaters, concert halls, stadiums, or other places of exhibition or entertainment

- Bakeries, grocery stores, clothing stores, hardware stores, shopping centers, or other sales or rental establishments

- Laundromats, dry cleaners, banks, barber shops, beauty shops, travel services, funeral parlors, gas stations, offices of accountants or lawyers, pharmacies, insurance offices, professional offices of a health care providers, hospitals, or other service establishments

- Terminal depots, or other stations used for specified public transportation

- Parks, zoos, amusement parks, or other places of entertainment

- Nurseries, elementary, secondary, undergraduate, or postgraduate private schools, or other places of education

- Day-care centers, senior citizen centers, homeless shelters, food banks, adoption agencies, or other social service center establishments

- Gymnasiums, health spas, bowling alleys, golf courses, or other places of exercise or recreation.[95]

EMS professionals should note that it is considered discriminatory under Title III for a covered entity to fail to remove structural, architectural, and communication barriers from existing facilities when the removal is "readily achievable," easily accomplished, and can be performed with little difficulty or expense. Factors to be considered include the nature and cost of the modification, the size and type of the business, and the financial resources of the business, and the like. If the removal of a barrier is not "readily achievable," the covered entity may make goods and services readily available and achievable through alternative methods to individuals with disabilities.

EMS professionals should be aware that employers may not use application or other eligibility criteria that screen out or tend to screen out individuals with disabilities unless they can prove that doing so is necessary to providing the goods or services that they provide to the public. Title III additionally makes discriminatory the failure to make reasonable accommodations in policies, business practices, and other procedures that afford access to and use of public accommodations to individuals with disabilities and employers from denying access to goods and services because of the absence of "auxiliary aids" unless the providing of such auxiliary aids would fundamentally alter the nature of the goods or services or would impose an undue hardship. The ADA defines "auxiliary aids and services" as:

A. qualified interpreters or other effective methods of making aurally delivered materials available to individuals with hearing impairments;

B. qualified readers, taped texts, or other effective methods of making visually delivered materials available to individuals with visual impairments;

C. acquisition or modification of equipment or devices; and

D. other similar services or actions.[96]

Title III does not specify the type of auxiliary aid that must be provided, but requires that individuals with disabilities be provided equal opportunity to obtain the same result as individuals without disabilities.

Title III provides an obligation to provide equal access, requires modification of policies and procedures to remove discriminatory effects, and provides an obligation to provide auxiliary aids in addition to other requirements. The safety and health exception and undue burden exception are available under Title III in addition to the "structurally impracticable" and possibly the "disproportionate cost" defenses for covered organizations.

TITLE IV—TELECOMMUNICATIONS

Title IV amends Title II of the Communication Act of 1934[97] to mandate that telephone companies provide "telecommunication relay services in their service areas by July 26, 1993." Telecommunication relay services provide individuals with speech-related disabilities the ability to communicate with hearing individuals through the use of telecommunication devices like the TDD system or other nonvoice transmission devices.

The purpose of Title IV is in large measure "to establish a seamless interstate and intrastate relay system for the use of TDD's (telecommunication devices for the deaf) that will allow a communication-impaired caller to communicate with anyone who has a telephone, anywhere in the country."[98]

Title IV contains provisions affording the disabled access to telephone and telecommunication services equal to that which the nondisabled community enjoys. In actuality, Title IV is not a new regulation but simply an effort to ensure that the general mandates of the Communication Act of 1934 are made effective. Title IV consists of two sections. Section 401 adds a new section (Section 225) to the Communication Act of 1934 and Section 402 amends Section 711 of the Communications Act.

Regulations governing the implementation of Title IV were issued by the Federal Communication Commission (FCC) in 1992. These regulations establish the minimum standards, guidelines, and other requirements mandated under Title IV in addition to establishing regulations requiring round-the-clock relay service operations, operator-maintained confidentiality of all messages, and rates for the use of the telecommunication relay systems that are equivalent to current voice communication services. Title IV additionally prohibits the use of relay systems under certain circumstances, encourages the use of state-of-the-art technology where feasible, and requires public service announcements and other television programs that are partially or fully funded by the federal government to contain closed captioning.

TITLE V—MISCELLANEOUS PROVISIONS

Title V contains a myriad of provisions addressing a wide assortment of related coverage under the ADA. First, Title V permits insurance providers to continue to underwrite insurance, to continue to use preexisting condition clauses, and to classify risks as long as consistent with state-enacted laws. Title V also permits insurance carriers to provide bona fide benefit plans based upon risk classifications but prohibits denial of health insurance coverage to an individual with a disability based solely on that person's disability.

Title V does not require special treatment in the area of health or other insurance for individuals with disabilities. An employer is permitted to offer insurance policies that limit coverage for a certain procedure or treatment even though this might have an adverse impact on the individual with a disability.[99] The employer or insurance provider may not, however, establish benefit plans as a subterfuge to evade the purposes of the ADA.[100]

Second, Title V provides that the ADA will not limit or invalidate other federal or state laws that provide equal or greater protection to individuals with disabilities. Additionally, the ADA does not preempt medical or safety standards established by federal law or regulation nor does it preempt state, county, or local public health laws. However, state and local governments and their agencies are subject to the provisions of the ADA, and courts may provide the same remedies (except for punitive damages at this time) against state or local governments as any other public or private-covered entity.

In an effort to minimize litigation, Title V promotes the use of alternate dispute resolution procedures to resolve conflicts under the ADA. As stated in Section 513, "Where appropriate and to the extent authorized by law, the use of alternate dispute resolution, including settlement negotiations, conciliation, fact-finding, mini-trials, and arbitration, is encouraged to resolve disputes under the ADA."[101] Safety and health professionals should note, however, the fact that the use of alternate dispute resolution is voluntary and, if used, the same remedies must be available as provided under the ADA.

PROGRAM DEVELOPMENT

Given the fact that many EMS professionals could be provided responsibilities in the development and management of the organization's ADA compliance program, a general outline of the key areas to be considered when developing a plan of action follows:

1. Acquire and read the entire *Americans with Disabilities Act*. Acquire and review the rules and interpretations provided by the EEOC, the Department of Labor, and the Department of Federal Contract Compliance. Acquire the Health and Human Services List of Communicable Diseases. Keep abreast with governmental publications and case law as published. It may be prudent to have the organization's counsel or designated agency representative review and identify pertinent issues.

2. Educate and prepare the organizational hierarchy. Explain in detail the requirements of the ADA and the limited perameters of the "undue hardship" and "safety or health" exceptions. Ensure complete and total understanding regarding the ADA. Communicate the philosophy and express the organization's commitment to achievement of the goals and objectives of the ADA.

3. Acquire necessary funding to make the necessary accommodations and acquire the auxiliary aids. If necessary, search for outside agency funding and assistance. Review possible tax incentives available with the appropriate department or agency.

4. Designate an individual(s) (either an employee or consultant) who is well versed on the requirements of the ADA or establish an advisor group to serve as the ADA "expert" within the organization.

5. Establish a relationship with organizations serving individuals with disabilities for recruiting, advice, or other purposes.

6. Analyze the operations and identify applicable areas, practices, policies, procedures, and the like, requiring modification. Remember to include all public areas, parking lots, access ways, and all equipment. Document this analysis in detail.

7. Develop a *written* plan of action for each required area under the ADA. Set completion dates for each phase of the compliance plan in accordance with the mandated target date.

8. Develop and publish a written organizational policy incorporating all of the provisions of the ADA.

9. Review and, where applicable, renegotiate employment agency contracts, referral contracts, and other applicable contractual arrangements. Document any and all modifications.

10. Acquire the posting information and make certain this document is appropriately posted within the facility. Develop and place notices of ADA compliance on all applications, medical reports, and other appropriate documents.

11. Develop an employee and applicant self-identification program and communication system to permit employees and applicants to identify themselves as qualified individuals with disabilities and communicate the limitations of their disability. This program should be in writing and available for review by employees.

12. Implement the Plan of Action.

13. Review and modify selection policies and procedures including, but not limited to, the following:

A. interviewing procedures

B. selection criteria

C. physical and psychological testing procedures

D. alcohol and controlled substance testing programs

E. application forms

F. medical forms

G. filing procedures

H. disability and retirement plans

I. medical examination policies and procedures

J. physical and agility testing

K. other applicable policies and procedures.

14. Develop procedures to ensure confidentiality of medical records. All new procedures or modifications should be documented.

15. Review all current job descriptions and identify the essential functions for each position. Develop a *written job description* for each and every job in the organization. Remember, the *written job description* is evidence of the "essential functions" of the jobs and the first line of defense.

16. Review and modify the personnel and medical procedures and policies. Maintain all medical files separately and confidentially. Address option of a separate entity conducting medical review.

17. Plan and complete all physical accommodations to the workplace. Remember to analyze your complete work environment and the entire surrounding areas including parking lots, access-ways, doors, water fountains, rest rooms, etc. Document all physical accommodations made to the

workplace. Provide documentation of all bids, reviews, etc. for any accommodation not made due to undue hardship.

18. Document all requests for accommodations requested by job applicants or current employees. Document the accommodation provided or, if unable to accommodate, the reason for the failure to accommodate.

19. Analyze the workplace for the need for possible "auxiliary aids" and other accommodation devices. Prepare a list of vendors and services to be able to acquire all possible "auxiliary aid" within a reasonable time. Maintain documentation of all auxiliary aids requested and provided.

20. If the health or safety exception is relied upon for employment decisions or other situations, the manager or other individual making this determination should document all reasonable accommodations explored and all other information used to make this determination.

21. If the undue hardship or burden exceptions are to be used, all financial records, work force analyses, and other information used to make this decision should be documented and secured for later viewing.

22. Educate and train *all* levels within the organizational structure. Remember, if a member of the organizational team discriminates against a qualified individual with a disability, the organization will be responsible for his or her actions. Develop an oversight mechanism to ensure compliance.

23. Develop a mechanism to encourage employees to come forward in confidence and discuss their disabilities.

24. Evaluate and analyze the employee assistance programs, restricted duty or light duty programs, and other related programs. Organizations should address and plan for such situations as permanent light duty positions in advance.

25. If necessary, enter into negotiations with any labor organizations to reopen or otherwise modify collective bargaining agreements to ensure compliance with the provisions of the ADA. Evaluate all insurance plans, retirement plans, contracts with employment agencies, or other contractual arrangements to ensure compliance with the ADA. Documentation of any agreement should be included in the written contract.

26. Develop a *written* evaluation or audit instrument in order to properly gauge compliance efforts. Designate specific individual(s) responsible for the audit and corrective actions. Establish a schedule for conducting the ADA audit.[102]

EEOC GUIDANCE ON ADA EMPLOYMENT QUESTIONS

One of the most frequently asked questions by fire and emergency service personnel who are conducting interviews as part of the selection process is, "What questions are prohibited from being asked under the Americans with Disabilities Act." The Equal Employment Opportunity Commission (known as the "EEOC"), which is the governing agency for the ADA, recently revised their directions that provide substantial guidance as to the "Dos and

Don'ts" in asking questions regarding the ADA and specifically regarding requests for reasonable accommodation. A guidance document, published in an easy to read question-and-answer format, is available at your local EEOC office. Some of the new preemployment regulatory provisions and interpretations important to fire service organizations are excerpted in the following questions:

- *May an employer ask a particular applicant to describe or demonstrate how she or he would perform the job, if other applicants are not asked to do this?*

When the employer could reasonably believe that an applicant will not be able to perform a job function because of a known disability, the employer may ask that particular job applicant to describe or demonstrate how she or he would perform the particular function. An applicant's disability would be a "known disability" either because it is obvious (for example, the applicant uses a wheelchair), or because the applicant has voluntarily disclosed that he or she has a hidden disability.

- *May an employer ask applicants about their arrest or conviction records?*

Yes. Questions about an applicant's arrest or conviction records are not likely to elicit information about disability because there are many reasons unrelated to disability why someone may have an arrest or conviction record.

- *May an employer ask applicants about their certifications and licenses?*

Yes. An employer may ask an applicant at the preoffer stage whether he or she has certifications or licenses required for any job duties. An employer also may ask an applicant whether she or he intends to get a particular job-related certification or license, or why he or she does not have the certification or license. These questions are not likely to elicit information about the applicant's disability because there may be a number of reasons unrelated to disability why someone does not have—or does not intend to get—a certification or license.

- *May an employer ask whether an applicant can meet the employer's attendance requirements?*

Yes. An employer may state its attendance requirements and ask whether an applicant can meet them. An employer also may ask about an applicant's prior attendance record. (For example: How many days the applicant was absent from her or his last job.) An employer may also ask questions designed to detect whether an applicant abused his or her leave because these questions are not likely to elicit information about the disability. (For example: How many Mondays or Fridays were you absent last year on leave other than approved vacation leave?)

However, at the preoffer stage, an employer may *not* ask how many days an applicant was sick, because these questions relate directly to the severity of the individual's impairment. Therefore, these questions are likely to elicit information about a disability.

- *May an employer ask applicants about their workers' compensation history?*

No. An employer may *not* ask applicants about their job-related injuries or workers' compensation history. These questions relate directly to the severity of the applicant's impairment. Therefore, these questions are likely to elicit information about the disability.

- *May an employer ask applicants about their current* illegal *use of drugs?*

Yes. An employer may ask applicants about current illegal use of drugs because an individual who is currently illegally using drugs is *not* protected under the ADA (when the employer acts on the basis of the drug use).

- *May an employer ask applicants about their* lawful *drug use?*

No, if the question is likely to elicit information about the disability. Employers should know that many questions about current or prior lawful drug use are likely to elicit information about the disability, and are therefore impermissible at the preoffer stage. (For example, questions like "What medications are your currently taking? and "Have you ever taken AZT?" certainly elicit information about whether an applicant has a disability.)

- *May an employer require applicants to take physical agility tests?*

Yes. A physical agility test, in which an applicant demonstrates the ability to perform actual or simulated job tasks, is *not* a medical examination under the ADA.

- *May an employer require applicants to take physical fitness tests?*

Yes. A physical fitness test, in which an applicant's performance of physical tasks—such as running or lifting—is measured, is *not* a medical examination under ADA.

- *May an employer give psychological examinations to applicants?*

Yes, unless the particular examination is medical. This determination would be based on some of the factors listed above, such as the purpose of the test and the intent of the employer in giving the test. Psychological examinations are medical if they provide evidence that would lead to identifying a mental disorder or impairment (for example, those listed in the American Psychiatric Association's most recent *Diagnostic and Statistical Manual of Mental Disorders*).[103]

These are but a few of the important clarifications regarding the questions that can be asked at the preoffer, normally the interview, stage of the hiring process. As prudent fire service organizations you should acquire this information and all other information regarding this important aspect of the hiring and selection process and ensure that your procedures comply with this guidance. Prudent fire and emergency service organizations should also update their hiring and selection processes and procedures on at least an annual basis in order to be able to modify or adjust the procedures to comply with this changing area of the law. Remember: Ignorance of the law is never a good defense!

CHAPTER 4

Family and Medical Leave Act and EMS

Twenty thousand years ago the family was the social unit. Now the social unit has become the world, in which it may truthfully be said that each person's welfare affects that of every other.

—Arthur H. Compton

The thing that impresses me most about America is the way parents obey their children.

—Duke of Windsor

The Family and Medical Leave Act (known as the FMLA) often causes confusion for many EMS professionals with responsibilities for personnel issues. The FMLA is relatively new being enacted by Congress on February 3, 1993. The fundamental purpose of the FMLA was to balance the demands of the workplace with the needs of employees to deal with certain medical necessities (including maternity-related matters) and compelling family matters by providing a minimum employment standard for unpaid leave, and the right of the employee to reinstatement to their former position or an equivalent position at the conclusion of the qualified leave.

It is imperative that EMS professionals responsible for personnel issues possess a working knowledge of this new and important law. To assist in the acquisition of this requisite knowledge base, below is a synopsis prepared by the Department of Labor addressing the various requirements and often asked questions regarding the FMLA.

Family and Medical Leave Act of 1993*
(29 USC § 2601 et seq; 29 CFR 825)

WHO IS COVERED

The family and Medical Leave Act (FMLA) is intended to provide a means for employees to balance their work and family responsibilities by

*U.S. Department of Labor, as printed in *Small Business Handbook: Wage, Hour and Other Workplace Standards*, 1994, Department of Labor, Washington, DC.

taking unpaid leave for certain reasons. The Act is intended to promote both the stability and economic security of families, and the national interests in preserving family integrity. The FMLA is applicable to any employer in the private sector who is engaged in commerce or in any industry or activity affecting commerce, and who has 50 or more employees each working day during at least 20 calendar weeks or more in the current or preceding calendar year.

All public agencies (state and local government) and local education agencies (schools) are covered. These employers do not need to meet the 50 employee test. Most federal employees are covered by Title II of FMLA and are subject to regulations issued by the **Office of Personnel Management**.

In order to be "eligible" for FMLA leave, an employee must be employed by a covered employer and work at a worksite within 75 miles of which that employer employs at least 50 employees; must have worked at least 12 months (which do not have to be consecutive) for the employer; and, must have worked at least 1,250 hours during the 12 months immediately preceding the date of commencement of FMLA leave.

BASIC PROVISIONS/REQUIREMENTS

The FMLA provides an entitlement of up to 12 weeks of job-protected, unpaid leave during any 12 months for the following reasons:

- Birth and care of the employee's child or placement for adoption or foster care of a child with the employee;

- To care for an immediate family member (spouse, child, parent) who has a serious health condition; or

- For the employee's own serious health condition.

An employer must maintain group health benefits that an employee was receiving at the time leave began during periods of FMLA leave at the same level and in the same manner as if the employee had continued to work. Under most circumstances, an employee may elect or the employer may require the use of any accrued paid leave (vacation, sick, personal, etc.) for periods of unpaid FMLA leave. FMLA leave may be taken in blocks of time less than the full 12 weeks on an intermittent or reduced leave basis. Taking intermittent leave for the placement for adoption, or foster care of a child is subject to approval by the employer. Intermittent leave taken for the birth and care of a child is also subject to the employer's approval except for leave relating to the pregnancy which would be leave for a serious health condition.

When leave is foreseeable, an employee must provide the employer with at least 30 days notice of the need for leave or as much notice as is practicable. If the leave is not foreseeable, then notice must be given as soon as practicable. An employer may require medical certification of a serious health condition from the employee's health care provider, and may require periodic reports during the period of leave of the employee's status and intent to return to work, as well as "fitness-for-duty" certification upon return to work in appropriate situations.

When the employee returns from FMLA leave, the employee is entitled to be restored to the same or an equivalent job. An equivalent job is one with equivalent pay, benefits, responsibilities, etc. The employee is not entitled to accrue benefits during periods of unpaid FMLA leave, but must be returned to employment with the same benefits at the same levels as existed when leave commenced.

Employers are required to **post a notice** for employees that outlines the basic provisions of FMLA and are subject to a civil money penalty for willfully failing to post such notice. Employers are prohibited from discriminating against or interfering with employees who take FMLA leave.

ASSISTANCE AVAILABLE

FMLA is administered by the Employment Standards Administration's **Wage and Hour Division**. More detailed information, including copies of **explanatory brochures**, may be obtained by contacting the local **Wage and Hour offices**. In addition, Wage and Hour has developed the **Family and Medical leave Act**.

Advisor(http://www.dol.gov/elaws/), which is an Internet online system that answers a variety of commonly asked questions about FMLA including employee eligibility, valid reasons for leave, employee/employer notification responsibilities, and employee rights/benefits.

PENALTIES

Employees or any person may file complaints with the Employment Standards Administration, U.S. Department of Labor (usually through the nearest office of the Wage and Hour Division). The Secretary may file suit to insure compliance and recover damages if a complaint cannot be resolved administratively. Employees also have private rights of action without involvement of the Department to correct violations and recover damages through the courts.

RELATION TO STATE, LOCAL, AND OTHER FEDERAL LAWS

A number of States have family leave statutes. Nothing in the FMLA supersedes a provision of State law that is more beneficial to the employee, and employers must comply with the more beneficial provision. Under some circumstances, an employee with a disability may also have rights under the Americans with Disabilities Act (enforced by the **U.S. Equal Employment Opportunity Commission**).

DOL Home Page	OASP Home Page	Table of Contents	Overview
U.S. Department of Labor			

As can be seen from the above synopsis provided by the United States Department of Labor, most EMS organizations are required to provide FMLA leave to eligible employees. In theory, this does not appear to present a major problem for most EMS organizations; however, as a practical matter, FMLA leave requests have caused many conflicts between EMS organizations and individual EMS professionals.

It is important that EMS organizations be familiar with the requirements of the FMLA and the requirements for eligibility for an FMLA leave. When an individual requests an FMLA leave of absence, the first step in any assessment should be to ensure that the individual is eligible under the requirements of the FMLA, namely, to specify the reason for the leave, the number of hours worked, and so on.

EMS organizations should also be aware of the posting requirement and should be aware that additional information can be acquired at www.dol.gov and the United States Department of Labor offers a free advisory service for employers and individuals located at www.elaws.gov. An exceptional guide for EMS personnel in this area is the FMLA Supervisor's Guidelines below.

In summation, most FMLA leave requests can be effectively and efficiently managed by EMS organizations if the EMS professionals know this regulation and work with the requesting employee. However, when an EMS organization is unaware of and ignores this new law, substantial conflicts can result that usually result in legal actions. EMS organizations should be prepared for additional modifications and expansion of this family-oriented law in the near future.

Family and Medical Leave Supervisor's Guidelines

The FMLA imposes significant supervisory responsibilities in addition to the other daily responsibilities for answering requests for leave in an almost limitless number of circumstances. Supervisors are the front line in preserving management's right to provide only as much leave as is required by law.

Each supervisor is responsible for indicating to the employee, within two business days of learning about the nature of an employee's leave, whether this particular leave request is going to "count" as FMLA leave. In addition, the supervisor must provide a written "seven point notice" detailing the specifics of the leave. A template of the typical "seven point notice" is included in this instructional bulletin. Representative listings of what constitutes a "serious health condition" and what does not under certain circumstances represent a serious health condition are also provided for supervisory guidance. Please note that these lists are not inclusive or exclusive, but are merely general guides for supervisors so that they may be able to focus on the potential areas of FMLA leave designation.

Examples of Serious Health Conditions:	Conditions generally excluded from Serious Health Conditions (unless complications occur):
• heart conditions requiring bypass surgery • pregnancy • most types of cancers • miscarriage • back conditions requiring therapy or surgery • complications related to pregnancy • (e.g., severe morning sickness) • pneumonia • recovery from childbirth • emphysema • asthma • severe arthritis • diabetes • severe nervous disorders • epilepsy • injuries caused by serious accidents • (on or off the job) • migraines • long-term chronic conditions such as Alzheimer's or other diseases in terminal stage • kidney disease	• common cold • headaches (other than migraines) • flu • routine dental or orthodontia problems • earaches • stress • minor ulcers • absence due to substance abuse (as opposed to treatment for substance abuse)

"Think FMLA" under These Circumstances

You should use the following guidelines to determine whether an absence possibly can be attributed to a serious health condition. Any of the following should immediately cause you to "think FMLA" and start the clock running on appropriately designating leave:

• Employee or family member is hospitalized.

• Employee is absent more than 3 consecutive days (or the day before and after a weekend).

• Employee is pregnant.

- Employee or family member has a chronic serious illness (asthma, diabetes, etc.) or illness that requires multiple treatments (cancer, kidney disease, etc.)

The following checklist will help in determining the presence of a serious health condition:

❑ Does the condition involve inpatient care?
  an overnight stay in a hospital, or
  any period of incapacity of subsequent treatment in connection with an overnight stay?

If the condition involves inpatient care, it qualifies as a serious health condition protected by the FMLA.

❑ Does the condition involve continuing treatment?
  incapacity lasting more than 3 consecutive calendar days and that involves one of the following:
    2 or more treatments by or under the supervision, order, or referral of a health care provider;
    or
    1 treatment by a health care provider followed by a regimen of continuing treatment (e.g., prescription medications or therapy with specialized equipment, but not over-the-counter medications, bed-rest, fluid intake, or exercise).

NOTE: in the absence of complications, this does not include the common cold, the flu, earaches, upset stomach, minor ulcers, headaches other than migraine, routine dental or orthodontia problems, and periodontal disease.

❑ Does the condition involve pregnancy or prenatal care?
  incapacity due to pregnancy or for prenatal care?

❑ Is the condition chronic?
  incapacity or treatment for a chronic serious health condition that:
    requires periodic visits for treatment by or under the direct supervision of a health care provider; and
    continues over an extended period (including recurring episodes); and may be episodic (e.g., asthma, diabetes, epilepsy).

❑ Is the condition permanent or long-term?
  permanent or long-term incapacity for which treatment may be ineffective and which requires the supervision of, but not necessarily treatment by, a health care provider (e.g., Alzheimer's, severe stroke, terminal stages of disease).

❑ Does the condition require multiple treatments?
  absence to receive multiple treatments by or under the supervision, orders, or referral of a health care provider for one of the following:
    restorative surgery after an accident or injury;

or

a condition that is likely to result in incapacity of more than 3 consecutive calendar days without medical intervention or treatment (e.g., cancer, severe arthritis, kidney disease).

❑ Is this a period of recovery?

any period of recovery relating to the above treatments.

FMLA Employee Notification

1. The leave you have requested

   ❑ will

   ❑ will not

   be counted against your annual FMLA leave entitlement.

2. If this leave concerns a serious health condition, you are required to furnish medical certification (the certification form is included with this notice). Failure to produce such certification will result in denial of designation of this leave as Family and Medical Leave.

3. The following chart explains your leave-taking options for this period of Family and Medical Leave:

May use Sick Leave:	Must use Sick Leave:
birth of a child (only for the period of disability) another's illness	employee's illness
May use Vacation Leave:	**May use Leave Without Pay:**
birth of a child adoption another's illness employee's illness	birth of a child adoption another's illness employee's illness

4. Any share of health premiums which you paid before this leave must continue to be paid by you during this leave period. If your premium payment is more than 30 days late, the hospital is no longer obligated to maintain coverage, and will provide 15 days notice that coverage will cease.

5. If this leave request concerns a serious health condition, you will be required to produce a "fitness for duty" certification, signed by the

same health care provider who certified your serious health condition, before you will be allowed to return to work.

6. Upon reinstatement from FMLA Leave, you will be given the same or an equivalent job back.

7. If you do not return to work after this FMLA Leave, you will be liable for repayment of all health insurance premiums which were paid for you when you were on leave.

Family and Medical Leave Action Request

_____ SS#: _____
First Name   MI   Last Name

Dept#:_____ Dept Name:_____

Hrs/Week:_____

Explanation for Request for Family and Medical Leave:

   ❐ Birth of child   ❐ Care for child, spouse, or parent
   ❐ Care for child after birth   with serious health condition
   ❐ Adoption; Foster Care   ❐ Personal health condition

Start date:_____   Expected date of return to work:_____

How many hours/minutes of the following types of leave will be used during the family/medical leave period?

Vacation_____ Sick_____ Leave Without Pay_____

_____ Tele #:_____ Date:_____
Employee signature

_____ Tele #:_____ Date:_____
Immediate Supervisor signature

_____ Tele #:_____ Date:_____
Department Head or Designee signature

_____ Tele #:_____ Date:_____
Division Director or Designee signature

_____ Tele #:_____ Date:_____
Benefits Representative signature

Parking Arrangements Made?: ❐ Yes   ❐ No
_____

"SERIOUS HEALTH CONDITION" DEFINITION:
A Serious Health Condition means an illness, injury, impairment, or physical or mental condition that involves one of the following:

1. Hospital Care
Inpatient care (i.e., an overnight stay) in a hospital, hospice, or residential medical care facility, including any period of incapacity (see definition below) or subsequent treatment in connection with or consequent to such inpatient care.

2. Absence Plus Treatment
A period of incapacity of more than 3 consecutive calendar days (including any subsequent treatment or period of incapacity relating to the same condition), that also involves:

a. Treatment (see definition below) two or more times by a health care provider, by a nurse or physician's assistant under direct supervision of a health care provider, or by a provider of health care services (e.g., physical therapist) under order of, or on referral by, a health care provider, or

b. Treatment by a health care provider on at least one occasion which results in a regimen (see definition below) of continuing treatment under the supervision of the health care provider.

3. Pregnancy
Any period of incapacity due to pregnancy or for prenatal care.

4. Chronic Conditions Requiring Treatments
A chronic condition which:

a. requires periodic visits for treatment by a health care provider, or by a nurse or physician's assistant under direct supervision of a health care provider;

b. continues over an extended period of time (including recurring episodes of a single underlying condition); and

c. may cause episodic rather than a continuing period of incapacity (e.g., asthma, diabetes, epilepsy, etc.).

5. Permanent/Long-term Conditions Requiring Supervision
A period of incapacity which is permanent or long-term due to a condition for which treatment may not be effective. The employee or family member must be under the continuing supervision of, but need not be receiving active treatment by, a health care provider (e.g., Alzheimer's, a severe stroke, etc.).

6. Multiple Treatments (Non-Chronic Conditions)
Any period of absence to receive multiple treatments (including any period of recovery therefrom) by a health care provider or by a provider of health care services under orders of, or on referral by, a health care provider, either for restorative surgery after an accident or other injury, or for a condition that would likely result in a period of incapacity of more than 3 consecutive calendar days in the absence of medical intervention or treatment, such as cancer (chemotherapy, radiation, etc.), severe arthritis (physical therapy), or kidney disease (dialysis).

Certification of Health Care Provider

Family and Medical Leave Act of 1993—Federal Form WH-380

1. Employee's Name:

2. Patient's Name (if different from employee):

3. Above is a definition of what is meant by a "serious health condition" under the Family and Medical Leave Act. Does the patient's condition qualify under any of the categories described? If so, please check the applicable category.
   1. ❏   2. ❏   3. ❏   4. ❏   5. ❏   6. ❏   None of the above ❏

4. Describe the medical facts which support your certification, including a brief statement as to how the medical facts meet the criteria of one of these categories:

5. a. State the approximate date the condition commenced, and the probable duration of the condition (and also the probable duration of the patient's incapacity if different):

   b. Will it be necessary for the employee to work only inter-mittently or to work on less than a full schedule as a result of the condition (including the treatment described in Item 6 below)? Yes ❏   No ❏
   If Yes, give the probable duration:

   c. If the condition is a chronic condition (condition #4) or pregnancy, state whether the patient is presently incapaci-tated and the likely duration and frequency of episodes of incapacity:

6. a. If additional treatments will be required for the condition, provide an estimate of the probable number of such treat-ments.

If the patient will be absent from work or other daily activities because of treatment on an intermittent or part-time basis, also provide an estimate of the probable number and interval between such treatments, actual or estimated dates of treatment (if known), and period required for recovery, if any:

b. If any of these treatments will be provided by another provider of health services (e.g., physical therapist), please state the nature of the treatments:

c. If a regimen of continuing treatment by the patient is required under your supervision, provide a general description of such a regimen (e.g., prescription drugs, physical therapy requiring special equipment):

7. a. If medical leave is required for the employee's absence from work because of the employee's own condition (including absences due to pregnancy or a chronic condition), is the employee unable to perform work of any kind?
Yes ❏   No ❏

b. If able to perform some work, is the employee unable to perform any one or more of the essential functions of his or her job (the employee or employer will provide you with information about essential job functions)? Yes ❏   No ❏   If Yes, please list the essential function the employee is unable to perform:

c. If neither 7a nor 7b applies, is it necessary for the employee to be absent from work for treatment?

8. a. If leave is required to care for a family member of the employee with a serious health condition, does the patient require assistance or basic medical or personal needs or safety, or for transportation? Yes ❏   No ❏

b. If No, would the employee's presence to provide psychological comfort be beneficial to the patient or assist in the patient's recovery? Yes ☐   No ☐

c. If the patient will need care only intermittently or on a part-time basis, please indicate the probable duration of this need:

_____

Signature of Health Care Provider   Type of practice

_____

Address   Telephone #

To be completed by the employee needing family leave to care for a family member:
State the care you will provide and an estimate of the period during which care will be provided, including a schedule if leave is to be taken intermittently, or if it will be necessary for you to work less than a full schedule:

_____

Employee signature   Date

POLICY DEFINITIONS:
Incapacity:
For the purposes of the FMLA, means the inability to work, attend school, or perform any other regular daily activities due to a serious health condition, treatment therefor, or recovery therefrom.
Treatment:
Includes examinations to determine if a serious health condition exists and evaluations of the condition. Treatment does not include routine physical examinations, eye examinations, or dental examinations.
Conditions:
Information sought relates only to the condition for which the employee is taking FMLA leave.
Regimen:
A regimen of continuing treatment includes, for example, a course of prescribed medication (e.g., an antibiotic) or therapy requiring special equipment to resolve or alleviate the health condition. A regimen of treatment does not include the taking of over-the-counter medications such as aspirin, antihistamines, or salves; or bed-rest, drinking fluids, exercise, and other similar activities that can be initiated without a visit to a health care provider.

June MANUEL

v.

WESTLAKE POLYMERS CORPORATION.[*]

Civ. A. No. 94-0691.

United States District Court,
W.D. Louisiana,
Lake Charles Division.

Nov. 30, 1994.

Scott D. Wilson, Baton Rouge, LA, for plaintiff.

Robert E. Landry, Scofield Gerard Veron Hoskins & Singletary,
Lake Charles, LA, for defendant.

MEMORANDUM RULING

EDWIN F. HUNTER, Jr., Senior District Judge.

*1 June Manuel was fired by her employer, Westlake Polymers Corporation ("Westlake Polymers"), on February 7, 1994, for her continued failure to abide by the company's absenteeism policy. Shortly thereafter, on April 14, 1994, Manuel filed suit in federal court alleging that one of her leave periods (October 8-November 29, 1993) counted by the company as a step in its "no fault" absenteeism policy, was in fact due to "a serious medical condition", and thus protected under the Family and Medical Leave Act ("FMLA" or "the Act"). 29 U.S.C. § 2601, et seq. Both parties assert that there are no material issues of fact in dispute, and have each submitted respective motions for summary judgment, which are now pending. For reasons assigned below, Westlake Polymers' motion for summary judgment is GRANTED.

Background

Westlake Polymers hired Manuel as an operator in July, 1986. [FN1] Manuel exhibited a history of missing work days while employed at Westlake Polymers. In 1987, she missed 17 work days due to personal problems; in 1988—49 work days; in 1989 she only missed 4 days; in 1990 plaintiff missed 30 work days; in 1991—25 work

---

[*]U.S. Department of Labor, as printed in *Small Business Handbook: Wage, Hour and Other Workplace Standards*, 1994, Department of Labor, Washington, DC.

days. In 1992, Westlake Polymers established an absentee control program. The program was a "no fault" policy in which every absence, regardless of cause, was counted. [FN2] During 1992–93, Manuel periodically continued to miss work, and received several notices and/or counseling sessions regarding her continued absenteeism. [FN3]

On October 6, 1993, plaintiff sought treatment at the Southern Emergency Center in Lake Charles for an ingrown toenail which had troubled her. The treating physician, Dr. Robbins, advised Manuel that it was necessary to remove her toenail, and if the procedure were performed on Friday, October 8, she would be free to return to work the following Monday. Manuel contacted her supervisor, Sheldon Cooley, who gave her permission to take off work Friday, the 8th, for the procedure. However, Manuel was unable to return to work on Monday, due to infection and swelling of her toe. At that time, she contacted her supervisor and informed him of her inability to return to work. Plaintiff did not resume employment until November 30, 1993, the day after Westlake Polymers' physician examined Manuel and pronounced her fit for work.

After plaintiffs October/November, 1993, leave of absence, she was notified by Westlake Polymers that she had reached step three of the company's absentee control program. A final warning/suspension letter for unsatisfactory attendance was issued to plaintiff, together with a four day suspension. Also, her emergency vacation privileges were revoked. Approximately two months later in January, 1994, plaintiff missed three days of work due to the flu. [FN4] She attempted to secure permission from her supervisors for the absence, but it was denied. Shortly thereafter on February 7, 1994, plaintiffs employment with Westlake Polymers was terminated as a result of her chronic absenteeism.

Summary Judgment Principles

*2 Summary judgment is appropriate if the record discloses "that there is no genuine issue of material fact and that the moving party is entitled to judgment as a matter of law." Fed. R. Civ. P. 56(c). A party seeking summary judgment bears the initial burden of identifying those portions of the pleadings and discovery filed, together with any affidavits, which it believes demonstrate the absence of a genuine issue of material fact. Celotex Corp. v. Catrett, 477 U.S. 317, 325 (1986). Once the movant carries its burden, the burden shifts to the nonmovant to show that summary judgment should not be granted. Id. at 324–325. While we must "review the facts drawing all inferences most favorable to the party opposing the motion," Reid v. State Farm Mut. Auto Ins. Co., 784 F.2d 577, 578 (5th Cir. 1986), that

party may not rest upon mere allegations or denials in its pleadings, but must set forth specific facts showing the existence of a genuine issue for trial. Anderson v. Liberty Lobby, Inc., 477 U.S. 242, 256–57, (1986)
Rosado v. Deters, 5 F 3d 119, 122 (5th Cir. 1993).

Discussion

June Manuel contends that the counting of her October/November, 1993, absence as an additional step in Westlake Polymers' absentee control program violated provisions of the FMLA. On August 5, 1993, the Family and Medical Leave Act went into effect. [FN5] The FMLA provides affected employees with 12 work weeks of unpaid leave during any 12 month period for the birth of a child, the care of a relative, or as in this case, a serious health condition which prevents the employee from performing her job duties. 29 U.S.C. § 2612(a)(1). There is no question that the parties, herein, qualify as an "eligible employee" and an "employer" as defined under the Act. [FN6]

The dispute in this case centers around notice. The Act provides that when an employee, or immediate family member, suffers from a serious medical condition, requiring foreseeable, planned medical treatment, the employee,

shall provide the employer with not less than 30 days notice, before the date the leave is to begin, of the employee's intention to take leave under such subparagraph, except that if the date of the treatment requires leave to begin in less than 30 days, the employee shall provide such notice as is practical.
29 U.S.C. § 2612(e)(2)(B).

It is undisputed that plaintiff notified her supervisor of the need to miss work on October 8, 1993, due to her infected toe. Also, on Monday, October 11, plaintiff called Westlake Polymers and told them she would not be able to go into work since her toe was badly swollen, and she was on crutches. Plaintiffs ingrown toenail and infection were not foreseeable 30 days in advance. It is also evident that Manuel informed her employer when she became aware that she was going to miss some work days due to the infected toe. However, at no time did Manuel ever request or otherwise intimate to Westlake Polymers that she was taking FMLA leave. [FN7] This leads to the narrow question posited: must an employee specifically invoke the FMLA, or otherwise attempt to refer to the Act, when she takes leave due to an unforeseen, yet not patently obvious, serious medical condition?

*3 When a serious medical condition is foreseeable, the worker must inform her employer of her intention to exercise leave "under such subparagraph". 29 U.S.C. § 2612 (e)(2)(B). When a serious medical condition leave is unforeseeable, (as in this case) the employee shall provide such notice, "as is practicable". Id.

As authorized by Congress, [FN8] the Department of Labor implemented extensive regulations shoring up some of the gaps and ambiguities inherent in the FMLA. As customary, the regulations are posed in the form of questions, followed by a detailed series of responses. In this instance, separate sections focus upon foreseeable leave, and unforeseeable leave, respectively. The foreseeable leave section states that,

> An employee shall provide at least verbal notice sufficient to make the employer aware that the employee needs FMLA-qualifying leave, and the anticipated time and duration of the leave. The employee need not express certain rights under the FMLA or even mention the FMLA, but may only state that leave is needed for an expected birth or adoption, for example. The employer should inquire further of the employee if it is necessary to have more information about whether FMLA leave is being sought by the employee, and obtain the necessary details of the leave to be taken. In the case of medical conditions, the employer may find it necessary to inquire further to determine if the leave is because of a serious health condition and may request medical certification to support the need for such leave. (see § 825.305).

29 C.F.R. § 825.302(b).

Somewhat differently, "when the need for leave or its approximate time, is not foreseeable, an employee should give notice to the employer of the need for the FMLA leave as soon as practicable under the facts and circumstances of the particular case ..." 29 C.F.R. § 825.303(a). The language in § 825.303 raises the possibility that an employee is required to inform the employer of the "need for FMLA leave". [FN9]

In any event, we find that leave due to complications with an ingrown toenail does not constitute sufficient notice to apprise an employer of an employee's need to use FMLA-qualifying leave. 29 C.F.R. § 825.302(b). Plaintiff did not have an obviously serious injury, such as a broken leg, cancer, or heart attack, which would trigger an employer inquiry into whether the employee intended to use FMLA leave.

Moreover, the injury in this case was unforeseeable, and Westlake Polymers received no advance notice that Manuel would not return to work as scheduled on Monday, October 11. Under this extremely short notice period (i.e. the same morning leave commenced), and when the serious medical condition alleged is not the type which would normally require an employer to inquire whether FMLA leave is needed, it is not inconvenient nor unduly burdensome to require an employee in some manner to refer, or attempt to refer, to the Act. Manuel did not do so.

*4 Manuel claims that she was precluded from specifically referencing or alluding to the FMLA, since she was unaware of the Act, other than having heard on the news that Congress was considering its passage. The Act requires an employer to keep posted in conspicuous places at the work site pertinent provisions of the FMLA. 29 U.S.C. § 2619. The regulations enacted by the Department of Labor require that the employee have actual notice of the FMLA notice requirements if FMLA leave is to be impacted. 29 C.F.R. § 825.304(c). However, employees are deemed to have actual notice if the employer properly posted required provisions of the FMLA at the work site. Id. The uncontradicted evidence fully supports a finding that Westlake Polymers placed a notice detailing pertinent provisions of the FMLA in a locked bulletin board frequented by employees, including June Manuel.

In a separate section, the regulations require an employer to describe the FMLA entitlements and employee obligations in an employee handbook, if one exists. 29 C.F.R. § 825.301. [FN10] We can discern the purpose and intent of § 825.301(a) by looking to its related subparts. Sections 825.301(b) and (c) require an employer, who does not have a handbook to make available written notice of the FMLA provisions whenever an employee invokes the FMLA's protection. These sections indicate that the employer should provide supplementary FMLA information to an inquiring employee. This supports a finding that an employee handbook is not intended to be a source of primary notice, merely a secondary resource which fleshes out the details of the Act. This interpretation of § 825.301 leads to a consistent application of § 825.304, which provides that actual notice is satisfied with proper posting of the notice at the work site. Moreover, this is all that Congress required. 29 U.S.C. § 2619.

What are the consequences of plaintiffs failure to provide notice of her need for FMLA leave? When the leave is foreseeable, an employer may deny the onset of FMLA leave until 30 days after notice is eventually provided by the employee. 29 C.F.R. § 825.304(b). No statute or regulation directly addresses the effect of an employee's failure to give notice for an unforeseen injury. However, a consistent interpretation of 29 C.F.R. § 825.304(b) would excuse an employer from providing FMLA leave for an unforeseeable injury until such time as the employee makes her employer aware of her need for FMLA leave. [FN11] No such notice was provided in this case.

Plaintiffs failure to inform her employer of her need for FMLA leave precludes relief under the enforcement sections of the Act. Manuel's motion for summary judgment is DENIED. Westlake Polymers' motion for summary judgment is GRANTED. [FN12]

JUDGMENT

In accordance with today's memorandum ruling, it is ORDERED, ADJUDGED, and DECREED, that judgment be, and it hereby entered in favor of defendant, WESTLAKE POLYMERS CORPORATION, and against plaintiff, JUNE MANUEL, dismissing, with prejudice, plaintiffs claims against said defendant arising under the Family and Medical Leave Act. Plaintiff's remaining state law claims against said defendant, if any, are dismissed, without prejudice. The case is closed.

*5 THUS DONE AND SIGNED in Chambers at Lake Charles, on this 30th day of November, 1994.

FN1. She worked as an at-will employee until her termination.

FN2. The program imposed a four-step disciplinary system: the first violation resulted in an oral reprimand; the second transgression warranted a warning letter; step three drew a one-week suspension and a final warning; and the last step resulted in the employee's termination.

FN3. Manuel received notices and/or counseling sessions on February 12, July 13, September 8, and December 30, 1992, and April 13, 1993.

FN4. Plaintiffs three day absence from work does not constitute a serious medical condition cognizable under the FMLA. See, 29 C.F.R. § 825.114 (must miss at least four days of work or seek inpatient care to qualify).

FN5. The FMLA did not go into effect until February 5, 1994, for companies which had collective bargaining agreements with their employees. There is no evidence that Westlake Polymers negotiated a collective bargaining agreement with its employees. Consequently, the August 5, 1993, effective date for the FMLA governs in this instance.

FN6. An "eligible employee" must have been employed by the same employer for at least 12 months prior to the leave, and performed at least 1250 hours of service with that employer during the previous 12 month period. 29 U.S.C. § 2611(2)(A). An "employer" is defined as any person "engaged in commerce or in any industry or activity affecting commerce who employs 50 or more employees for each working day during each of 20 or more calendar work weeks in the current or preceding calendar year," 29 U.S.C. § 2611(4)(A)(i).

FN7. In fact, Manuel never referenced, mentioned, or otherwise hinted at exercising FMLA leave until she filed the instant suit against Westlake Polymers.

FN8. 29 U.S.C. § 2654.

FN9. We note that this is only one possible interpretation of that section. The drafters may merely have intended to qualify the noun, leave, as opposed to injecting a substantive requirement that the employee refer to the FMLA.

FN10. Westlake Polymers did have an employee handbook, but it did not address the FMLA.

FN11. Any other conclusion is untenable. To permit a plaintiff to maintain an enforcement action under the FMLA when she has not provided her employer with notice, would render meaningless the notice requirements.

FN12. We decline to exercise supplemental jurisdiction over plaintiff state law claims, if any. 28 U.S.C. § 1367; Rhyne v. Henderson County, 973 F.2d 386, 395 (5th Cir. 1992)(dismissed of state law claims is proper after district court has dismissed original jurisdiction claims). Plaintiff's state law claims are dismissed, without prejudice.

CHAPTER 5

Wage and Hour Issues

Even Noah got no salary for the first six months—partly on account of the weather and partly because he was learning navigation.

—Mark Twain

Of course, it is not the employer who pays wages. He only handles the money. It is the product that pays wages and it is management that arranges the production so that the product may pay the wages.

—Henry Ford

Why does your EMS personnel show up to work every day? Is it only the love of the job or is there more? Would your qualified personnel leave your organization if they were offered a salary increase in the private sector of 10 percent? 50 percent? 100 percent? Would your qualified personnel leave your organization if another organization offered them a better medical benefits package? How about stock options? Better job security? How can you keep your most valuable assets from abandoning your EMS organization?

The proper management of what and how your employees are paid as well as their fringe benefits is one, if not "the," most important issue for many EMS organizations. The loss of qualified personnel represents not only the loss of your organization's monetary investment and possibly a loss in productivity and quality, but also represents the loss of the individual's expertise, technical knowledge, and individual efficacy.

In today's workplace, the cost of selecting, hiring, and training qualified EMS personnel can involve an investment of thousands of dollars for the EMS organization. When a qualified individual leaves the organization either voluntarily or involuntarily, the investment the EMS organization has made in the qualified individual goes out the door with the employee.

Additionally, the labor market today is extremely tight. In many places in the country, unemployment is extremely low and thus the pool of potential employment candidates is exceptionally shallow. In many areas, the specific technical expertise required to perform the job cannot be acquired from the employment pool of candidates, thus driving the cost of labor higher and increasing the investment by the organization in the employee's training, relocation, salary, benefits, and so on.

WHAT IS AN EMS JOB WORTH?

What a job is worth depends on whose perspective you are analyzing. From the employer's perspective, the marketplace determines the wage, or the relative value or specific education or expertise of the individual can determine the wage. From the employee's perspective, the wage is determined by both monetary and nonmonetary factors and the working condition and wage must equalize for the employee to remain with the company (i.e., poor working conditions require a higher wage to maintain the employee versus a lower wage but better working conditions). Additional factors to consider include:

Employer's Perspective

- Cost of labor usually determined by supply and demand
- More expertise required results in higher costs
- Labor is one of the main costs of producing the product or providing a service
- Employer is in business to make a profit or provide a service
- Governmental requirements govern labor issues
- Labor must be productive and qualified
- Need return on labor investment to the company or community
- Control of the workplace

Employee's Perspective

- Appropriate return for labor investment
- Good working conditions
- Job security
- Benefits
- Time to enjoy fruits of labor
- Peripherial issues, i.e., child care, elder care, transportation, etc.
- Quality of life

WAGE AND SALARY ADMINISTRATION

Many EMS organization go to a great deal of effort and expense to design and implement strategic plans for the future. Especially important is the growing need to obtain and retain quality employees. As the cost of recruitment rises and a fully qualified work force decreases in many sectors, an effective wage and salary plan is critical.

For many years, compensation plans were very rigid and inflexible. Most classes of employees were analyzed and treated identically and significant compensation growth generally occurred only when someone moved up the corporate ladder.

Today, flexibility and creativity are critical. Recruiting top performers and retaining quality employees require organization to rethink compensation programs and the needs and wants of a more educated work force. In addition, many employees today want flexibility in time management. In some cases, employees desire a trade-off between flexibility in hours worked and their compensation packages.

PREPARING A SALARY PROGRAM TO FIT YOUR EMS ORGANIZATION

When reviewing your EMS organization's compensation program, consider the following organizational issues:

- What are your business objectives and long-range plans? Are they in writing?

- Is accountability figured into your program? Managers and executives should be held accountable and their compensation package should reflect this philosophy.

- Is your organizational design structured in a way that allows management to carry out its business objectives in an orderly manner?

- Are various employee groups assigned to an organization unit and evaluated together?

- Is your organizational structure as simple as it can be and still well managed? (This will keep the number of compensation components to a minimum and allow your compensation review and package to be kept workable while keeping costs down.)

- Are the number of levels of authority kept to a minimum?

- Have you reviewed expected growth and recruiting needs?

- Are your position titles accurate and kept to a minimum?

- Have you performed exit interviews to determine whether your compensation package was a major cause and effect of turnover? If your compensation package is inadequate, "former" employees will be more than happy to let you know.

HOW TO ADMINISTER AN EFFECTIVE COMPENSATION PROGRAM

In today's highly volatile labor market (volatile in the sense that people are less likely to stay with the same company for their entire careers) competitive compensation packages are a key factor in recruitment and retention of quality employees. If your compensation package is competitive, it will allow you to:

- Hire qualified people. The salary a job pays and the perks attached to a position are probably the most important elements in an applicant's decision to take a job.

- Retain a full staff. The salary a job pays is one of the most important elements in keeping people. People will usually stay with a company if they are paid competitively.

- Motivate your people. A good pay system, coupled with a performance appraisal program, will motivate people. Again, the merit increase must be competitive in your industry and location, and it must be earned. Some companies are going to unscheduled pay increases in order to emphasize that the raise is in recognition of good performance.

- Experience lower turnover. If pay is perceived as being too low and noncompetitive, unless the company is in an area of high unemployment, the employee will most likely quit or, at the very least, will be demotivated and less productive.

It's important to have a flexible and timely orientation to salary administration. Designing a salary program that fits your organization needs today is fine, but you can't walk off smugly and think that the same program will be effective in six months or one year. There's a new work ethic, and organizations today find it tougher to attract and retain a highly technical, professional work force. Even during periods of high unemployment, people with key skills and top track records will migrate for more money, more opportunity to achieve, more paid time off, and so on.

If your salary program pays attention to only one or two items, and those items are not the ones your key people are looking for, you won't achieve your goal of attracting and retaining a productive work force.

PAY TERMINOLOGY, DEFINITIONS, AND PURPOSES

Automatic Pay Increases and General Adjustments

Some organizations have automatic pay increases at specified intervals. These organizations have a fixed-rate type of pay structure. This results in employees in certain job classifications with the same number of years of service to the organization making the same salary. This is typical of the civil service.

Base-Rate Structure

An organization that has no type of compensation other than pay shows only a base pay structure. If there are additional forms of compensation, they may be reflected in total compensation. Many companies pay bonuses at certain levels, and it's important when making external comparisons through surveys to be sure you compare base pay to base pay, and that the bonuses and other perks are listed separately.

Benchmark Jobs

When using a point method of measuring jobs, evaluations of a selected group of representative jobs help to clarify various factors and establish a framework for evaluating and comparing jobs throughout the organization. If you are installing a job evaluation system from scratch, establishing such benchmark jobs saves time, effort, and cost by providing points of comparison throughout the organization. Benchmark jobs should be easy to define, noncontroversial, and representative of the organization in general.

Bonus

A bonus can be almost anything other than base pay or perks. Most bonuses are cash, usually determined at the end of the fiscal year after profit-and-loss statements are completed. Other bonus payments might be in the form of company stock, stock options, and so on.

Call-back Pay

This is hourly pay guaranteed for a certain minimum number of hours when an hourly worker is called to work at a time other than the ordinary shift.

Call-in Pay

This is hourly pay guaranteed for a specified number of hours if the worker is called to work on a day that is not an ordinary workday.

Career Ladders

These are successive promotional steps in an occupational or professional area that allow movement up through the organization. There is normally at least a 15 percent increase in pay between each step.

Career Planning

Job descriptions and performance appraisals form the basis for planned career development in most organizations, and include identifying needed skills and abilities for higher level jobs and scheduling the training needed to prepare for those jobs.

Centralized vs. Decentralized Compensation Program

A centralized salary program is designed, implemented, and administered at the corporate level. A centralized compensation program is less complex, easier, and less costly to administer in one location. The main characteristic is its uniformity throughout the organization—it can address the diverse needs of separate groups, but it has the same overall guidelines. A centralized compensation effort provides more control over internal equity and uniform administration. A company that has union contracts may decentralize hourly pay. Hourly pay administration will follow union contract provisions and can follow administrative guidelines without regard for the type of company organization.

Compa-ratio

When you talk about compa-ratio, you simply mean a person's current salary as a percentage of the midpoint of their salary range.

Compensation Survey

Companies that wish to compare their salary range and actual pay practices participate in compensation surveys. The surveys include companies in their industry and their location. It is important to compare actual benchmark jobs—apples to apples, so to speak—when using the data of any survey. When participating in a compensation survey, it's a good idea to have a third party collect the data and produce the survey so that raw data are not exchanged. There might be antitrust implications.

Compression

Compression is the narrowing of pay differentials between employees who should be paid at varying levels. Three of the most common situations where compression can occur follow.

- Subordinate vs. supervisor

- New hire vs. senior employee

- Superior performer vs. average performer

The obvious problems associated with inequities caused by salary compression are poor morale and performance, unwillingness to accept promotions, and higher turnover.

COLA

An increase based on measure of cost of living (nationally) used in union contracts.

Cost-of-Living Allowances or Geographic Differentials

Some corporations pay cost-of-living allowances to employees they ask to relocate to areas of this country or overseas where the cost of living is significantly higher than the cost of living at their current location.

Deferred Compensation Plan

This is compensation awarded to an employee, but payment is deferred to a later date. Deferred compensation is usually in the form of cash or stock. Some plans require purchase by the employee and might be (1) employee savings plans, (2) stock purchase plans, and (3) stock options. Some plans that do not require purchase by the employee are (1) stock bonuses, (2) profit-sharing plans, and (3) deferred cash compensation. Deferred compensation plans are desirable because of their tax advantages.

Equity

There are two main kinds of equity—internal and external. The perceptions that employees have of equity are so variable they are difficult to define. Equity seems to exist as an individual perception that is influenced by a variety of factors, a perceived sense of rewards. Equity is seen by most people as the balance between output and the pay received for the job done. It is also a perception that individuals are paid fairly within their work group, their total organization, and externally compared to other companies in the same industry.

Exempt Employees

Exempt employees are salaried and hold managerial, supervisory, administrative, professional, or sales positions. They are exempt from the overtime provisions of the Fair Labor Standards Act.

Guide Charts

The guide chart profile method of job evaluation was developed by Edward N. Hay Associates to provide a systematic, easily administered approach to evaluating jobs at all levels in all organizations. The evaluations may form the basis for pay comparisons.

Two Principles Are Fundamental to the Guide Chart Method:

1. A thorough understanding of the content of the job to be measured

2. The direct comparison of one job with another job to determine relative value

Three Job Elements Are Reviewed:

1. *Know-how* is the amount of knowledge and skills needed for satisfactory job performance.

2. *Problem solving* is the amount of original thinking required by the job for analyzing, evaluating, reasoning, and arriving at an effective conclusion.

3. *Accountability* is the responsibility for actions and for the consequences of those actions, usually expressed in dollar figures.

Incentives

Incentives are frequently part of an executive's total compensation package. Incentives may include such items as added compensation, commissions, bonus plans, prizes, awards, stock options, profit sharing, and so on.

Management by Objectives

In 1943, Peter Drucker coined a new phrase, "Management by Objectives," as a new approach to performance appraisal. In his book, *The Practice of Management*, Drucker said:

> Business performance requires that each job be directed toward the objectives of the whole business, and in particular each manager's job must be focused on the success as a whole. The performance that is expected of the manager must be derived from the performance goals of the business; the results must be measured by the contribution they make to the success of the enterprise.

Maturity Curve Data

Maturity curve data are a comparison of pay levels with years of experience. We traditionally look at technical people such as scientists and engineers in relation to the number of years since they received their bachelor's degree. This kind of analysis is a normal characteristic of most engineering salary surveys. Maturity curve data are not normally found in other salary surveys, but are available from professional organizations.

Merit Increases

A merit increase system rewards employees for job performance and ties job performance to the percentage increase in pay.

Nonexempt Employees

Nonexempt employees are hourly paid people who hold white- or blue-collar jobs and are paid overtime for working more than 40 hours in a week. The tests that determine whether a job is exempt or nonexempt are set out in the Fair Labor Standards Act.

Report-in Pay

This is hourly pay guaranteed when work is called off because of something like bad weather or machine breakdown.

Salary Budget

The human resource manager normally prepares a budget for the organization's pay increases. Personnel and payroll policies and the company's total financial philosophy are taken into account. The formal budget is normally established after a survey of the external competitive situation and a review of the company's resources and financial condition.

TRASOP and ESOP

The 1975 Tax Reduction Act provided a 10 percent tax credit for capital investment with an additional 1 percent tax credit available to companies using that 1 percent to establish an employee stock ownership plan. An Employee Stock Ownership Plan (ESOP) is a special form of employee benefit plan that is primarily for the purpose of providing participating employees with stock in their company. The additional investment credit for contributions to a Tax Reduction Act Employer Stock Ownership Plan ("TRASOP") terminated with respect to qualified investments made after December 31, 1982.

HOW TO SAVE BIG MONEY WHEN DESIGNING A NEW SALARY PROGRAM OR REVISING AN ESTABLISHED PROGRAM

- Design an organization that is tightly structured with a minimum of management levels, one that includes only the numbers of people needed to get the job done effectively.
- Eliminate jobs and titles such as "assistant to" and other "gofer"-type jobs. If the job is needed, it should have full authority to act.

QUESTIONS AND ANSWERS ON COMPENSATION TOPICS

Q: What are the key elements of a successful compensation program?

A: External competitiveness, internal equity, pay for performance, the ability to be flexible and innovative in pay approaches, and an effective employee communications program.

Q: How does an organization keep up with the constantly rising expectations of the work force? More pay, more benefits, shorter work weeks, etc.?

A: Organizations could handle big increases in pay and continuing increases in benefits when cheap energy, significant advances in technology, low inflation rates, and little foreign competition were the order of the day, but now that these influences have nearly all turned around, organizations do not have the big pie to split with employees, and a new era is dawning where both employees and organizations will have to identify new ways to relate to expectations. The way to do this is to examine total compensation versus pay alone. Look at benefits also.

Here are some compensation and benefit ideas that organizations are using to attract and retain people.

- Lump-sum increases
- More time off with pay
- More perks like company cars and stock programs, like TRASOPs and ESOPs
- Giving management employees and other professionals a "piece of the action"
- Deferred compensation
- Incentives
- Day-care
- Dental, vision, and legal insurance
- Job-sharing
- Flexitime or four-day work weeks

Complicated programs like TRASOPs and ESOPs require competent consultants for design and implementation.

The secret lies in the area of tailoring programs specifically to the organization, keeping the organization as lean as possible, while maintaining a competitive position in your particular industry. Success in the compensation field will depend on the manager's ability to be flexible, creative, and open-minded to change and innovative techniques.

Q: How do you handle the question of inflation and your salary program?

A: Most fined EMS organizations have not found a workable way to deal with inflation in their merit budgets. We've just hoped inflation would go away. The real question here may be a more serious one, however, assuming inflation won't go away, but will continue at a rate of, say, 5 percent; and if your organization is lucky and increasing in earnings (Public Sector) or time base (Public Sector) at 15 percent per year, you are still only holding your own or achieving a small percent upward movement. When using competitive market surveys, pay increases from inflation tend to be rolled in so that market rate will actually reflect the impacted inflation. EMS organizations as well as private sector organizations will have to look for ways to address inflation aside from "pay for performance" or men budgets. The average company or public sector organizations may not be able to address inflation but instead may find ways to cut expenses, including cutting executive bonuses in order to fund a men budget that allows the organization to maintain a "stay-even" pay policy as opposed to an "external competitiveness at all costs" policy. Some private and public sector organizations are moving to provide more perks in the way of added benefits such as child day-care, more employee say in work schedules (flextime or four (4)-hour days), or company cars, instead of higher pay, which keeps putting the employee in a higher tax bracket anyway. EMS professionals will have to come up with new ideas and innovations in pay and benefits in order to meet the challenge of competitive compensation now and in the future.

Q: Why don't promotions come faster, and why aren't there more in our organization?

A: Most public and private sector organizations are structured in pyramidal shapes—there are too many middle managers and top executives in their late twenties, thirties, and forties who will be there for another ten or twenty years, thus slowing promotional opportunities for a bright, young, well-educated work force.

Q: What is the best method of job evaluation for a company that has a large percentage of professional, technical, and managerial personnel?

A: There are so many ways to evaluate jobs. EMS professionals need to understand the organization, its needs and goals, and its personality. The most objective evaluation method is the Hay Guide Chart Profile Method, designed many years ago by Edward N. Hay and Associates of Philadelphia, Pennsylvania. Hundreds of medium and large companies in the United States today use the Hay job evaluation method. Implementing the Hay system facilitates job correlation when using and participating in salary surveys. There are other proprietary systems used by consultants such as Towers, Perrin, Forster, and Crosby.

Q: What is the major function of the compensation manager?

A: The position of an EMS compensation manager is a fairly new one in most organizations. As regulations become more complex and companies grow in size and diversity, the compensation function becomes more important to the success of an organization's plans. There are eight main responsibilities in the compensation function:

1. Planning and control of compensation and merit budgets

2. Policy and procedure development

3. Maintaining internal equity

4. Maintaining external competitiveness

5. Wage and salary recordkeeping, policy control, and administrative responsibilities

6. Advisory and counseling responsibilities related to recruiting, promotions, and organization restructuring

7. Establishing and maintaining a valid system of job evaluation

8. Establishing an effective program for communication of compensation programs.

EQUAL PAY ACT

LEGISLATIVE PURPOSE

A significant amendment to the FLSA occurred in 1963. Congress passed the Equal Pay Act prohibiting unequal wages for women and men who work in the same establishment for equal work on jobs that require equal skill, effort, and responsibility and that are performed under similar working conditions.

Initially, the Act was enforced by the Department of Labor; however, on July 1, 1979, by Executive Order, the enforcement responsibilities were transferred to the U.S. Equal Employment Opportunity Commission (EEOC). In October 1986, the EEOC published its own regulations, which no longer followed those filed earlier by the Department of Labor.

COVERAGE

With a few inconsequential exceptions, the Equal Pay Act now covers most employees, including executive, administrative, and professional employees as well as U.S. government employees who had initially been exempted from coverage. The Equal Pay Act is designed to eliminate any wage rate differential based on sex; nothing in the law is intended to prohibit differences in wage rates that are based not at all on sex, but wholly on other factors. The equal pay standards do not rely upon job classifications or titles, but depend rather on actual job requirements and performance. The focus of any equal pay inquiry is the job itself and the worker's hour-by-hour duties and responsibilities. Men are protected under the law equally with women. While the Equal Pay Act was motivated by concern for the weaker bargaining position of women, the law by its expressed terms applies to both sexes.

ESTABLISHMENT

The law uses "establishment" to mean a distinct place where employees work. Therefore, the obligation to comply with the equal pay provisions must be determined separately with references to those employees at that particular location. Thus, where there are disparities in wage rates among various branch operations of a business, it is not relevant as the EEOC inquiry will be limited to a single location. Further, the "establishment" limit in the law does not preclude protection for employees whose employment is outside a "fixed location" (e.g., an outside salesperson).

WAGES

Wages paid an employee include all payments made to the employee as remuneration for employment. Vacation and holiday pay, premium payments of any kind, and fringe benefits are also included. [Note, however, that payments that do not constitute remuneration for employment are not "wages" (e.g., expense reimbursements).]

FRINGE BENEFITS

Fringe benefits are considered to be remuneration for employment; therefore, it is unlawful for an employer to discriminate between men and women performing equal work with regard to fringe benefits. Fringes include medical, hospital, accident, and life insurance, retirement benefits, profit sharing, bonus plans, leave, and the like. Among the key points in the EEOC regulations are the following:

1. Where an employer conditions benefits to employees and their spouses and families on whether the employee is the "head of the household" or "principal wage earner" in the family unit, the overall implementation of the plan will be closely scrutinized.

2. It is unlawful for an employer to make available benefits for the spouses or the families of employees of one gender when the same benefits are not made available for the spouses or families of employees of the opposite gender.

3. It shall not be a defense to a charge of sex discrimination in benefits, under the Equal Pay Act, that the cost of such benefits is greater with respect to one sex than the other.

4. It is unlawful to have a pension or retirement plan that establishes different optional or compulsory retirement ages based on sex, or which otherwise differentiates benefits on the basis of sex.

In the intervening years since the Equal Employment Opportunity Commission has taken over the enforcement of the Equal Pay Act, the Supreme Court has ruled in two decisions that retirement benefits constitute "wages." In these new rules, the EEOC makes clear that wages have been consistently defined for Equal Pay Act purposes as "all payments made to an employee as remuneration for employment." Therefore, the specific references to "fringe benefits" in the new regulations is intended simply to resolve any lingering doubts that they are covered by the Equal Pay Act.

DETERMINING "EQUAL WORK"

Congress intended that jobs requiring equal pay should be substantially equal with respect to skill, effort, and responsibility and performed under similar working conditions.

In determining whether employees are performing equal work within the meaning of the Equal Pay Act, the amounts of time that employees spend in the performance of different duties are not the sole criteria. It is also necessary to consider the degree of difference in terms of skill, effort, and responsibility. These factors are related in such a manner that a general standard to determine equality of jobs cannot be set up solely on the basis of a percentage of time. Consequently, a finding that one job requires employees to expend greater effort for a certain percentage of their working time than employees performing another job, would not in itself indicate that the two jobs do not constitute equal work.

Similarly, the performance of jobs on different machines or equipment would not necessarily result in a determination that the work so performed is unequal within the meaning of the statute if the equal pay provisions otherwise apply. If the difference in skill or effort required for the operation of such equipment is inconsequential, payment of a higher wage rate to employees of one sex because of a difference in machines or equipment would constitute a prohibited wage-rate differential.

Where greater skill or effort is required from the lower paid sex, the fact that the machinery or equipment used to perform substantially equal work is different does not defeat a finding that the Equal Pay Act has been violated. Likewise, the fact that jobs are performed in different departments or locations within the establishment would not necessarily be sufficient to demonstrate that unequal work is involved where the equal pay standard otherwise applies. This is particularly true in the case of retail establishments. Unless a showing can be made by the employer that the sale of one article requires such a higher degree of skill or effort than the sale of another article as to render the equal pay standard inapplicable, it will be assumed that the salesman and saleswomen concerned are performing equal work.

Although the equal pay provisions apply on an establishment basis (the jobs to be compared are those in the particular establishment), all relevant evidence that may demonstrate whether the skill, effort, and responsibility required for the jobs in the particular establishment are equal should be considered, whether this relates to the performance of like jobs in other establishments or not.

The law uses three separate tests, those of equal skill, effort, and responsibility. Each of them must be present in order for the equal pay law to apply.

1. *Equal Skill.* Here, the analysis includes experience, training, education, and ability. Skill should be measured in terms of the performance of the job. Possession of a skill not needed to meet the requirement of the job cannot be a relevant factor in determining the quality of skill. It is, after all,

the job that is being scrutinized and not the worker. Similarly, the efficiency of the employee's performance on the job is not itself an appropriate fact to consider in evaluating an individual's skill.

2. *Equal Effort.* The measure of the physical or mental exertion needed for the performance of a job is the key here. Jobs may require equal effort for performance even though the effort may be displayed differently in two otherwise similar jobs. Differences only in the kind of effort required of the job in such a situation will not justify wage differentials among employees.

The occasional or sporadic performance of an activity that may require extra physical or mental exertion is not alone sufficient to justify a finding of unequal effort. Suppose, however, that men and women are working side by side in a factory line assembling parts. Suppose further that one of the men who performs the operations at the end of the line must also lift the assembly, as he completes his part of it, and place it on a waiting pallet. In such a situation, a wage rate differential might be justified for the person (but only for that person) who is required to expend the extra effort in the performance of the job, provided that the extra effort is substantial and is performed over a considerable portion of the work cycle.

3. *Equal Responsibility.* For this test, the degree of accountability in the performance of the job with the emphasis on the importance of the job obligation is paramount. To illustrate this test, let us say that there are sales clerks, engaged primarily in selling identical or similar merchandise, who are given different responsibilities. Suppose that one employee of such a group is authorized and required to determine whether to accept payment for purchases by personal checks from customers. The person having the authority to accept personal checks may have a considerable additional degree of responsibility, which may materially affect the business operations of the employer. In this situation, payment of a higher wage rate to this employee would be permissible.

SIMILAR WORKING CONDITIONS

Employees performing jobs requiring equal skill, effort, and responsibility are likely to be performing them under similar working conditions. However, in situations where some employees whose work meets these standards have working conditions substantially different form those required for the performance of other jobs, the equal pay principle would not apply. For example, if some salespersons are engaged in selling a product exclusively inside a store and others employed by the same establishment spend a large part of their time selling the same product away from the establishment, the working conditions would be dissimilar.

Also, where some employees do repair work exclusively inside the shop and others spend most of their time doing similar repair work in customers' homes, there would not be a similarity in working conditions. On the other hand, slight or inconsequential differences in working conditions that are essentially similar would not justify a differential in pay. Such differences are not usually taken into consideration by employers or in collective bargaining in setting wage rates.

EXCEPTIONS TO EQUAL PAY STANDARD

The Equal Pay Act provides three specific exceptions and one broad exception to its general standard requiring that employees doing equal work be paid equal wages, regardless of sex. Under these exceptions, where it can be established that a differential in pay is the result of a wage payment made under a *seniority system, a merit system, a system measuring earnings by quantity or quality of production, or a system in which the differential is based on any factor other than sex,* the differential is expressly excluded from the statutory prohibition of wage discrimination based on sex. *The legislative intent was stated to be that any discrimination based upon any of these exceptions shall be exempted from the operation of the statute.* These exceptions recognize that there are factors other than sex that can be used to justify a wage differential, even as between employees of opposite sexes performing equal work on jobs that meet the statutory tests of equal skill, effort, responsibility, and similar working conditions. An employer who asserts an exception to equal pay has the burden to provide the facts establishing this affirmative defense.

Additional duties may not be a defense to the payment of higher wages to one sex where the higher pay is not related to the extra duties. The Commission will scrutinize such a defense to determine whether it is bona fide. For example, an employer cannot successfully assert an extra duties defense where:

1. employees of the higher paid sex receive the higher pay without doing extra work;

2. members of the lower paid sex also perform extra duties requiring equal skill, effort, and responsibility;

3. the extra duties do not in fact exist;

4. the extra task consumes a minimal amount of time and is of peripheral importance; or

5. third persons (i.e., individuals who are not in the two groups of employees being compared) who do the extra task as their primary job are paid less than the members of the higher paid sex for whom there is an attempt to justify the pay differential.

The term "red circle" rate is used to describe certain unusually higher wage rates that are maintained for reasons unrelated to sex. An example of bona fide use of a "red circle" rate might arise in a situation where a company wishes to transfer a long-service employee, who can no longer perform his or her regular job because of ill health, to different work that is now being performed by opposite gender employees.

Under the "red circle" principle the employer may continue to pay the employee his or her present salary, which is greater than that paid to the opposite gender employees, for the work both will be doing.

Under such circumstances, maintaining an employee's established wage rate, despite a reassignment to a less demanding job, is a valid reason for the differential even though other employees performing the less demanding work would be paid at a lower rate. Here the differential is based on a factor other than sex. However, where wage rate differentials have been or are being paid on the basis of sex to employees performing equal work, rates of the higher paid employees may not be "red circled" in order to comply with the Equal Pay Act. To allow this would only continue the inequities that the Equal Pay Act was intended to cure.

EQUAL PAY RECORDKEEPING

All records required by the FLSA described in this chapter (next section) must also be made available to EEOC representatives. In addition, every employer subject to the Equal Pay Act shall maintain and preserve, for at least two years, any records relating to the payment of wages, wage rates, job evaluations, job descriptions, merit systems, seniority systems, collective bargaining agreements, and any description of wage differentials to employees of the opposite sex in the same establishment based on a factor other than sex.

EQUAL PAY ENFORCEMENT

The Equal Pay Act is enforced by the Equal Employment Opportunity Commission. Its representatives have full investigatory powers to:

1. enter and inspect the place of employment, review records, and interview employees;
2. advise employers regarding any changes necessary or desirable to comply with the law (if a violation of the law is found, the EEOC will attempt to negotiate a settlement to give the employees back wages due and raise pay levels);
3. subpoena witnesses and order production of documents;
4. supervise back wage payments; and
5. initiate and conduct litigation.

The names of complaining parties are not to be discussed unless necessary in a court proceeding.

The penalties for Equal Pay violations are covered by the FLSA, and they are discussed in the next section. Once a prohibited sex-based wage differential has been proved, an employer can come onto compliance only by raising the wage rate of the lower paid sex. The Equal Pay Act

prohibits an employer from attempting to cure a violation by hiring or transferring employees to perform the previously lower-paid job at the lower
rate.

FAIR LABOR STANDARDS ACT

IN GENERAL

The Fair Labor Standards Act establishes a minimum wage rate and an
overtime wage rate for employees engaged in interstate commerce or the
production of goods for interstate commerce. The act also imposes restrictions on the employment of children under 18 years of age.

COVERAGE

An employee is covered by the minimum wage and overtime provisions of FLSA if his or her work is performed in the United States or a U.S.
possession or territory, a true employment relationship exists between the
employee and the employer, and the employee is either:

- engaged in interstate commerce or the production of goods for interstate
  commerce; or

- employed by an enterprise that is engaged in interstate commerce or the
  production of goods for interstate commerce.

FLSA's child labor restrictions prohibit the employment of "oppressive
child labor" in commerce, the production of goods for commerce, or any
covered enterprise. In general, child labor is defined as oppressive when a
minor is below the minimum age for a particular occupation.

EXEMPTIONS

Certain employees are explicitly exempt from FLSA's minimum wage,
overtime, and child-labor provisions. Some exemptions apply to all of the
provisions, while others apply only to one or two of the provisions. In general,
exemptions are provided for:

- white-collar workers, for example, executives, administrators, professionals, and outside sales persons;

- workers in specific industries, for example, transportation, hospitals, sea-
  sonal businesses, communications, and agriculture;

- specifically exempt workers, for example, commissioned retail salespersons, family members, fishermen, taxicab drivers, and newspaper delivery
  persons; and

- employees working under special certificates, for example, full-time students, learners, student learners, apprentices, disabled employees, and messengers.

MINIMUM WAGE REQUIREMENTS

Employees covered by FLSA must be paid at least $5.25 per hour under the Act's minimum wage provisions. (Note: Minimum wage subject to increase by Congress.) Although FLSA states the minimum wage as an hourly rate, an employer can choose to pay an employee on a salary, commission, or other basis, as long as the employee's average hourly wage for any given workweek equals the minimum wage.

Some states and even local governments mandate higher minimum wages than required by the FLSA.

OVERTIME REQUIREMENTS

FLSA requires employers to pay covered employees time and one-half their regular rates for each hour, or fraction thereof, worked in excess of 40 during any given workweek. The act does not require that employers pay the overtime premium for hours worked in excess of a daily maximum, nor does it specify overtime pay for work performed on weekends or holidays. However, employers are free to pay employees overtime pay for hours worked in excess of a daily maximum or for work performed on weekends and holidays. In addition, employers are permitted to define a shorter workweek—for example, 37 hours—and pay overtime for hours worked in excess of the shorter workweek.

FLSA does not set any limits on the number of hours that an employee can work in a given week. However, other laws governing specific industries, such as the transportation industry, do set weekly maximum hour limits.

CHILD LABOR REQUIREMENTS

FLSA imposes certain restrictions on the employment of children under 18 years old. In general, the minimum age for employment under FLSA is 16, but special exemptions allow employment as early as age 14 in nonhazardous jobs and as early as age 10 in agriculture if the employment does not interfere with the minor's schooling. Minors under 15 years old also can be employed in conjunction with certain work experience programs.

FLSA sets a higher minimum age of 18 years for occupations listed in Department of Labor regulations as hazardous for the employment of minors or detrimental to their health or well-being. Regulations also list those occupations in retail and service industries that are considered permissible for minors ages 14 to 16.

Regulations under FLSA limit working hours for minors under age 16, requiring that employment be confined to periods that do not interfere with schooling or the health and well-being of the child. Working hours for minors 16 and over are not limited.

State laws in some instances require employers to meet more stringent standards, and many states limit working hours of all minors.

ENFORCEMENT AND PENALTIES

Employers that violate FLSA can be subject to criminal, civil, or administrative sanctions. The Wage and Hour Division, part of the Department of Labor's Employment Standards Administration, is responsible for investigating possible violations of FLSA and has broad powers to enter and inspect an employer's facilities. Wage-hour inspectors generally can review whatever records are pertinent to FLSA compliance and can question employees about the employer's wage and hour practices.

Criminal sanctions can be levied against employers who willfully violate FLSA. An employer can be fined up to $10,000, or, for a second conviction, be fined up to $10,000 and/or imprisoned up to six months. In addition, civil remedies can be pursued by employees or by the labor secretary on behalf of employees. Employers found to have violated overtime or minimum wage rules can be liable for unpaid wages or overtime compensation, plus liquidated damages of an equal amount. The labor secretary also can pursue injunctions to prevent an employer from violating FLSA employment from selling, distributing, or transporting goods and materials produced under conditions that violate those standards.

RECORDKEEPING

Employers covered by FLSA must maintain, for at least two years, employment and earnings records, wage rate tables, and work time schedules. For three years, they must keep payroll records, contracts and plans, and sales and purchase records.

Willful failure to keep such records or deliberately falsifying records is a criminal offense.

INDEPENDENT CONTRACTORS

CLASSIFICATION

Whether an individual is classified as an employee or an independent contractor has far reaching consequences for determining a business's responsibility for the individual under the Fair Labor Standards Act, for determining liability under the Federal Insurance Act (FICA) and the Federal Unemployment Tax Act (FUTA), for determining income tax withholding responsibilities, and for determining liability for providing benefits to an individual under evolving sections of the Internal Revenue Code such as those applicable to employee leasing.

While similar, the definitions of, and the procedures for, determining whether an individual is an independent contractor or employee are different for the purposes of FLSA and for most tax purposes.

FLSA DETERMINATIONS

It is no easy matter to determine when an individual is an independent contractor. There have been many legal challenges over the years by employers, and the Supreme Court has been asked on a number of occasions to resolve controversies arising out of the dilemma to define who is an "independent contractor" and who is an "employee."

The U.S. Supreme Court has been careful to point out that there is no rule or test that can determine whether an individual is an independent contractor or an employee for purposes of the FLSA. It is the totality of the activities that is the controlling factor. Some of the circumstances that the Supreme Court has considered significant follow.

1. The nature of the relationship of the services to the principal's business. In this connection, it has been judicially commented upon that routine work that requires industry and effiency is not indicative of independence and nonemployee status.

2. The permanency of the relationship. The less permanent, the more persuasive it is that it is not an employer-employee relationship. The courts have stated, "It is not significant how one could have acted under the contract terms. The controlling economic realities are reflected by the way one actually acts."

3. The amount of individual investment in facilities and equipment. Obviously, the greater the dollar commitment of the individual, the more likely there will be a determination of independent contractor status.

4. The opportunities for profit and loss. There must be more than mere compensation for time spent at work. At the very least, there must be opportunities of profit or loss flowing from the operations of independent business people in open market competition.

5. The degree of independent business organization and operation. This is a crucial test and goes to the heart of the question of whether there is the requisite degree of independence. The employer does not have to actually control the details and ways of accomplishing tasks in order for individuals to be considered "employees." There need only be the right to exercise that control.

6. The degree of independent initiative or judgment. If the task performed is identical to one performed by an employee, and no amount of personal initiative would change the condition of work or the job to other than an employee's, then there is no basis to find an independent contractor relationship.

INTERNAL REVENUE SERVICE DETERMINATIONS

In the Tax Equity and Fiscal Responsibility Act of 1982, Congress provided for two categories of statutory nonemployees—qualified real estate agents and direct sellers. (A "direct seller" is any salesperson who sells consumer products in the home or in a place other than in a permanent retail establishment.) In other employment situations, the Internal Revenue Service uses common law principles.

Under the common law test, an individual generally is an employee if the person for whom the individual performs services has the right to control and direct that individual, both as to the result to be accomplished by the work and to the details and means by which that result is accomplished. Thus, the most important factor under the common law is the degree of control, or rights of control, which the employer has over the manner in which the particular work is to be performed.

In determining whether the necessary degree of control exists in order to find that an individual has common law employee status, the courts and the Internal Revenue Service ordinarily consider all of the facts of a particular situation, which are then evaluated and weighed in light of the presence or absence of the various pertinent characteristics. The decision as to the weight to be accorded rests upon both the activity under consideration and the purpose underlying the use of the factor as an element of the classification decision.

REPORTING REQUIREMENT

To satisfy the reporting requirement, a taxpayer must have timely filed Form 1099-NEC, accompanied by Summary and Transmittal Form 1096, with respect to the individuals in question for all taxable years after December 31, 1978.

A Form 1099-NEC must be prepared with respect to each worker who was paid compensation in the amount of $600 or more and, together with Form 1096, must be filed by February 28 of the year following the calendar year in which the compensation is paid. Reasonable extensions of time for filing these may be granted by the IRS if requested on or before the due date. In addition, the IRS has announced that it will not deny relief under Section 530 to taxpayers who mistakenly, but in good faith, timely file Form 1099-Misc (Statements for Recipients of Miscellaneous Income) instead of Form 1099-NEC.

SUMMATION

The area of independent contractors can often be very confusing. It is highly recommended that your legal counsel or tax advisor provide guidance in this important area.

OTHER TYPES OF WORKERS

While independent contractors by definition remain outside the scope of employer-employee relationships, there has been an enormous increase in the use of part-time, temporary, and leased personnel who have become part of the contingent work force. Indeed, government data confirm that the contingent work force is growing at a faster rate than the entire labor force. Approximately 25 percent of the work force is contingent.

1. **Temporary Employees**—Known by a variety of names ("temporaries," "part-timers," "casuals," "nonregulars"), these individuals may be on the payroll or working for a temporary service, in which case they become the employees of that company. Temporary service employees receive their entire compensation and benefit package from their employers. The question of who actually employs temporary employees is important in circumstances where the employee files a discrimination complaint, or if the employee is discharged or is the subject of any disciplinary action.

2. **Leased Employees**—It is estimated that there are now between 200 and 300 employee-leasing companies in business with some 500,000 workers under lease. Rapid future growth is predicted because of the myriad of federal laws and regulations. Small employees, especially, like the fact that leasing allows them to obtain for their workers the kinds of benefits that a large company can provide because of the greater leverage the leasing company has.

JOB DESCRIPTIONS AND JOB EVALUATIONS—HOW TO CHOOSE THE BEST SYSTEM FOR YOUR ORGANIZATION AND HOW TO DESIGN A SIMPLE BUT EFFECTIVE PROGRAM

Job descriptions and effective job evaluations are the underpinnings of a good compensation program. A small EMS organization might be able to get by with a hit-and-miss, case-by-case type of system, but once your EMS organization starts to grow, a complete system should be designed to fit the needs of your particular organization.

The job description is the single most important document in the compensation program. To approach the task of writing job descriptions in a logical, organized manner, one must first ask three questions before beginning to prepare job descriptions.

1. How are the job descriptions to be used?

2. What kind do we want?

3. Are we capable of maintaining and updating the job description file?

THE USES OF JOB DESCRIPTIONS

How the job description is to be used should determine the kind you want. Job descriptions can be used for many functions, from placement and training to labor relations and salary surveying. Attitudes toward job descriptions are changing, however, and many experts believe it's best to tailor job descriptions to one or two basic uses. Many EMS and HR professionals believe that job descriptions should be primarily designed for compensation and legal defense purposes only. For these purposes, job descriptions should be designed to compare jobs internally, to price jobs in salary surveys by comparing internal and external positions, and to explain the job to others or defend the company against violations of the Equal Pay Act, Title VII of the Civil Rights Act, Age Discrimination in Employment Act, and the Rehabilitation Act.

Writing job descriptions with an eye toward legal defense is important because when a charge of wrongdoing is filed against your company, a poorly written job description too often supports the allegations of the aggrieved employee or inspecting governmental agency.

PREPARING JOB DESCRIPTIONS

The first step in preparing your job descriptions is the collection of data. This should be done systematically, by gathering important facts about the job. There are four key data elements: skill requirements, effort, responsibility, and working conditions. In order to include all of the key data elements, review the seven-point data collection process that follows.

1. Principal job duties and responsibilities. Determine and record any function that takes up 5 percent or more of the employee's time.

2. Output. Determine what results are expected by the job, both quantitative and qualitative.

3. Reporting relationships. Determine all reporting relationships, upward and downward. Include an accurate and current organizational chart.

4. Skill requirements. Determine all skill, ability, or training requirements, including formal education (degree), specialized training (certification), specialized skills (licensing), and amount of experience.

5. Effort. Include the physical and mental effort required to perform the job

6. Responsibilities. Determine and record in detail how much independent judgment is allowed and used, the impact of the job on the organization, whether the job holder has responsibility for the supervision of others, and whether he or she has responsibility for policy design and administration.

7. Working conditions. Include any unpleasant or dangerous working conditions, travel required (determine percentage of time), or abnormal working times or workdays.

METHODS OF COLLECTING DATA

There are several methods available to the job analyst for collecting the key data elements for job descriptions. Interviews are often conducted on a one-to-one basis with the job incumbent. This method produces high-quality data but is very expensive. It's most suitable for collecting data on senior management jobs. Direct observation also produces high-quality data. But it's time consuming and methods oriented, slanted to the incumbent's way of doing things. The direct observation method is recommended for use with short-cycle, production-type jobs.

The fastest and least expensive method of data collection is the questionnaire. It's also considered the best general-purpose method. If possible, have the entire group of employees that hold the job fill out the questionnaire at the same time. This gives a fuller picture of how the job is performed and doesn't damage morale by singling out employees to be surveyed.

When the data collection is completed, and you begin to write the job descriptions, remember to:

- keep in mind the primary use of the job description (compensation, legal defense),

- make sure all personnel-shop jargon is removed, and

- review the description in light of legal requirements.

Job descriptions and the law. To help make sure job descriptions won't run afoul of the law, remember to focus on job content, not the incumbent. Keep your job descriptions up to date with periodic review. Do an immediate follow-up when job duties change. Keep your records accurate. Don't include unreasonable requirements or expectations. Some specific tips follow.

- Make sure your job descriptions don't include such phrases as, "This job requires a young, aggressive . . . " or "A training position for a recent college graduate." Such statements in your job descriptions could get you into trouble under the Age Discrimination in Employment Act.
- Keep educational and experience requirements job related. The EEOC considers such requirements to be employment "tests," and they are subject to the uniform guidelines on testing. Requirements that aren't job related can get you into trouble under Title VII of the Civil Rights Act.
- Make sure your job descriptions' references to health requirements, working conditions, and effort are proper and accurate. Job descriptions that don't fully explain physical activities won't help you if you're charged with violating the Rehabilitation Act or ADA.

When developing your wage and salary programs, use only complete and accurate descriptions of job content. When the content of two or more jobs is similar, grade and range should be similar.

THE THREE MOST COMMON METHODS
OF JOB EVALUATION

1. The *classification method* of job evaluation is used by most civil service systems. Before the jobs are evaluated, a decision is made as to the number of pay grades that are needed, and then job descriptions are written for each class of jobs in the structure.

2. The *ranking method* of job evaluation is one of the easier methods. A list of jobs to be evaluated is established, and the jobs are then ranked in relation to each other on an overall basis. The overall judgment is made on the value of each job in relation to all other jobs on the list. This method works best in smaller companies.

3. The *point method* of job evaluation reviews three or four job factors that are common to all the jobs being evaluated and then rates each job in relation to each factor on a numerical scale. Points are given for each factor, looking at the degree to which the job possesses each factor. There are usually four or five factors reviewed. They might be education, know-how, safety, responsibility for budgeted dollars, management skills, and so on. The points are added, and a total point factor is assigned for each job. Jobs are then related to each other on the basis of the total point scores, and total points can be related to wage and salary ranges. To arrive at a salary range, points usually apply to a dollar formula, which will place the job at a particular place on a salary policy line.

For example: Job points = 500 policy line formula = $50 per point + $10,000. Multiply through, and you get a salary range midpoint of $35,000 for a job worth 500 points.

If the measured worth of a job fits an established job grade schedule, a range of point totals (e.g., 401 to 500 points) could be assigned a specific salary grade (e.g., a grade 12 in a 20-grade system).

MAKING JOB EVALUATION SIMPLE BUT EFFECTIVE

There seems to be a trend today of hiring qualified people and implementing your own salary programs in house. The area, however, where we do see outside consultants used most in human resource management is job evaluation. Consultants in this area are expensive, but there are good reasons for considering an outside expert.

- Trial and error is an expensive way to attempt to install a salary program. The errors can cost more than the consultant.
- The consultant can devote full time to the project, and if there are time constraints this is a real plus.
- Top management's commitment is essential to the successful installation of a job evaluation program, and executives may be more amenable to an outside expert with prestige in the field.
- You can utilize the expert to the fullest extent in the job evaluation process by seeing that your staff is trained as the installation is implemented.

- The consultant should provide an operating guide for use of the system, and cooperation between your staff and the consultant can ensure that the program and the guide are tailored specifically to your company.

The fact that the consultant is an impartial third party should aid the installation. One of the foremost consultants in the job evaluation field today is Edward N. Hay Associates of Philadelphia, Pennsylvania. They install the Hay Guide Chart Profile method of job evaluation, which is a popular method in many larger organizations throughout the country. There are many other proprietary systems available.

THE HAY GUIDE CHART PROFILE METHOD OF JOB EVALUATION

The two key elements for measuring job content under the Hay Guide Chart method are (1) a thorough understanding of the content of the job to be measured, and (2) the comparison of one job with another in order to determine the relative value.

It's almost impossible to measure an entire job against another entire job, so elements that are present in all jobs are measured. These elements are:

- **Know-how.** The sum total of all knowledge and skills, however acquired, needed for satisfactory job performance.

- **Problem solving.** The amount of original, self-starting thinking required by the job for analyzing, evaluating, creating, reasoning, and arriving at conclusions.

- **Accountability.** The person's responsibility for actions and for the consequences of those actions.

The most important aspect of the Hay job evaluation method is understanding the job. This understanding usually comes from the job description, so it's important that the job description be current and complete, and capture the total essence of the job—what it's expected to accomplish, why it's needed, what results are to be achieved, and so on.

Whether you use the Hay job evaluation or another system of your own design, there are several essential elements to consider.

ESSENTIAL ELEMENTS OF JOB EVALUATION

Job evaluation is a systematic method for comparing jobs in an organization to determine a reasonable and effective order or hierarchy. A good job evaluation program will give you an accurate measure of differences in accountabilities and duties of the jobs in your company.

Differentiate the jobs in your EMS organization so that reasonable salary differentials can be made between them. Job evaluation is not meant to judge the performance of the employee being observed. Its purpose is to measure what is done, not how well one particular person performs.

To the basic management problem of pay the goal of job evaluation is to offer a solution equity. When employees feel there is no logical connection between their compensation and their jobs, dissatisfaction and poor performance can easily result. Job evaluation works on the premise that a basic pattern controls the wage relationships between jobs in every company. Job evaluation helps you discover what that pattern is and produces an explainable system for comparing the relative worth of similar or widely differing jobs—some jobs are routine and observable, with easily defined tasks, whereas other jobs require the performance of nonobservable, highly cognitive tasks.

The following are important goals and benefits of a sound job evaluation program:

• To simplify and make rational the relatively chaotic wage structure likely to result from chance, custom, and individual biases; to eliminate favoritism and potentially unlawful or discriminatory pay rates and relationships between jobs (internal equity).

• To provide a factual guideline for judging the relevance of job applicants' backgrounds to available jobs. (Knowing what the job consists of can be a valuable aid in performance review. The quality of performance can be measured.)

• To attract and hold capable employees by setting pay in line with rates for comparable jobs in other firms (external equity).

• To provide work incentives and boost morale. (Only by studying jobs can you recognize superior performance.)

• For unionized firms, to provide a rational basis for setting negotiated rates.

• For nonunionized firms, to remove a common cause of low morale and dissatisfaction when employees perceive an inequity exists. If there is a perception of inequity, it might encourage unionization drives.

• To safeguard a company's prerogative to grant salary increases during periods of government wage control (income policy).

• To develop a policy of equal pay for equal work consistent with federal law.

How can you determine whether your firm is in sufficient need of a job evaluation plan to justify a large commitment in capital and manpower? Here are some rules of thumb that may help you decide.

• *How large is your company or organization?* If your CEO can't have personal knowledge of all the jobs in the organization, salary decisions must be delegated to others. Job evaluation will keep these decisions objective, consistent, and justifiable. Many experts feel that the critical point is somewhere between 500 and 1,000 employees. However, many smaller offices and manufacturing firms install programs covering only 50 or 100 people. It depends on the complexity of the organization and the jobs.

• *How fast is your firm growing?* Regardless of size, you may need a job evaluation plan because of your company's growth or expansion. If former organizational patterns, recruiting techniques, or pay practices are no longer applicable, a job evaluation program can provide a flexible system in which to grow.

- *Are you having a recruiting or turnover problem?* if you find your company is attracting low-quality job applicants or losing many employees, your pay rates may be to blame. Inconsistency in pay, both internally (among jobs in your organization) and externally (when compared with your competitors), may be the culprit.
- *How is employee morale?* Even if recruiting or turnover problems haven't materialized, productivity and costs can be adversely affected if employees are dissatisfied with existing pay relationships.

If your answers to these questions indicate that you need a formal program, your next step is to make all of the top decision makers in your organization share your awareness. The decision to undertake a job evaluation program must be arrived at by the top operating officers of the firm without undue sales pressure from you, and with full knowledge of all that is involved. The initiator of the program, whether a Human Resource executive or some other manager, should never try to minimize the costs of the job evaluation program.

A lack of honesty at this stage can undermine the program later. The plan will cost money, it will take managers and staff away from their normal duties, and it will interfere with the operating routine of the workers. To indicate otherwise, either directly or indirectly, in an effort to sell the program is unwise. The decision to install a job evaluation program must be made with the full knowledge by all concerned that there will be inconveniences. The job of the initiator is to show that the benefits of the plan will far outweigh any temporary annoyances. The formation of a top management committee to approve the establishment of the job evaluation plan can be of great help in gaining acceptance of the concept. Participation in the plan should begin at this level and continue downward to the lowest levels of the organization.

If your company or organization has a compensation specialist, he or she can be invaluable in the early stages of the plan. The human resources or accounting department should be intimately involved with the plan and can offer strong support to the claim that the plan will be soundly administered after its installation.

Tips for EMS Organizations

Be sure your job evaluation program is tailored to your company or organization. Some industry associations and other EMS organizations have developed job evaluation plans that can be used as a template so the provided wheel does not have to be recreated. However, a template should be customized to meet the perimeters of your organization.

There are some potential pitfalls in developing and implementing career ladders:

1. Always obtain management approval before communicating plans for career ladders to the employees affected. Should implementation of plans be delayed or approval denied, the expectation of employees will not be disappointed.

2. Once career ladders are implemented, it is essential that EMS managers and supervisors be trained in understanding and using the promotional guidelines. As a means of maintaining internal equity among employees in the same professional area, career ladder guidelines must be applied fairly and consistently.

JOB ANALYSIS AND THE UNIFORM GUIDELINES ON EMPLOYEE SELECTION PROCEDURES

EMS organizations subject to the requirements of job analysis under the Uniform Guidelines on Employee Selection Procedures should pay special attention to job analyses as a key element in the justification of any selection procedure, especially if actual selection reflects an adverse impact on any race, sex, or ethnic group. Consider these guidelines:

Any measure, combination of measures, or procedure used as a basis for any employment decision. Selection procedures include the full range of assessment techniques, from traditional paper and pencil tests, performance tests, training programs, or probationary periods and physical, educational, and work experience requirements through informal or casual interviews and unscored application forms.

Where selection procedure has a differential impact, its continued use may be justified only by a showing of job relatedness or business necessity. Federal EEO enforcement agencies generally require demonstration of job relatedness through a formal study that shows validity for the selection procedure. The guidelines specify the collection of information about the job, generally in the form of job analysis, as one of numerous conditions for an acceptable validity study.

THERE ARE RESEARCHED SYSTEM OF JOB ANALYSIS—YOU DON'T HAVE TO REINVENT THE WHEEL!

Current systems for conducting a job analysis generally fall into two broad categories.

1. Systems that provide a standardized set of descriptors and are programmed to provide output in quantitative terms that can be compared with a database established by a compendium of research studies.

2. Methods that require origination of job elements, task inventories, or other descriptors, but with the analysis programmed to provide results according to a prescribed matrix. Several are listed below.

- The *Position Analysis Questionnaire* is a standardized instrument developed by Ernest J. McCormick and his associates at the Occupational Research Center, Department of Psychological Sciences, Purdue University, West Lafayette, Indiana. Dr. McCormick and two of his principal research associates have founded an organization called PAQ Services, Inc., to provide data processing and to conduct further research on the instrument.
- The *Occupation Analysis Inventory* (OAI) is a standardized instrument developed by Joseph W. Cunningham and his associates at the Center for Occupation Education, North Carolina State University, Raleigh, North Carolina.
- The *Skills and Attributes Inventory* (*SAI*) is a standardized instrument developed by Melany E. Baehr and her associates at the Industrial Relations Center, University of Chicago, Chicago, Illinois.
- *Functional Job Analysis* is a method attributed principally to Sidney A. Fine and his associates at the W.E. Upjohn Institute for Employment Research, Kalamazoo, Michigan. The results are exemplified in the Dictionary of Occupational Titles, published by the U.S. Department of Labor.
- *Job Element Method* was developed principally by Ernest Primoff at the U.S. Civil Service Commission. The method is the foundation for the "J coefficient," whereby job elements are translated directly into selection characteristics.
- *Health Services Mobility Study Method* (HSMS) was developed by Eleanor Gilpatrick of Hunter College and the Research Foundation, City University of New York, under contract to the U.S. Department of Labor. Originally envisaged as a means of providing upward mobility for nonprofessionals in hospital settings, the end product is a carefully integrated system for any setting.
- *Air Force Comprehensive Occupational Data Analysis Program* (CODAP) was developed by Raymond E. Christal and his associates at the Personnel Research Division, Air Force Human Resources Laboratory, Lackland Air Force Base, Texas. Organizations outside the Air Force are beginning to use the system.

WHY HAVE PERFORMANCE APPRAISALS
FOR EMS PERSONNEL?

The performance appraisal provides EMS organizations with a unique opportunity to tie the employee's accountabilities and achievements to the organization's objectives and strategic plans.

If the EMS organization designs a performance appraisal form around the major accountabilities of the job rather than the minute tasks and personality traits that appear on many performance appraisals, this action, in and of itself, can be used as a motivational tool.

DESIGNING AN EFFECTIVE APPRAISAL PROGRAM
AND PARTICIPATIVE PERFORMANCE

An effective performance appraisal program can help your EMS organization achieve corporate goals through the active management of the human resource. To be effective, though, the program must be accepted by management and by all employees; it must be participative in order to be successful with the contemporary worker.

The program should also tie performance and development of the employee together. The form should provide a place to identify development needs in the current job, and for the next job, when the time is right to start preparing the employee for promotion. More specifically, the program must:

1. identify and communicate organizational goals to all employees. The EMS professional should do this with each individual during the appraisal;

2. identify the employee's current accountabilities and then establish clear, realizable goals which can serve as a motivational tool for your employees.

3. convert the organizational objectives and accountabilities to the employee's objectives during the appraisal. Show how the employee's contribution will help the organization achieve its business plans;

4. provide coaching and counseling in order to assist every employee in using his or her talents and capabilities to the fullest in performing the current job and in preparing for greater responsibility; and

5. be a successful tool for compensation administration.

The key to making performance appraisals effective but painless is for EMS managers to meet with their subordinates at the beginning of each year to discuss the subordinates' goals and objectives for the accountabilities and to agree on the coming year. Once agreement is reached, managers have a responsibility to monitor progress during the year to make sure that subordinates are on track and to coach and assist subordinates in achieving their goals. Coaching should be a daily occurrence. At the end of the year when the performance appraisal is due, it has been done throughout the year, so that the actual sit-down appraisal—filling out the forms and discussing the subordinate's performance for the year—is easy and painless. You have been discussing it right along. There should be no surprises. This three-part motivational plan includes:

1. Agreement at the beginning of the year on accountabilities and objectives

2. Review of accountability achievement and timing throughout the year

3. Completion of performance appraisal

Train EMS supervisors to treat performance appraisal as a unique opportunity to coach and develop subordinates and to tie individual goals and objectives to the organization's business plans. The new worker wants to feel a sense of self-fulfillment and to make a contribution. A workshop for managers on coaching and developing subordinates would be a good place to start.

WAGE AND SALARY SURVEYS—HOW TO USE THEM—HOW TO START ONE

Your EMS organization can have the most sophisticated compensation program there is, but if you don't pay competitively and keep your eye on the market, your pay could fall below prevailing salaries in your industry, and you could lose people. You can find out what other companies are paying by participating in a salary survey. There are several ways to obtain survey data.

1. Participate in a survey group in your industry. Contact your industry association.

2. Participate in the American Compensation Association survey. If you have primary responsibility for compensation, it would be to your advantage to join the ACA. The data you'll receive and the contacts you'll make will be invaluable.

3. If you use a consultant like Edward N. Hay Associates to install your job evaluation program, you can obtain the Hay All-Industry Salary Survey.

4. Other consultants like Towers, Perrin, Forster, and Crosby also provide salary surveys.

5. Create your own survey by forming a survey group.

Whatever methods your organization uses to gather survey data, the organization should get two sets of figures: first, base rates and salary structures set for each job, and second, average base-rate salaries earned by employees currently holding the jobs.

Jobs and pay relationships are changing continually. Information the organization gathers today won't be accurate next year. To be most useful, salary surveys should be continually reviewed and revised. The organization's other concern must be with the jobs themselves: are they truly comparable to jobs in your company? Titles alone aren't guarantees. Detailed job descriptions will increase your chances of getting market information that's valid and reliable as well as up to date.

Why make your own survey? Published surveys can be valuable inputs to your pay decisions, but they're not the answer to all your survey problems. You need facts and figures from companies in your own recruiting area. Chances are you'll have to do a survey yourself sooner or later, and you'll have to train one or two staffers to work with you.

PRELIMINARY CONSIDERATIONS

The first and most important consideration in planning a survey is to determine its purpose: Will the data be used to establish a new salary program, to assess your competitive position, to verify your hunch that excessive turnover may be caused by low pay, to get data on which you can base your position in collective bargaining sessions, or for other reasons? Once the specific purpose is identified, you'll need to make some key determinations as listed below.

COMPENSATION INFORMATION REQUIRED

You'll need information on basic compensation (wages) and supplemental compensation (benefits). In obtaining basic wage information, the base salary or base rate should be used.

PROS AND CONS: USING OUTSIDE SURVEYS VERSUS DOING IT YOURSELF

Using surveys your organization purchased or participated in has many advantages: they're relatively inexpensive, involve only supplying your own data and interpreting survey results, and usually have a large number of participants. In addition, purchased surveys are professionally conducted and summarized.

They also have a great many disadvantages: your organization can't choose key jobs, questions, or companies; your organization can't identify individual companies; your organization can't weight the data according to the importance to your unique situation; and your organization may have to resummarize the data so that they meet your company or organizational requirements.

But conducting your own survey is time consuming—your organization will have to contact each prospective respondent (and you can expect many to refuse to participate for one reason or another), it's difficult to get a statistically sound sample size, your organization will have to compute and summarize the data for all participants, and your organization will have to distribute the results.

What it comes down to is a trade-off between getting exactly what your organization wants, and getting results quickly, easily, and cheaply. If your organization absolutely demands personalized information, a do-it-yourself survey is the only answer.

If, on the other hand, your organization feels that participating in another company's survey or buying one designed for a work force similar to yours is adequate, you can save yourself a lot of time and expense. The choice is yours.

HEALTH BENEFITS AND OTHER EMPLOYEE PROGRAMS

HEALTH INSURANCE

The acquisition and cost of health insurance benefits for employees and their families have become a major issue for most employers. In recent years, the costs of health insurance benefits have skyrocketed causing many employers to reduce benefits, require employees to pay a portion of the costs, or even discontinue or refuse to offer health insurance benefits.

Health insurance coverage and costs have become a major public policy issue in the United States. Congress has intervened creating several laws, including ERISA and COBRA (see ERISA and COBRA sections), that provide specific requirements in the health insurance area. Additionally, employers and health care providers have instituted other methods of attempting to control costs including preadmission testing, outpatient surgery, employee wellness programs, and others.

Health insurance is a major issue with most employers and is usually within the realm of responsibility of the human resource or personnel department. In smaller EMS organizations, a designated individual should possess a level of competency in this very important area.

COBRA COVERAGE

Continuation of Health Coverage under COBRA

Continuation of health care provisions was enacted as part of the Consolidated Omnibus Budget Reconciliation Act of 1985 (COBRA). These provisions cover group health plans of employers with 20 or more employees on a typical day in the previous calendar year. COBRA gives participants and beneficiaries an election to maintain, at their own expense, coverage under their health plan at a cost that is comparable to what it would be if they were still members of the employer's group. Employers and plan administrators have an obligation to determine specific rights of beneficiaries with respect to election, notification, and type of coverage options (see 29 USC §§ 1161 through 1168). Plans must give covered individuals an initial general notice informing them of their rights under COBRA and describing the law. Plan administrators are required to provide specific notices when certain events occur. In most instances of employee death, termination, reduced hours of employment, entitlement to Medicare, or bankruptcy, it becomes the employer's responsibility to provide a specific notice to the plan administrator.

The Department of Labor's regulatory and interpretative jurisdiction over COBRA provisions is limited to the COBRA notification and disclosure provisions. Instead it is the Internal Revenue Service that has regulatory and interpretative responsibility for all provisions of COBRA not under the Department's jurisdiction. In addition, ERISA provisions relating to participation, vesting, funding, and benefit accrual, contained in parts 2 and 3 of Title I, are generally administered and interpreted by the IRS.

Who Gets COBRA Benefits and What Is Covered?

There are three elements to qualify for COBRA benefits. COBRA establishes specific criteria for plans, beneficiaries, and events that initiate the coverage. Group health plans for employers with 20 or more employees on more than 50 percent of the working days in the previous calendar year are subject to COBRA. The term "employees" includes all full-time and part-time employees, as well as self-employed individuals. For this purpose, the term employees also includes agents, independent contractors, and directors, but only if they are eligible to participate in a group health plan.

A qualified beneficiary generally is any individual covered by a group health plan on the day before a qualifying event. A qualified beneficiary may be an employee, including the employee's spouse and dependent children, and in certain cases, a retired employee, including the retired employee's spouse and dependent children. "Qualifying events" are certain types of events that without COBRA coverage would otherwise cause an individual to lose health coverage. The type of qualifying event will determine who the qualified beneficiaries are and the required amount of time that a plan must offer the health coverage to them under COBRA. A plan, at its discretion, may provide longer periods of continuation coverage. Some of those qualifying events have included voluntary or involuntary termination of employment for reasons other than "gross misconduct," or a reduction in the number of hours of employment. The types of qualifying events for spouses would include termination of the covered employee's employment for any reason other than "gross misconduct," reduction in the hours worked by the covered employee, the covered employee's becoming entitled to Medicare, divorce or legal separation of the covered employee, or death of the covered employee. Qualifying events for dependent children are the same as those of the spouse except for the loss of "dependent child" status under plan rules.

Notice and Election Procedures

COBRA outlines procedures for employees and family members to elect continuation coverage and for employers and plans to notify beneficiaries. The qualifying events contained in the law create rights and obligations for employers, plan administrators, and qualified beneficiaries. Qualified beneficiaries have the right to elect to continue coverage that is identical to the coverage provided under the plan. Employers and plan administrators have an obligation to determine the specific rights of beneficiaries with respect to election, notification, and type of coverage options.

Notice Procedures

An initial general notice must be furnished to covered employees, their spouses, and newly hired employees informing them of their rights under

COBRA and describing provisions of the law. COBRA information also must be contained in the summary plan description (SPD) that participants receive. ERISA requires employers to furnish modified and updated SPDs containing certain plan information and summaries of material changes in plan requirements. Plan administrators must automatically furnish the SPD booklet 90 days after a person becomes a participant or beneficiary begins receiving benefits or within 120 days after the plan is subject to the reporting and disclosure provisions of the law.

Specific notice requirements are triggered for employers, qualified beneficiaries, and plan administrators when a qualifying event occurs. Employers must notify plan administrators within 30 days after an employee's death, termination, reduced hours of employment, or entitlement to Medicare. Multiemployer plans may provide for a longer period of time.

A qualified beneficiary, usually the employee, must notify the plan administrator within 60 days after events such as divorce or legal separation or a child's ceasing to be covered as a dependent under plan rules. Disabled beneficiaries must notify plan administrators of Social Security disability determinations. A notice must be provided within 60 days of a disability determination and prior to expiration of the 18-month period of COBRA coverage. These beneficiaries also must notify the plan administrator within 30 days of a final determination that they are no longer disabled.

Plan administrators, upon notification of a qualifying event, must automatically provide a notice to employees and family members of their election rights. The notice must be provided in person or by first class mail within 14 days of receiving information that a qualifying event has occurred. There are two special exceptions to the notice requirements for multiemployer plans. First, the time frame for providing notices may be extended beyond the 14- and 30-day requirements if allowed by plan rules. Second, employers are relieved of the obligation to notify plan administrators when employees terminate or reduce their work hours. Plan administrators are responsible for determining whether these qualifying events have occurred.

Election Decisions

The election period is the time frame during which each qualified beneficiary may choose whether to continue health care coverage under an employer's group health plan. Qualified beneficiaries have a 60-day period to elect whether to continue coverage. This period is measured from the later of the coverage loss date or the date the notice to elect COBRA coverage is sent. COBRA coverage is retroactive if elected and paid for by the qualified beneficiary.

A covered employee or the covered employee's spouse may elect COBRA coverage on behalf of any other qualified beneficiary. Each qualified beneficiary, however, may independently elect COBRA coverage. A parent or legal guardian may elect on behalf of a minor child. A waiver of coverage may be revoked by or on behalf of a qualified beneficiary prior to the end of the election period. A beneficiary may then reinstate coverage. Then, the plan need only provide continuation coverage beginning on the date the waiver is revoked.

Covered Benefits

Qualified beneficiaries must be offered benefits identical to those received immediately before qualifying for continuation coverage. For example, a beneficiary may have had medical, hospitalization, dental, vision, and prescription benefits under single or multiple plans maintained by the employer. Assuming a qualified beneficiary had been covered by three separate health plans of his former employer on the day preceding the qualifying event, that individual has the right to elect to continue coverage in any of the three health plans.

Noncore benefits are vision and dental services, except where they are mandated by law, in which case they become core benefits. Core benefits include all other benefits received by a beneficiary immediately before qualifying for COBRA coverage.

If a plan provides both core and noncore benefits, individuals may generally elect either the entire package or just core benefits. Individuals do not have to be given the option to elect just the noncore benefits unless those were the only benefits carried under that particular plan before a qualifying event. A change in the benefits under the plan for active employees may apply to qualified beneficiaries. Beneficiaries also may change coverage during periods of open enrollment by the plan.

Duration of Coverage

COBRA establishes required periods of coverage for continuation health benefits. A plan, however, may provide longer periods of coverage beyond those required by COBRA. COBRA beneficiaries generally are eligible to pay for group coverage during a maximum of 18 months for qualifying events due to employment termination or reduction of hours of work. Certain qualifying events, or a second qualifying event during the initial period of coverage, may permit a beneficiary to receive a maximum of 36 months of coverage.

Coverage begins on the date that coverage would otherwise have been lost by reason of a qualifying event and can end when the last day of maximum coverage is reached, premiums are not paid on a timely basis, the employer ceases to maintain any group health plan, coverage is obtained with another employer group health plan that does not contain any exclusion or limitation with respect to any preexisting condition of such beneficiary, or a beneficiary is entitled to Medicare benefits.

Special rules for disabled individuals may extend the maximum periods of coverage. If a qualified beneficiary is determined under Title II or Title XVI of the Social Security Act to have been disabled at the time of a termination of employment or reduction in hours of employment and the qualified beneficiary properly notifies the plan administrator of the disability determination, the 18-month period is expanded to 29 months.

Although COBRA specifies certain maximum required periods of time that continued health coverage must be offered to qualified beneficiaries, COBRA does not prohibit plans from offering continuation health coverage that goes beyond the COBRA periods.

In fact some plans allow beneficiaries to convert group health coverage to an individual policy. If this option is available from the plan under COBRA it must be offered to you. In this case, the option must be given for the beneficiary to enroll in a conversion health plan within 180 days before COBRA coverage ends. The premium is generally not at a group rate. The conversion option, however, is not available if the beneficiary ends COBRA coverage before reaching the maximum period of entitlement.

Paying for Cobra Coverage

Beneficiaries may be required to pay the entire premium for coverage. It cannot exceed 102 percent of the cost to the plan for similarly situated individuals who have not incurred a qualifying event. Premiums reflect the total cost of group health coverage, including both the portion paid by employees and any portion paid by the employer before the qualifying event, plus 2 percent for administrative costs. For disabled beneficiaries receiving an additional 11 months of coverage after the initial 18 months, the premium for those additional months may be increased to 150 percent of the plan's total cost of coverage.

EMPLOYEE WELLNESS PROGRAMS

EMS personnel are often under a tremendous amount of stress and may possess a poor life style. Studies have shown that roughly 50 percent of large case costs could be mitigated substantially by improvement in four areas of wellness—smoking cessation, proper diet, regular exercise, and moderate consumption of alcohol. To foster these improvements, the EMS organization can offer employees wellness-oriented programs. These include on-site screening for major diseases and employer education programs aimed at informing employees about life style choices that lead to optimum health. EMS organizations that invest in these programs feel that the long-term payoff will be a work force with improve life style habits, which will, in turn, lower health care costs.

EMPLOYEE ASSISTANCE PROGRAMS

A wide range of problems, not indirectly associated with a person's job function, can have an effect on that individual's job performance. Significant changes in any of the following areas can indicate that an employee is troubled.

- Low productivity

- Poor work quality

- Interpersonal conflicts with co-workers, customers, or clients (e.g., inappropriate hostility, anger, withdrawal, or exhibition of inappropriate attitudes or behaviors)

- Excessive waste

- Excessive accidents or mistakes or both

- Excessive absenteeism (especially on Mondays)

- Poor judgment

- Reduced efficiency

- Disappearance from work

- Extending or not returning from lunch or other breaks

- Consistently missing deadlines

- Minimal contact with co-workers, especially supervisors

Typical problems employees may have include:

- Alcohol and/or drug dependency

- Family (which includes marital, children, extended families, parents, etc.)

- Financial

- Legal

- Work related

In most instances, employees overcome such personal problems independently and the effect on job performance is negligible. In other instances, normal supervisory assistance serves as motivation or guidance by which such problems can be resolved, thereby returning job performance back to an acceptable level. In some cases, however, neither the efforts of the employee nor those of the supervisor have the desired effect and unsatisfactory job performance persists.

Many employers, recognizing that almost any human problem can be successfully treated if it is identified in its early stages, and if referral is made to an appropriate professional care facility, are now offering an Employee Assistance Program (EAP). Such EAPs are designed to help employees resolve personal problems that may adversely affect their jobs or lives.

EAP services are normally available to employees on a voluntary, self-referral basis through an outside agency or by supervisory referral to the EAP agency. Resources through the EAP agency include professional counseling, doctors, and information resources to which employees may not have access or about which they may not be aware. Employers with EAPs make it clear to employees that neither a request for treatment nor program participation will jeopardize the employee's job security or advancement opportunities.

WORKERS' COMPENSATION VERSUS HEALTH INSURANCE BENEFITS

The primary distinction between workers' compensation coverage for an employee and health insurance coverage is the place of the injury or illness. As discussed in Chapter 7—Workers' Compensation—this state-mandated program covers work-related injuries and illnesses that "arise out of or in the course of employment," that is, within the duties of the job. Whereas health insurance coverage usually encompasses all injuries or illnesses within the scope of the policy that happen outside of the job.

In many organizations, the human resource (HR) department or other designated EMS professional is responsible for the proper management of the workers' compensation and health insurance functions. Thorough and careful analysis of the facts and circumstances surrounding the injury or illness will normally provide the proper direction for the filing for either workers' compensation benefits or health insurance benefits.

LONG-TERM DISABILITY

Under some health insurance plans, employees can be offered long-term benefits to compensate for loss of income in the event of a totally disabling injury or illness. Long-term disability policies are usually voluntary and supplemental to the health insurance policy and normally require the employee to be totally disabled to qualify for benefits.

FRINGE BENEFIT PROGRAMS

401K PLANS

Many employers are offering employees methods through which to save monies for retirement or other reasons on a tax-deferred or tax savings basis. These plans can include, but are not limited to, 401(k) savings plans, 403B savings plans, IRA/SEP plans, and other vehicles. HR professionals should be aware that each plan possesses specific rules and requirements.

STOCK OPTIONS

In publically held companies, employees are often permitted to join stock option programs whereby the employer provides a matching amount of stock or permits the employee to purchase stock at a discount. There are a wide variety of stock option programs. The HR professional should be thoroughly familiar with all rules and requirements of her or his individual company's plan if offered.

CHILD CARE

With our changing work force, many companies are offering reduced cost or free child care for their employees.

RETIREMENT BENEFITS

America's population is aging. In 1988, 30 million people were older than 64; of these, 12 million were 75 or older. (Sixty-five is the retirement age treated as "normal" in many pension systems, and the "normal" age under current Social Security rules. Most American workers cannot be retired on account of age; until enactment of a 1986 law, mandatory retirement was increased to age 70. The age for receiving full Social Security benefits is scheduled to rise gradually from 65 to 67, a change that will affect persons born in 1938 and later.)

As the population ages (a result of longer life expectancy and of demographic cycles), more of the nation's income must be devoted to retirees. Retirees consume their savings. In addition, they live on income transfers from government and on pension payments earned during their years at work. In 1989, Social Security paid about $242 billion in old age and survivors benefits to about 35.5 million retirees and dependents. Supplemental Security Income (SSI), a federal program for the needy, paid $3.4 billion to 1.4 million elderly persons. Other programs, providing food stamps, fuel assistance, and housing benefits, also transferred money to the elderly poor. In 1988 nearly 14 million elderly persons received about $137 billion in income from private sector pension plans. About the same number of people receive public pensions under civil service, military, and railroad retirement systems. In 1987, the assets of these plans were greater than 42 trillion, more than two-thirds of that in private plans.

Social Security (technically, Old Age and Survivors Insurance) payments are thus the largest part of the income of America's elderly. Entitlement is earned by labor force participation and benefit levels are related to the wages on which the Social Security tax (FICA) was paid. Thus Social Security is very much a work-based and work-tiered system of retirement income. Pensions are obviously earned through work. Pension law was largely a matter of state law (and most of that created by common law court adjudications) until 1974, when Congress preempted the field with the Employee Retirement Income Security Act. This complicated law, partly located within the Internal Revenue Code (because the law establishes conditions that pension plans must meet to be eligible for income tax treatment benefiting both the employing companies and the pension recipients), has become an important area of legal specialization. This chapter will not make you a specialist on either "government" Social Security law or "private" pension law, but it will introduce you to important issues and especially to some of the interconnections between the two systems, which after all are performing the single task of providing retirement income to former workers.

PENSION PLANS

There are two general types of pension plans:

Defined Benefit Plans

Promise employees specific monthly benefits at retirement. They may state the exact dollar amount (e.g., $1,150 a month) or they may provide a formula to calculate the benefits (e.g., $15 per month for every year of service with the employer).

Defined Contribution Plans

Provide benefits based on employer contributions and investment earnings of the pension trust. An individual account is established for each employee. The employer may promise to contribute a specific amount of money (e.g., five percent of the employee's annual earnings), as in a money purchase plan, or contributions may vary with the company's profits, as in a profit-sharing plan. However, no exact benefit is promised at retirement.

Defined contribution plans include target benefit plans, thrift and savings plans, 401(k) arrangements, and employee stock ownership plans (ESOPs).

In recent years, many private and public sector organizations have begun supplementing existing defined benefit plans.

Plan Requirements

To protect the rights of plan participants, ERISA imposes certain requirements for pension plans. (Author's note: The following text is taken from the *Employer's Pension Guide*, a publication of the Department of Labor, the Internal Revenue Service, and the Pension Benefit Guaranty Corporation. It is a very useful reference.)

Plan Purpose

A pension plan must be operated solely in the interest of participants and beneficiaries. Pension funds must be held in a trust fund separate from an employer's assets or be used to purchase insurance policies that are held as plan assets. Trust fund assets or insurance policies must be used exclusively to provide benefits for plan participants and, with very few exceptions, may not be returned to the employer while the plan is in operation.

Virtually any transaction involving an employer and the assets of any pension plan maintained by the employer is prohibited. For example, an employer is not allowed to borrow money from its pension fund, even if it is willing to pay a higher interest rate than the plan could obtain in the open market. However, a plan may hold a limited amount of the employer's stock as part of the plan's assets.

If a company is sold or merged, the assets of the pension plan do not become the property of the new company, but must remain in the trust fund for the benefit of the plan participants.

Participation

Generally, employees must be allowed to participate in a plan if they are at least age 21 and have completed one year of service with the employer. However, two years of service may be required if a plan provides for full and immediate vesting. An employee may not be excluded from a pension plan because of age, even if he or she is hired within a few years of retirement age.

Vesting

Being "vested" means an employee has completed the years of service required under the plan to attain a permanent legal right to receive his or her pension, whether or not the employee continues to work for the same employer. Despite the years of service requirement, an employee is entitled to 100 percent of his or her accrued benefit upon attaining the normal retirement age under the plan. For this purpose, the plan cannot define a normal retirement age that is later than age 65 or the time a person has five years of participation. In addition, an employee must always be fully vested in his or her own contributions to the plan. This means that if the employee leaves the company, he or she is entitled to the money he or she contributed, plus interest.

Single-employer pension plans must provide vesting for employees *at least as rapidly* as either of the following two methods:

Cliff Vesting—employees are fully vested after five years of service.

Graded Vesting—employees are at least 20 percent vested after three years of service and receive at least an additional 20 percent vesting for each of the next four years, with full vesting coming after no more than seven years.

If the plan's vesting schedule is changed, individuals with three or more years of service must be able to remain under the prior schedule if they wish to do so.

Years of Service—Ordinarily, for vesting purposes, a year of service is defined in the plan as a 12-month period during which an employee performs at least 1,000 hours of service, which generally are defined as:

- hours for which an employee is paid or entitled to be paid (including pay for vacation and sick leave); and

- hours for which an employee is awarded back pay.

Pension plans also are permitted to use an "elapsed time" method of counting service. Under this system, the total period of time from the date of employment to the date of severance is computed, regardless of actual hours worked.

Exclusions—Service that may be excluded when demanding employee vesting includes years of service before age 18; periods during which an employee declined to contribute to a plan for which employee contributions were required; periods when the employer did not maintain the plan or a predecessor plan; years during which an employee has a break in service; and certain periods preceding breaks in service.

Break in Service—A plan may regard a year in which an employee does not complete more than 500 hours of service as a "break in service," and this may result in an employee receiving credit for less service for vesting purposes.

However, if an employee takes leave because of pregnancy, birth, or adoption of a child, or to care for the child immediately following birth, or adoption, up to 501 hours of that leave must be counted as hours of service to the extent that such hours prevent the occurrence of a break in service.

Absence due to certain military service also cannot be counted as a break in service.

Disclosure Requirements

There are certain disclosure requirements to which plan sponsors and plan administrators must comply under ERISA. The plan administrator must automatically provide employees with the following information:

Summary Plan Description—A booklet or similar document written in easily understandable language that includes such information as how the plan operates; when employees are eligible to receive their pensions; how they can calculate the amount of their benefits; and how to file claims. This information must be provided free of charge within 90 days after an employee becomes a participant in the plan. All updated versions of the Summary Plan Description that reflect changes in the plan also must automatically be provided to the plan participants.

Summary of the Annual Report—A summary of the annual report—information on the financial activities of the plan—must be provided to participants annually. (The full annual report also must be provided to any participants who request it in writing.)

Survivor Coverage Data—Information on the plan's survivor coverage, and how it affects employees and their spouses, must be provided to participants.

Benefit Statement—In general, the plan administrator must furnish to any participant or beneficiary who so requests *in writing*—but not more frequently than once a year—a statement of the participant's total accrued benefit and the earliest date on which he or she will become vested.

Additionally, administrators of all pension plans covered by ERISA must file an annual report with the IRS using the Form 5500 series. The IRS transmits the report to the Department of Labor and specific information from the report is sent to the Pension Benefit Guaranty Corporation.

The primary statutes referred to under the category of "employee benefits law" include the Employee Retirement Income Security Act ("ERISA") and the Consolidated Omnibus Budget Reconciliation Act ("COBRA"). The breadth of ERISA is extensive. COBRA, on the other hand, is more specific, as it applies to health benefits and the continuation of those benefits under certain circumstances.

ERISA PLANS

BASIC PROVISIONS/REQUIREMENTS OF ERISA

ERISA sets uniform minimum standards to ensure that employee benefit plans are established and maintained in a fair and financially sound manner. In addition, employers have an obligation to provide promised benefits and satisfy ERISA's requirements on managing and administering private pension and welfare plans. The Department's Pension and Welfare Benefits Administration (PWBA), together with the Internal Revenue Service (IRS), carries out its statutory and regulatory authority to ensure that workers receive the promised benefits.

The Department has principal jurisdiction over Title I of ERISA, which requires persons and entities who manage and control plan funds to manage plans for the exclusive benefit of participants and beneficiaries; carry out their duties in a prudent manner and refrain from conflict-of-interest transactions expressly prohibited by law; comply with limitations on certain plans' investments in employer securities and properties; fund benefits in accordance with the law and plan rules; report and disclose information on the operations and financial condition of plans to the government and participants; and provide documents required in the conduct of investigations to ensure compliance with the law.

By contrast the IRS administers Title II of ERISA, which includes vesting, participation, nondiscrimination, and funding standards.

WHO IS COVERED?

The provisions of Title I of ERISA cover most private sector employee benefit plans. Employee benefit plans are voluntarily established and maintained by an employer, an employee organization, or jointly by one or more such employers and an employee organization. Employee benefit plans that are pension plans are established and maintained to provide retirement income or to defer income to termination of covered employment or beyond. Employee benefit plans that are welfare plans are established and maintained to provide health benefits, disability benefits, death benefits, prepaid legal services, vacation benefits, day care centers, scholarship funds, apprenticeship and training benefits, or other similar benefits.

In general, ERISA does not cover plans established or maintained by governmental entities or churches for their employees, or plans that are maintained solely to comply with applicable workers' compensation, unemployment, or disability laws. ERISA also does not cover plans maintained outside the United States primarily for the benefit of nonresident aliens or unfunded excess benefit plans.

REPORTING AND DISCLOSURE

The administrator of any employee benefit plan must furnish participants and beneficiaries with a summary plan description (SPD), describing in understandable terms, their rights, benefits, and responsibilities under the plan. Plan administrators are also required to furnish participants with a summary of any material changes to the plan or changes to the information contained in the summary plan description. Generally, copies of these documents must be filed with the Department.

In addition, the administrator must file an annual report (Form 5500 Series) each year containing financial and other information concerning the operation of the plan. Plans with 100 or more participants must file the Form 5500. Plans with fewer than 100 participants must file the Form 5500-C at least every third year and may file a form 5500-R, an abbreviated report, in the two intervening years. The forms are filed with the Internal Revenue Service, which furnishes the information to the Department of Labor. Welfare benefit plans with fewer than 100 participants that are fully insured or unfunded (i.e., benefits are provided exclusively through insurance contracts where the premiums are paid directly from the general assets of the employer or the benefits are paid from the general assets of the employer) are not required to file an annual report under regulations issued by the Department. Plan administrators must furnish participants and beneficiaries with a summary of the information in the annual report.

RETIREMENT BENEFIT PLANS

Under ERISA and the Internal Revenue Code, tax-deductible employer contributions must be held in trust to provide pension benefits. (*See* 29 U.S.C. 1103, I.R.C. 401(a).) The employer, as a plan sponsor, must meet annual, minimum funding obligations so that the plan will have the wherewithal to provide retirement benefits. (*See* 29 U.S.C. 1082, I.R.C. 412.)

At a minimum, employers must annually contribute an amount equal to the cost of the plan (which is essentially the cost of funding the benefits earned during the current year) plus an amount necessary to amortize past service liability (i.e., the cost of funding benefits attributable to service before the employer began to maintain the plan). *See* 29 U.S.C. 1082, I.R.C. 412. (Generally, the maximum amortization period is 30 years, although for certain plans and benefits the period is as long as 40 years.) Contributions to single employer plans must be made in quarterly installments, 29 U.S.C. 1082(e), and the sponsoring employer as well as every member in its controlled group—*see* 29 U.S.C. 1082(c)(11) and I.R.C. 414(b),(c),(m),(o)—are liable for the contributions.

CONTRIBUTIONS VERSUS CREDITORS

A pension plan is not a gift, but a contract entered into by the employer unilaterally or through negotiation with the employees' representative. See *Allied Structural Steel Co. v. Spannaus*, 438 U.S. 234 (1978); *Inland Steel Co. v. NLRB*, 170 F.2d 247 (7th Cir. 1948), *cert. denied*, 336 U.S. 960 (1949); 29 U.S.C. 186(c)(5). As a form of deferred compensation that an employer can fund over a period of up to 40 years, a pension plan is the functional equivalent of a loan. In essence, plan participants lend to their employers the difference between (a) the present value of all the benefits for which they have already rendered service and (b) the amount the employer contributes to the plan. Among the immediate beneficiaries of this extension of credit— that is, the participants' agreement to accept deferred compensation—are the employer and its creditors, who use and receive the revenue that would otherwise have gone into current wages.

Unfortunately, recent bankruptcy decisional law has eroded the principle that employers are obligated to fund the pension benefits that their employees have earned, that is, for which the employers have already received full consideration. [See *In re Chateaugay Corp.*, 12 Employee Benefits Cas. 1441 (Bankr. S.D.N.Y. 1990), *aff'd*, 14 Employee benefits Cas. 1225 (S.D.N.Y. 1991). Forgotten or ignored are the earlier decisions in which the judiciary recognized that an employer's obligation to provide pension benefits is entitled to priority, as in, for example, *Bowen v. Hockley*, 71 F.2d 781 (4th Cir. 1934). Accord *Wood v. Camden Iron Works*, 221 F. 1010 (D.N.J. 1915).]

FIDUCIARIES, ETHICS, AND DUTIES

Part 4 of Title I sets forth standards and rules governing the conduct of plan fiduciaries. In general, persons who exercise discretionary authority or control regarding management of a plan or disposition of its assets are "fiduciaries" for purposes of Title I of ERISA. Fiduciaries are required, among other things, to discharge their duties solely in the interest of plan participants and beneficiaries and for the exclusive purpose of providing benefits and defraying reasonable expenses of administering the plan. In discharging their duties, fiduciaries must act prudently and in accordance with documents governing the plan, to the extent such documents are consistent with ERISA. Certain transactions between an employee benefit plan and "parties in interest," which include the employer and others who may be in a position to exercise improper influence over the plan, are prohibited by ERISA. Most of these transactions are also prohibited by the Internal Revenue Code ("Code"). The Code imposes an excise tax on "disqualified persons"—whose definition generally parallels that of parties in interest—who participate in such transactions.

EXEMPTIONS FROM ERISA

Both ERISA and the Code contain various statutory exemptions from the prohibited transaction rules and give the Departments of Labor and Treasury, respectively, authority to grant administrative exemptions and establish exemption procedures. Reorganization Plan No. 4 of 1978 transferred the authority of the Treasury Department over prohibited transaction exemptions, with certain exceptions, to the Labor Department.

The statutory exemptions generally include loans to participants, the provision of services necessary for operation of a plan for reasonable compensation, loans to employee stock necessary for operation of a plan for reasonable compensation, loans to employee stock ownership plans, and investments with certain financial institutions regulated by other state or federal agencies. (See ERISA Section 408 for the conditions of the exemptions.) Administrative exemptions may be granted by the Department on a class or individual basis for a wide variety of proposed transactions.

RELATION TO STATE, LOCAL, AND OTHER FEDERAL LAWS

Part 5 of Title I provides that the provisions of ERISA Titles I and IV supersede state and local laws that "relate to" an employee benefit plan. ERISA, however, saves certain state and local laws from ERISA preemption, including state insurance regulation of multiple-employer welfare arrangements (MEWAs). MEWAs generally constitute employee welfare benefit plans or other arrangements providing welfare benefits to employees of more than one employer, not pursuant to a collective bargaining agreement.

In addition, ERISA's general prohibitions against assignment or alienation of pension benefits do not apply to qualified domestic relations orders. Plan administrators must comply with the terms of orders made pursuant to state domestic relations law and award all or part of a participant's benefit in the form of child support, alimony, or marital property to an alternative payee (spouse, former spouse, child, or other dependent).

SOCIAL SECURITY INSURANCE

One of the major social issues in the United States today is the funding of Social Security Insurance. EMS organizations should be aware that Social Security possesses two (2) major areas that affect many employees, namely Social Security (also known as "Old Age and Survivor's Insurance") benefits (including Medicare/Medicaid) and Social Security Disability Insurance (known as "SSDI").

GOVERNMENT DISABILITY PLANS

EMS organizations should be aware of the Social Security Disability Program (42 U.S.C. § 423 *et. seq.*) that provides benefits to individuals who are "permanently and totally disabled." Under SSD, an individual is required to prove (1) that he has worked at covered employment for the requisite number of quarters; (2) that his inability to work is "medical" in nature; and (3) that he is totally disabled. SSD often comes into play for EMS professionals for employees incurring permanent injuries or illnesses from sources outside the workplace.

LIFE INSURANCE

Many companies offer paid life insurance benefits or supplemental life insurance policies for their employees. EMS professionals are usually responsible for the on-site management of these programs and the oversight responsibility for the overall programs.

TYPES

There are varying types of life insurance policies covering a wide variety of types of coverages. EMS professionals are usually responsible for managing life insurance policies at the company location and often are called upon to assist the employee with policy issues or to assist the family in collecting benefits. EMS professionals should possess a working knowledge of the policies offered by their organization.

LEAVING A JOB

One of the critical times for your human resource department or designated EMS professional is when an employee is leaving the employ of your organization. Whether the individual is leaving voluntarily or involuntarily, human resources is usually the key department to assist the individual in acquiring pertinent information regarding transfer of such "things" as retirement benefits, health insurance, life insurance, and so on.

SEVERANCE PAY

Under most circumstances, a severance pay policy is held to be an "employee welfare benefit plan" and as such subject to ERISA. Even in those cases where the severance plan is unfunded and an administrator is difficult to ascertain, the courts have ruled that severance pay was a plan (thereby preempting a state law contract claim for vested severance pay). The most important aspect of an ERISA severance pay plan is the fact that severance never vests under ERISA (until severance occurs, that is). Severance pay can create quite a problem when a corporate transfer of assets takes place, or when a company files bankruptcy or downsizes. A prudent EMS professional would do well to examine the severance plan, first deciding whether it is necessary at all. In many instances the corporate executives may be the primary proponents of such a plan, and uniform application throughout the company would be required in order to avoid a charge of arbitrary and capricious decision making by the administrator. Get rid of the severance policy, or at least remove some of its teeth.

The personnel department should consider implementing the following course of action with regard to any antiquated severance pay policies:

1. Turn it into an ERISA plan by including it in literature, identifying the administrator, and defining its terms within a memorandum to all employees.

2. Include a specific provision within the terms that upon sale or transfer of the company severance shall not be due any employee who is offered employment of any sort from the successor company, whether or not that employee takes the job and without regard to any reduction in pay or benefits via the successor company.

3. These modifications should be made well in advance of an impending shutdown or corporate sale. Although the severance plan cannot vest, and the administrator has the right to unilaterally modify or eliminate the plan; any changes made immediately preceding the sale of its operations could be considered an arbitrary and capricious act on the part of the administrator.

BENEFITS ADMINISTRATION

In the past decade or so, government intervention into the employee benefits arena has been unprecedented. Inflation and rising health-care costs are additional problems that organizations must deal with when administering their benefits programs.

EMS organizations have had to become more knowledgeable about benefits administration and benefits. Consultants have flourished in an atmosphere of continued regulation and inflation.

KEY ISSUES THAT HAVE HAD AN IMPACT ON THE ADMINISTRATIVE COST OF BENEFITS IN RECENT YEARS

- The Employee Income Security Act (ERISA) was passed by Congress in 1974. Litigation over coverage of pregnancy as a disability led to the Pregnancy Disability Act of 1978. Pregnancy now establishes eligibility for benefits on equal terms with other disabilities. Both a company's health insurance plan and short-term disability income plans are affected. Before the new law was enacted, approximately 60 percent of the established short-term disability plans had no provision for pregnancy benefits.
- Amendments to the Age Discrimination in Employment Act (ADEA) have now extended the protections for individuals over 70.
- The Health Maintenance Organizations (HMO) Act was enacted in 1973. There are hundreds of qualified HMOs throughout the country and most companies make employees aware of the HMO option.
- Current rates of inflation.
- Increased cost of new health and medical technology.

As benefits costs continue to go up, EMS organizations will have to look for innovative ways to provide new benefits and to alter current programs to fit the needs of their particular work force.

Installing a benefit program is a seven-step process. Prudent EMS organizations might consider the following:

1. Review the benefits currently in place

2. Assess their adequacy

3. Review the cost of each benefit

4. Conduct an employee survey to identify benefit needs and desires of the work force

5. Ensure compliance of the benefit programs with federal regulations, including sex and age discrimination legislation

6. Have a benefits consultant review the programs to ensure compliance and to provide advice regarding cost-effectiveness

7. Install needed programs and communicate their purpose to employees

BASIC BENEFITS FURNISHED BY MANY EMS ORGANIZATIONS

Medical Coverage

Most EMS organizations provide a base medical-hospital-surgical plan and a supplemental major medical plan for employees and their dependents. Most base benefit plans include the following:

Surgical charges are fully reimbursed at "reasonable and customary" rates, except in some states where fee schedules are in place.

Most companies pay full charges for a semiprivate room.

Most companies pay all costs for up to four months of hospitalization.

The normal major medical plan follows.

- $100–$500 deductible

- Coinsurance, where 80 percent is paid by the company and 20 percent by the employee

- Maximum major medical benefits of $250,000 to $1,000,000

- Most plans today also cover mental illness and treatment for drug or alcohol addiction, normally only at a 60 percent level

- Most companies still pay the total cost of medical coverage for the employee while the employee pays for dependent coverage

- The trend is to add dental and vision insurance and cover prescription drugs

Pension Plans

Most medium-sized and larger EMS organizations provide a fully paid pension plan to all employees; inflation is one of the most serious concerns of employees, and most companies are maintaining parity with inflation before retirement and making other adjustments from time to time as inflation accelerates. Vesting for pension plans occurs after 10 years of service.

Most companies also have some type of capital accumulation plan such as a thrift plan or savings plan. Employees contribute an amount up to 6 percent of their income, and the company matches that amount fifty cents on the dollar. Some companies are increasing their matching amount. Most companies now use a Social Security offset.

Life and Accident Insurance

Most EMS organizations provide death benefits and accidental death and dismemberment insurance. The typical life insurance plan is based on a formula that is twice the annual salary or a percentage of the annual salary, and some companies provide an additional amount if the employee elects to pay a portion of the cost. For example:

- Company provides $50,000, free to employee

- Employee takes an additional $50,000, employee pays premium

- Company provides additional $50,000, free to employee

Accidental death and dismemberment insurance is provided by most organizations and is company paid. Many companies also provide a portion, usually one-third, of the employee's preretirement life insurance, to be continued at company expense.

Disability

Long-term disability benefits are normally 60 percent of base pay reduced by any other benefit such as Social Security or unemployment. Long-term disability benefits usually start after twelve to twenty-six weeks of total disability or at such time as the company's short-term disability benefits run out. More companies are moving to a rehabilitation clause in their long-term disability benefit to curb accelerating costs. A rehabilitation clause might read as follows:

> The company at its discretion may require disabled employees to join a rehabilitation program that will be paid for by the company and is intended to improve the employee's condition and allow the employee to return to the work force in some productive role. If an employee is requested to enter a rehabilitation program, he or she must do so in order to continue receiving long-term disability pay.

Severance Pay

Not all EMS organizations have a severance pay policy, but many do. The pay is usually determined by a formula based on years of service, with a restriction or maximum limit; for example, two weeks severance for each year with the company, to a maximum of twenty-six weeks.

Some companies limit severance pay to salaried or management employees only, but most companies today feel that their severance pay policy should be available to all employees.

Time Off with Pay

Most EMS organizations give employees paid vacations, holidays, and time off to take care of family and civic responsibilities.

Vacations—These are normally two weeks after one year, three weeks after five years, and four weeks after ten years. Some companies require fifteen years of service before giving four weeks of vacation.

Holidays—Ten to eleven paid holidays seem to be standard today. Holidays are New Year's Day, President's Day, Good Friday, Memorial Day, Independence Day, Labor Day, Thanksgiving Day, the day after Thanksgiving, and Christmas Day. One or two *floating holidays* are given by many companies. The day before Christmas is usually given as one of the floating holidays.

Most companies give up to three days of leave for an employee to attend the funeral of a member of his or her immediate family. Paid time off for voting and for some civic responsibilities is also a common benefit.

OTHER BENEFIT TRENDS

Trends are toward flexible benefits to allow an employee a choice of benefits based on individual need, and more companies seem to be leaning toward flexible work schedules.

COMMUNICATING THE VALUE OF EMPLOYEE BENEFIT PROGRAMS

Often, employees tend to take benefits for granted. Usually the only time you hear an employee make disparaging remarks about benefit programs is when a specific feature of a plan isn't as good as someone else's.

With the tremendous increases in the costs of benefits, more and more organizations are looking for innovative, visible ways to communicate the benefits of their total compensation and benefits programs.

One of the most commonly used tools for communicating employee benefits is the annual employee benefits letter. Every spring, hundreds of thousands of employees receive a tastefully designed computer-printed statement of their company benefits. The statements report what each employee is receiving and how much. Companies hope that this statement will begin to instill a feeling for the real cost and value of the benefits long taken for granted by employees.

Most companies have ambivalent feelings about communicating all the details of their compensation program but less reticence about benefit communications, because benefits aren't as confidential a subject and because ERISA regulations mandate benefits communication anyway.

Benefits play an extremely important part in attracting and retaining top-level people, and companies miss the boat when they don't communicate the value and cost of their benefits programs.

SAMPLE EMPLOYEE BENEFITS STATEMENT

- Employee's name, address, and Social Security number.

- Employee's gross wages for the previous year and current salary. A cost breakdown of the various benefits the employee has that are paid in W-2 earnings.

- These benefits might include regular earnings, overtime earnings, accident/illness benefits, shift premiums, allowances, military pay, jury duty, funeral pay, holiday pay, vacation pay, service awards, suggestion awards, company car, relocation expenses, club memberships, lunch and coffee breaks, cash bonus, stock bonus, scholarships for employees' children, social and recreational programs, health and fitness programs, physical exams, paid parking, food services, medical facilities, employee newsletters, matching donations to colleges and universities.

Translating as many as possible of the benefit costs into a monetary value to the employee is certainly one of the best ways to sell employees on the true worth of your programs.

Benefits paid but not included in W-2 earnings include company contributions to

> Pension plan, hospitalization, life and accidental death insurance, dental insurance, vision insurance, stock purchase, thrift, or other savings plans, Social Security tax on wages and salaries, cost of premium on Workers' Compensation, cost for tax on wages for Unemployment Compensation, cost of tuition refund program, cost of safety equipment

Because benefits are linked to salaries that escalate with inflation, pension and insurance payouts are moving up almost 10 percent a year, and benefits specialists say a middle manager can easily have benefits that exceed $500,000.

SUMMARY

The areas of wages and benefits are of utmost importance to most EMS personnel and thus should be provided top consideration by every EMS organization. The laws governing these important areas have become complicated and thus if your EMS organization does not possess the necessary expertise to effectively manage these important areas, acquisition of assistance from outside of the EMS organization may be required. Remember, the greatest assets your organization possesses are its human assets!

CHAPTER 6

Negligence Issues

Laws are not invented; they grow out of circumstances.
—Azarias

The law does not generate justice, the law is nothing but a declaration and application of what is already just.
—P. J. Proudhon

In the past, EMS organizations were often placed within the category of a governmental agency and thus, under the concept "the king can do no wrong." Public sector EMS organizations were rarely, if ever, found liable under a tort liability theory. Through the years, this well established principle of law that public sector EMS organizations were considered to be a governmental undertaking, that is, an undertaking that could only be performed by an agency of the government, has began to erode. Under the general rule, public sector EMS organizations owe a duty to the community as a whole and thus were not designed to protect an individual's interest [as contrasted to private sector EMS organizations that possessed a specific contractual duty]. The duty owed by the public sector EMS organization was considered to be limited in nature and restricted to protecting the community in total. In the concept of immunity, fire service organizations, as a governmental undertaking, were virtually immune to any type of tort liability for losses of individuals. This age-old concept, that an EMS organization owed a duty to all but owed a duty to no one in particular, has received extensive criticism and is slowly deteriorating. Through the years, courts have established many exceptions to this general rule of nonliability. For example, many courts have established exceptions to the rule concerning construction and maintenance of facilities, repair of equipment, and operation of vehicles. The basic premise in which public sector EMS organizations can determine the extent of their immunity from tort liability usually focuses on the exercise of professional judgment or lack thereof. In general, the court decisions regarding public sector EMS organization liability or immunity tend to fall into the following basic concept: When EMS organization activity is within the area of proprietary functions (i.e., no professional experience is required), usually immunity is not present for the EMS organization. Thus, the public sector EMS organization and the municipality and the other governmental agency may be liable under the same tort liability theories as private sector organizations.

For activities that are within the realm of a governmental function, that is, those that require the use of a professional judgment of EMS personnel, the EMS organization, municipalities, or any other government agency could be responsible under the doctrine of respondeat superior (i.e., the EMS organization was responsible for the wrongful acts of its personnel). This theory of tort liability has been utilized when an EMT (Emergency Medical Technician) or other agent of the EMS organization was in privity with the fire service organization or where the employee or agent detrimentally relied upon the word or actions of the EMS organization. Immunity for the public sector EMS organization was utilized when the activities of the organization fell within the categories of the judicial, quasi-judicial, legislative, or quasi-legislative character thus safe guarding the EMS organization from potential liability. In general, if when the activity fell within the exercise of governmental judgment, the EMS organization, municipality, or other governmental agency was usually immune to tort liability.

As noted above, municipal immunity is based on the theory that "the king can do no wrong." Through varying exceptions that have been carved out of this general rule, the concept of immunity has been transferred to the fire service and EMS organizations. The issue of tort liability for fire service or EMS organizations, municipalities, and other governmental agencies can be a confusing situation. The confusion stems from a clash between theories of law that are fundamental to the subject. Thus, if we start with the basic rule that public sector EMS organizations, as an extension of the government, cannot be sued and then add the exceptions that have been carved out of the general rule by the courts, by the statutes, or by other rules that need to be applied to the situation, we usually can ascertain the position that an EMS organization is in following an incident. It should be noted that this myriad of rules varies from state to state and from municipality to municipality and that there may be a substantial number of variations to the rules of liability in any given jurisdiction. It also should be noted that our society is trending toward individual rights rather than governmental protections and thus new and novel theories for recovery for an injured individual may be also available.

Review of the cases in various jurisdictions that have considered the question of municipal liability for EMS organizations has revealed several general reasons leading to the conclusion that EMS organizations are either liable under a theory of tort liability or immune from tort liability actions or inactions. The question with regard to EMS liability under a tort theory revolved around whether the EMS organization possessed a duty to the individual. Listed below are some decisions that may provide guidance in this area.

1. Where a municipality is not required by statute to establish and maintain a fire service organization, there is generally no statutory obligation, and thus no duty, to protect any person or property.

2. Where a statute has been established by a legislature requiring a municipality to establish and maintain a fire service organization, a duty may exist to protect the public and/or an individual or individual's person or property.

3. Where a contractual obligation to provide fire services is established, a duty is normally created through this contractual obligation. In the absence of a contractual obligation to provide these services, usually no duty to perform has been created. EMS organizations, as an extension of a governmental entity, should be free to exercise their discretion and choice of tactics as long as appropriate, without worry of possible allegations of negligence in their decision making. As long as the public sector EMS organization is within the scope of its authority and using professional judgment in its activities, states retain qualified immunity for these "governmental activities." In most jurisdictions, the doctrine of sovereign immunity is based upon the characteristics of the activity (i.e., governmental vs. proprietary, congressional vs. administerial). Most states have developed statutory protections for specified government activities. Statutory immunities are normally narrowly construed and will provide immunity only within the activities specified within the statute.

In the area of EMS personnel liability, a definite distinction must be made between criminal liability and civil liability. In virtually all situations, the individual EMS professional is responsible for his or her own criminal acts. In the area of civil liability, the lines are often blurred depending upon the facts of the situation.

As a general rule for civil liability, EMS personnel are provided the same immunity as the EMS organization. Under the concept of respondeat superior, so long as the EMS professional is functioning within the scope of her or his employment, the EMS organization usually is the named responsible party. However, when an individual is outside the scope of employment or purposefully or willfully endangers another through his or her actions or omissions, personal, civil, and potentially criminal liability may result. Under many federal and state statutes, civil criminal liability may result where the individual willfully disregards a duty as proscribed by law (example: under OSHA, EPA, and other regulations).

Additionally, as we are aware, civil actions seeking monetary damages and the "deep pocket" in most civil actions involve the public sector EMS organization or municipality rather than the individual. However, when the individual is beyond the scope of duty and injury or harm occurs, potential personal liability may attach.

A substantial number of EMS organizations, such as the fire service, through charter provisions or by-laws or by separate contract, indemnify their officers for errors and omissions made while performing within the scope of their employment. Indemnity, by definition, is "a collateral contract or assurance, by which one person engages to secure another against anticipated loss or to prevent him from being damnified by the legal consequences of an act or forbearance on the part of one of the parties or of some third party. Terms pertaining to liability for loss shifted from one person held legally responsible to another person."[1] In an EMS situation, indemnification means that the EMS organization will bear the costs of legal fees, any civil penalties, and damages for the officer if he or she is named personally in the action that is basically against the fire service organization or municipality.

The greatest potential for civil liability falls for EMS personnel within the category of tort liability (i.e., negligence). With the ever-expanding trends to provide exceptions to the immunity doctrine and our litigious society, EMS personnel may increasingly become a target for civil actions just as officers and managers have in the private sector. EMS organizations should take the necessary precautions to protect their organization and themselves through appropriate planning, preparation, and decision making.

The question of whether or not a public sector EMS organization is liable tends to fall within the following categories:

1. Was the activity in which the harm occurred a proprietary function in which no judgment was required?

2. Was the activity in which the harm occurred a governmental function?

3. Was the activity in which the harm occurred within the category of judicial, quasi-judicial, legislative, or quasi-legislative function?

4. Was the activity in which the harm occurred outside of any or all of the above functions?

These categorizations are necessary in evaluating potential civil liability because of the potential protections afforded through immunity. However, as noted above, the concept of immunity is fast deteriorating due to the number of exceptions being provided by the courts.

The second category of questions that should be asked in evaluating potential civil liability surround the facts of the situation that resulted in the harm:

1. Was a duty created by statute or other law that required EMS organizations to respond? Was a special duty created through actions? Was that duty breached?

2. What was the nature of the duty violated (proprietary—governmental—ministerial)?

3. Was the negligent individual an employee, an agent, or otherwise employed by the EMS organization?

4. Was the EMS employee acting beyond the scope of his or her responsibility or authority?

5. If the EMS employee was acting outside the scope of authority, did the EMS organization or municipality subsequently ratify the act?

6. Was the EMS organization, it's officers, agents, or employees, negligent?

7. Was the injured employee another employee of the EMS organization or municipality? That is, do Workers Compensation laws apply?

8. Did the injured individual assume the risk or extend the harm?

As with individual liability, the major area of potential liability for EMS organizations is under the theory of tort liability (i.e., negligence). Most EMS organizations possess a duty created by statute, law, or the creation of a special relationship and when that duty is breached and harm occurs, the potential of civil liability is present. Activities such as tactics and strategies and 911 system failures are only a few of the activities performed by EMS organizations which are highly susceptible to potential liability when the activity malfunctions and harm occurs.

In most states, statutory immunity of varying types has been enacted to protect fire service and EMS organizations from civil liability. However, through performing activities outside of the statutory protection (i.e., outside the scope) and specific exceptions that have been found by various courts, statutory immunity against civil liability is eroding and limited at best.

For EMS vehicles, the first factor generally considered was whether the injury was caused by the negligence of the operator of the vehicle. Under the doctrine of respondeat superior, EMS organizations are generally responsible for the negligent acts or omissions of their employees operating response vehicles. However, many states have provided specific statutory immunity under specified circumstances.

Some states have required the operator of the vehicle to be an employee of the fire service or EMS organization and be driving an authorized emergency vehicle in order to be afforded protection.[2] Other states provide requirements that the vehicle be responding to an emergency call or fire alarm and some states require the siren to be sounding and warning lights displayed. Given the expansive nature of the decisions regarding fire service and response vehicles, prudent EMS organizations should become knowledgeable about the statutory protections provided, if any, and the case law in the jurisdiction regarding the operation of vehicles.

Of importance in mutual aid situations is the fact that the protections provided by statute do not normally go beyond the boundaries of the jurisdiction. Mutual aid agreements can be informal agreements or written agreements to provide assistance in emergency situations. The fire service organization must possess the authority to enter into such agreements and often mutual aid agreements are not considered binding unless the fire service or EMS organization negotiates the terms and conditions of the agreement. Of importance in any mutual aid agreement should be the protections provided under statutory immunity when the fire service or EMS organization is outside of the jurisdiction and indemnification and hold-harmless agreements in the event of personal injury or property loss.

In the areas of dispatch, the general consensus of the courts at this time is that the fire service and EMS organization are immune from liability.[3] However, where the fire service or EMS organization is negligent to exercise reasonable care, liability can be found. Cases where fire service and EMS organization have been held liable include failure to respond to several calls to 911, failure to respond to a fire call, failure to inspect valves, and additional areas.

Fire stations and emergency response apparatus are often categorized as "attractive nuisances" under the Attractive Nuisance Doctrine.[4] This doctrine, designed to protect small children, specified that a fire service and EMS organization, as the possessor of the property, may be liable for physical harm to children trespassing thereon caused by an artificial condition (i.e., bells, whistles, red paint, etc.) if:

1. the place where the condition exists is one upon which the fire organization knows or has reason to know that children are likely to trespass;

2. the condition is one which the fire service or EMS organization knows or has reason to know and which the fire service organization realizes or should realize involves an unreasonable risk of death or serious bodily harm to such children (for example, backing a vehicle from the station);

3. the children, because of their youth, do not discover the condition or realize the risk involved in intermeddling with it or in coming within the area made dangerous by it; and

4. the fire service or EMS organization fails to exercise reasonable care to eliminate the danger or otherwise protect the children.[5]

Though fire service and EMS organizations are generally immune from liability for truly discretionary undertakings or determinations, that exemption may be nullified where a special relationship has developed between the fire service and EMS organization and the injured individual. Typically, this occurs when a fire service and EMS organization undertakes a discretionary activity. The fire service or EMS organization subsequently ceases performance or does not perform without notifying the individual; the theory of detrimental reliance upon the activity is thus established.

There are several factors courts consider in determining whether the creation of a "new duty relationship" has been established. (i.e., a duty in which an individual may rely on their detriment to a fire service or EMS organization). The courts in several jurisdictions have found that a special relationship exists and thus a special duty created by the fire service and EMS organization in the following circumstances:

1. An individual must have direct contact with the fire or EMS organizational and the duties/identity must be reciprocally identified. The individual must be readily distinguished from the public as a whole.

2. The fire service or EMS organization was in a position of superior knowledge or authority, which could reasonably induce reliance by the individual on the statements of the fire service or EMS organization or its agents.

3. If the city's safety code required the fire service or EMS organization to perform specific acts upon finding a hazard, failure to perform these acts were considered gross negligence.

4. Fire service and EMS organizations communicating the assumption of corrective actions obligated the fire service or EMS organization to the individual. This communication can either be by words or by actions to establish a special duty to the fire service organization to protect the individual. The fire service or EMS organization will be considered to owe a particular individual a special duty of care when it's officers or agents, in

a position of authority to act or not to act, have or should have had knowledge of a condition that violates safety standards prescribed by statute or regulation and that presents serious risk of harm to a specified individual or property. When a fire service or EMS organization can reasonably foresee this danger, the fire service or EMS organization has a duty to exercise reasonable care for that specific individual's benefit.

In our world today, EMS organizations possess the potential for tort liability and immunity of any type is the exception to the rule. In order for EMS organizations to evaluate the potential risk from tort liability in any given situation, the following questions have been provided to perform a simple analysis of the risks in any given situation:

1. Has the duty been created by statute or duty actions or inactions of the fire service organization to respond to an individual's need?

2. Was the duty violated during a proprietary rather than a governmental activity, or with an administerial rather than a discretionary function?

3. Was the individual performing the negligent act or omission an employee or agent of the fire service or EMS organization?

4. Was the act ultra vires (beyond the individual's scope of authority or responsibility as provided by the fire service or EMS organization)?

5. Was the EMS professional's act subsequently ratified by the acts of the fire service and EMS organization or municipality?

6. Does the fire service or EMS organization or municipality have a duty to protect the particular individual that incurred the injury or property damage reasonably and detrimentally relied upon the affirmative representations of the fire service/EMS organizations, the employees, or the agents of the fire service/EMS organization?

7. Did the fire service/EMS organization, employees, or its agents perform the duty required by statute?

8. Was the fire service/EMS organization guilty of negligence and was the employee free from contributory negligence?

9. Was the assumption of the risk doctrine applicable?

10. Is the fellow servant rule applicable?

11. Do the provisions of the individual state's workers' compensation laws apply to the situation?

12. Does the individual state's statutory immunity apply to this situation?

The law of torts can be categorized by either (1) the nature of the defendant's conduct (i.e., intentional torts, negligence, product liability) or (2) the nature of the harm resulting to the injured individual, the damage to the property, or the harm to intangible personal interest.

INTENTIONAL HARM TO PERSONS

The torts involving intentional harm to persons are assault, battery, false imprisonment, and intentional infliction of emotional distress.

ASSAULT

The tort of assault is to redress the intentional invasion of a person's personal interest and freedom from apprehension of imminent harmful or offensive contact. The components of an assault include the intent to commit a harmful or offensive touching or creating apprehension of the same to the apprehension of offensive touching or harm in which the subjective mental state is in question. To establish the tort of assault, the plaintiff must prove that he was placed in apprehension of imminent harm or offensive touching. This is a subjective standard. An act that is intended to put another in apprehension of immediate bodily harm and succeeds in doing so may be considered assault. Assaults can result if the plaintiff is unaware of the threat and words alone cannot make an individual liable for an assault unless, together with other acts or circumstances, they put the plaintiff in reasonable apprehension of reasonable harm or offensive contact. It should be noted that a touching is not required for an assault.

BATTERY

The interest addressed in a battery action is the right of a person to be freed from intentional or offensive bodily contact. The basic components of a battery include (1) the intent to commit harmful or offensive touching or creating an apprehension of the same, (2) an actual touching of the individual, and (3) an absence of consent by the individual who was touched. In a battery action, the intent may be transferred from one individual to another and the direct application of force may be utilized. The touching must be of a harmful or offensive nature. The touching, which is not permitted by the norms of modern custom even though not harmful in nature, will suffice in most circumstances[6] (e.g., removal by the defendant of the plaintiff's false teeth, by force). The contact is offensive if it offends a person's reasonable sense of personal dignity (e.g., spitting upon or slapping a person). An individual being touched must be aware of the touching (e.g., not if the individual is asleep or unconscious) and must not consent to the touching. For a touching to actually be battery, the plaintiff must establish that he or she did not consent to the touching. A touching obtained by duress is ineffective. Only consent obtained by fraud, misrepresentation, or mistake is ineffective. In these situations, the traditional rules are that a doctor may extend an operation only when an emergency exists in that a failure to extend the operation would endanger the patient's life or health; or whether a later operation might unduly endanger the life or the health of a patient; or it is impractical to obtain the consent of the patient's family.[7] The states have adopted a more liberal view in light of the conditions in which the operations are now performed. Thus, in *Kennedy v. Parrott*,[8] the court held that in the absence of proof to the contrary, consent to an operation will be construed as general in nature, and the surgeon may extend the operation to remedy any abnormality or disease conditions in the area of the original incision wherever she, in the exercise of her sound professional judgment, determines the correct surgical procedures dictate and require an extension of the operation beyond the originally contemplated period. The test applied by most courts is whether a reasonable person in the possession of the patient would grant consent to the extension if he were able to choose.

The area of malpractice involving the extension of an operation without the consent of the patient (where an action sounds like a battery because the absence of consent makes the touching unpermitted) should be compared with the medical malpractice where a patient claims that she or he consented to a medical treatment by doctors who withheld material information concerning the risk of such treatment. In the United States today, lack of consent cases are treated as negligence cases rather than as battery.

FALSE IMPRISONMENT

The interest protected by false imprisonment is the individual's freedom from confinement or from restraint of movement. The elements of the false imprisonment action include (1) intent, (2) confinement, (3) consciousness of confinement, and (4) absence of consent. False imprisonment is an intentional tort (i.e., there is no such tort as a negligent false imprisonment tort). As with the action for battery, a distinction must be made between intent and motive. In the absence of privilege, if a defendant intentionally confines a plaintiff without his or her consent, the plaintiff may recover even if the person acted with good motive. In the area of confinement, the jury finds that the defendant imposed a restraint on his movement. An action will not lie in false imprisonment where a defendant merely impedes the individual's progress in one direction or confines him within an area where there is a reasonable exit. Insufficient false imprisonment may result by taking a person into custody under an assertive lawful authority that was in fact unlawful. No force or threat of force is necessary. The individual must be conscious in order to knowingly be confined. As with all of the intentional torts, the false imprisonment action also lacks consent.

INTENTIONAL INFLICTION OF EMOTIONAL DISTRESS

"One who, by extreme or outrageous conduct, intentionally or recklessly causes severe emotional distress to another, is subject to liability for such emotional distress and if bodily harm results from it, for such bodily harm." [Restatement (Second) of torts Section 46.] The elements for intentional infliction of emotional distress include intent, the impact of the distress must be severe, and a special relationship must exist between the parties. In most states, the intentional infliction of emotional distress may be based not only on the subjective intent or substantial certainty of the result but also on reckless disregard of probable consequences of the defendant's behavior. Additionally, in most states, the emotional distress must manifest itself in a severe form. Causing embarrassment or humiliation is normally inadequate for emotional distress. A special relationship is required between the parties to have intentional infliction of emotional distress. Courts allow recovery from common carriers, innkeepers, and public utilities for emotional distress to patrons resulting from gross insults of a highly offensive nature.[9] The liability for insulting language has been extended to owners of a place of business open to the public.[10] Liabilities for emotional distress can be inflicted on bystanders to the situation. Whether or not the defendant directs extreme or offensive conduct toward a third person, he may be responsible for liability to the third person if he intentionally or recklessly causes severe emotional distress to a member of the immediate family who was present at the time, whether or not such distress results in bodily harm to the third person who is present at the time, if such distress results in bodily harm.[11]

The defenses to intentional torts are varied. These defenses are usually available to actions of intentional torts to individuals who are privileged or who possess immunity. A privilege is a justification to a defendant's conduct that actually negates the tortious quality. An immunity goes not to the nature of the conduct but only to whether or not the defendant may be sued for such conduct. In the area of privilege, the defenses include self-defense, defense of others, defense of property, and arrest without a warrant. In the area of immunity, the defenses include interspousal immunity, parent and child immunity, charitable immunity, and governmental immunity. As a defense, a person who is threatened with bodily harm may meet his aggressor's force to repel the attack. This means that an individual may use whatever force necessary to repel an attack from an aggressor. A person's right to use force in self-defense is not limited to the situation where he is limited to injury or death.[12] However, unless the defendant was attacked with force apparently sufficient to warrant death or serious bodily harm, he may not use self-defense force calculated to cause death or serious bodily harm [Restatement (Second) of torts Section 65]. In some states, the individual has the obligation to retreat when being attacked with deadly force. With defense of a third person, a person is privileged to use reasonable force in defense of this individual. It does not generally require, as a condition of this privilege, that a person being defended be a member of the actor's household or one who is under a legal or social duty to protect. Where the actor or the individual makes a mistake as to the need to defend the third person, states are split on the issue of liability. The majority view is that the actor takes the risk that the person he is defending would not be privileged in defending himself in like manner. The minority view is that the standard of liability for the actor who mistakenly goes to the defense of a third person should be the same as when he makes a mistake in believing that self-defense is necessary. Reasonable mistake would preclude liability. Thus, the amount of force to be used by the individual assisting the third person would be to the individual being attacked. For defense of property, force is not permitted. There is no privilege to use any force calculated to cause death or serious bodily harm to repel a threat to land or chattel unless, as noted below, there is also a correlated threat to the person or others safety.[13] Force, in the recapture of chattel (personal property), is permitted when there is a wrongful taking and there is fresh pursuit. A common situation involving the use of force to recapture property wrongfully is a shoplifting situation. The law usually recognizes the privilege of merchants to detain a person when the merchant has reasonable grounds to believe that the person is stealing or attempting to steal his property. The detention, however, must be a reasonable period of time and must be conducted in a reasonable manner. The purpose of this privilege is to permit the owner to recover the goods. After the goods are recovered, if the defendant continues to detain the individual to obtain a signed confession, an action for false imprisonment may follow.[14] In most states, merchant privilege is normally covered by statute.

In summation, public and private sector EMS organizations and individual employees of EMS organization run a risk of a potential lawsuit virtually every day given the actions or inactions taken in the performance of the job. In the past, lawsuits against EMS organizations were unheard of. However, in today's litigious society, prudent EMS organizations should take a proactive approach to prepare for the inevitable legal battles, whether frivolous or valid. Today, it's not a matter of "if" a lawsuit will happen, it's a matter of "when."

CHAPTER 7

Workers' Compensation

Put all good eggs in one basket and then watch that basket.
—Andrew Carnegie

Before you invest—investigate.
—Salmon P. Halle

Many EMS professionals have found that the day-to-day administration of their organization's workers' compensation program and components thereof has fallen upon their shoulders due to the end result of work-related accidents (i.e., an injured employee). There are many similarities between the management of a workers' compensation program and basic "people management" but there are also many significant differences. A workers' compensation program is generally a reactive mechanism to compensate employees with monetary benefits after an accident has occurred. However, most management systems are designed by nature to be proactive programs, that is, to make something, build something, and the like. EMS professionals who wear the dual "hats" of production, safety, and personnel as well as workers' compensation must be able delineate which "hat" they are wearing at any given time. They must also effectively manage the individuals, the situation, and the potential liabilities surrounding the workers' compensation program.

The rising cost of workers' compensation for most employers has resulted in a significantly increased focus by management in this area. EMS organizations, always cognizant of the bottom line, have found that their workers' compensation costs have significantly risen due to many factors including, but not limited to, increased injuries and illnesses, increased medical and rehabilitation costs, increased time loss and benefits, and other factors. With this increased focus, EMS professionals are often thrust into the administrative world of workers' compensation with little or no training or education regarding its rules, regulations, and requirements. In the management arena, many of the potential liabilities encountered in the area of workers' compensation are a direct result of acts of omission rather than commission. EMS professionals should understand the basic structure and mechanics of the workers' compensation system and the specific rules, regulations, and requirements under their individual state system.

Workers' compensations systems are fundamentally a no-fault mechanism through which employees, who incur work-related injuries and illnesses, are compensated with monetary and medical benefits. Either party's potential negligence is not an issue as long as this is the employer/employee relationship. In essence, workers' compensation is a compromise in that employees are guaranteed a percentage of their wages (generally two-thirds) and full payment for their medical costs when injured on the job. Employers are guaranteed a reduced monetary cost for these injuries or illnesses and are provided a protection from additional or future legal action by the employee for the injury. The typical workers' compensation system possesses the following features.

1. Every state in the United States has a workers' compensation system. There may be variations in the amounts of benefits, the rules, administration, and so on, from state to state. In most states, workers' compensation is the exclusive remedy for on-the-job injuries and illnesses.

2. Coverage for workers' compensation is limited to *employees* who are injured *on the job*. The specific locations as to what constitutes the work premises and on the job may vary from state to state.

3. Negligence or fault by either party is largely inconsequential. It does not matter whether the employer is at fault or the employee is negligent, the injured employee generally receives worker's compensation coverage for any injury or illness incurred on the job.

4. Worker's compensation coverage is automatic, that is, employees are not required to sign up for workers' compensation coverage. By law, employers are required to obtain and carry worker's compensation insurance or be self-insured.

5. Employee injuries or illnesses that "arise out of 'and/or' are in the course of employment" are considered compensable. These definition phrases have expanded this beyond the four corners of the workplace to include work-related injuries and illnesses incurred on the highways, at various in- and out-of-town locations, and other such remote locals. These two concepts, "arising out of" the employment and "in the course of" the employment are the basic burdens of proof for the injured employee. Most states require both. EMS professionals are strongly advised to review the case law in their state to see the expansive scope of these two phrases. That is, the injury or illnesses must "arise out of," that is, there must be a casual connection between the work and the injury or illness and it must be "in the course of" the employment; this relates to the time, place, and circumstances of the accident in relation to the employment. The key issue is a *"work connection"* between the employment and the injury or illness.

6. Most workers' compensation systems include wage-loss benefits (sometimes known as time-loss benefits), which are usually between one-half to three-quarters of the employees' average weekly wage. These benefits are normally tax free and are commonly called temporary total disability (TTD) benefits.

7. Most workers' compensation systems require payment of all medical expenses, including such expenses as hospital expenses, rehabilitation expenses, and prosthesis expenses.

8. In situations where an employee is killed, workers' compensation benefits for burial expenses and future wage-loss benefits are usually paid to the dependents.

9. When an employee incurs an injury or illness that is considered permanent in nature, most workers' compensation systems provide a dollar value for the percentage of loss to the injured employee. This is normally known as permanent partial disability (PPD) or permanent total disability (PTD).

10. In accepting workers' compensation benefits, the injured employee is normally required to waive any common law action to sue the employer for damages from the injury or illness.

11. If the employee is injured by a third party, the employer usually is required to provide workers' compensation coverage but can be reimbursed for these costs from any settlement that the injured employee receives through legal action or other methods.

12. Administration of the workers' compensation system in each state is normally assigned to a commission or board. The commission or board generally oversees an administrative agency located within state government that manages the workers' compensation program within the state.

13. The Workers' Compensation Act in each state is a statutory enactment that can be amended by the state legislatures. Budgetary requirements are normally authorized and approved by the legislatures in each state.

14. The workers' compensation commission or board in each state normally develops administrative rules and regulations (that is, rules of procedure, evidence, and so on) for the administration of workers' compensation claims in the state.

15. In most states, any employers with one or more employees are normally required to possess workers' compensation coverage. Employers are generally allowed several avenues through which to acquire this coverage. Employers can select to acquire workers' compensation coverage from private insurance companies or from state-funded insurance programs, or they can become "self-insured" (that is, after posting bond, the employer pays all costs directly from its coffers).

16. Most state workers' compensation provides a relatively long statute of limitations. For *injury* claims, most states grant between one and ten years in which to file the claim for benefits. For work-related *illnesses*, the statute of limitations may be as high as twenty to thirty years from the time the employee first noticed the illness or the illness was diagnosed. An employee who incurred a work-related injury or illness is normally not required to be employed with the employer when the claim for benefits is filed.

17. Workers' compensation benefits are generally separate from the employment status of the injured employee. Injured employees may continue to maintain workers' compensation benefits even if the employment

relationship is terminated, the employee is laid off, or other significant changes are made in the employment status.

18. Most state workers' compensation systems possess some type of administrative hearing procedures. Most workers' compensation acts have designed a system of administrative "judges" (normally known as administrative law judges or ALJ) to hear any disputes involving workers' compensation issues. Appeals from the decision of the administrative law judges are normally to the workers' compensation commission/board. Some states permit appeals to the state court system after all administrative appeals have been exhausted.

EMS professionals should be very aware that the workers' compensation system in every state is administrative in nature. Thus there is a substantial amount of required paperwork that must be completed in order for benefits to be paid in a timely manner. In most states, specific forms have been developed.

The most important form to initiate workers' compensation coverage in most states is the first report of injury or illness form. This form may be called a "First Report" form, an application for adjustment of claim, or may possess some other name or acronym like the SF-1 or Form 100. This form, often divided into three parts in order that information can be provided by the employer, employee, and attending physician, is often the catalyst that starts the workers' compensation system process. If this form is absent or misplaced, there is no reaction in the system and no benefits are provided to the injured employee.

Under most workers' compensation systems, there are many forms that need to be completed in an accurate and timely manner. Normally specific forms must be completed if an employee is to be off work or is returning to work. These include forms for the transfer from one physician to another, forms for independent medical examinations, forms for the payment of medical benefits, and forms for the payment of permanent partial or permanent total disability benefits. Managers responsible for workers' compensation are advised to acquire a working knowledge of the appropriate legal forms used in their state's workers' compensation program.

In most states, information regarding the rules, regulations, and forms can be acquired directly from the state workers' compensation commission or board. Other sources for this information include your insurance carrier, a self-insured administrator, or the state-fund administrator.

EMS professionals should be aware that workers' compensation claims often possess a "long tail," that is, stretch over a long period of time. Under the Occupational Saftety and Health Administration (OSHA) recordkeeping system, which most companies possess because of OSHA regulations, every year injuries and illnesses are totalled on the OSHA Form 200 log and a new year begins. This is not the case with workers' compensation. Once an employee sustains a work-related injury or illness, the employer is responsible for the management and costs until such time as the injury or illness reaches maximum medical recovery or the time limitations are exhausted.

When an injury reaches maximum medical recovery, the employer may be responsible for payment of permanent partial or permanent total disability benefits prior to closure of the claim. Additionally, in some states, the medical benefits can remain open indefinitely and cannot be settled or closed with the claim. In many circumstances, the workers' compensation claim for a work-related injury or illness may remain open for several years and thus require continued management and administration for the duration of the claim process.

Some states allow the employer to take the deposition of the employee claiming benefits, while others strictly prohibit it. Some states have a schedule of benefits and have permanent disability awards based strictly on a percentage of disability from that schedule. Others require that a medical provider outline the percentage of *functional* impairment due to the injury/illness [in the Americans Medical Association (AMA) Guidelines]; then using this information as well as the employee's age, education, and work history, the ALT determines the amount of *occupational* impairment based upon which permanent disability benefits are awarded. Still other states have variations on those systems.

In summation, EMS professionals who are responsible for the management of a workers' compensation program should become knowledgeable in the rules, regulations, and procedures under their individual state's workers' compensation system. EMS professionals who possess facilities or operations in several states should be aware that although the general concepts may be the same, each state's workers' compensation program possesses specific rules, regulations, schedules, and procedures that may vary greatly between states. There is no substitute for knowing the rules and regulations under your state's workers' compensation system.

The potential liabilities for an EMS professional in handling a workers' compensation program are many and varied. Above all, the EMS professional should realize that most workers' compensation systems are no fault systems that generally require the employer or the employer's insurance administrator to pay all required expenses regardless of whether the employer or employee was at fault, whether the accident was the result of employee negligence or neglect, or whether the injury or illness was the fault of another employee. Most workers' compensations systems are designed to be liberally construed in favor of the employee.

Many EMS professionals who have been taught to use a proactive method of identifying the underlying causes of accidents and immediately correcting the deficiency may find that management of the workers' compensation function can often be very time consuming, frustrating, and show little progress. In situations of questionable claims, that is, whether the injury of illness was actually work related, EMS professionals should be aware that in many states, the employee has the right to initiate a workers' compensation claim with the workers' compensation commission or board and initiate or continue time-loss benefits and medical benefits until such time as the professional can acquire the appropriate evidence to dispute the claim benefits. This administrative procedure is often foreign to many EMS professionals and can be stressful and frustrating to a manager accustomed to a more direct management style. Above all, the EMS professional must realize that he or she must follow the prescribed rules, regulations, and procedures set forth under each state's workers' compensation system and any deviation thereof or failure to comply can place the company, the insurance carrier or administrator, and the manager at risk for potential liability.

In our modern litigious society, EMS professionals should be aware that they will often be interacting with the legal profession when managing an injured employee's workers' compensation claim. Although most workers' compensation systems are designed to minimize adversarial confrontations, in many states, attorneys are actively involved in representing injured employees with their workers' compensation claims. EMS professionals should be aware that the amount of money paid by the injured employee to the attorney, generally a contingent fee, is normally set by statute within the individual workers' compensation act.

EMS professionals should also be aware that when an injured employee is represented by legal counsel, often the direct lines of communication to the employee are severed and all communications must be through legal counsel. Circumvention of this communication bar by the manager often leads to confusion, mismanagement, and adversarial confrontations. EMS professionals should be aware of the rules and regulations of the individual state regarding contact and communication with an employee who is represented by legal counsel.

One of the major components in the management of a workers' compensation program is the communications with the medical professionals who are treating the injured or ill employee. The EMS professional should be aware that this can be an area of potential miscommunication and conflict. The goal of the EMS professional and the medical professional is normally the same, that is, making the injured employee well, but the methodology through which the goal is attained often conflicts. Although the potential liability in this area is not proscribed by statute, the manager should make every effort to ensure open and clear lines of communication to avoid any such conflicts. The potential liability in this area exists when there is a loss of trust between the safety and loss prevention professional and the medical community that can ultimately lead to additional benefit costs.

Given the many individuals who may be involved in a work-related injury situation (namely the injured employee, the attorney, the physician, the administrator, and the EMS professional, to name a few) the potential for conflict and thus litigation is relatively high. EMS professionals should know the rules and regulations of this administrative system and avoid areas of potential conflict.

The first and most common area of potential liability in the area of workers' compensation is simply not possessing or maintaining the appropriate workers' compensation coverage for employees. Often through error or omission, the employer either does not acquire the appropriate workers' compensation coverage or has allowed the coverage to lapse.[1] In most states, the employer's failure to possess the appropriate workers' compensation coverage will not deny the employee the necessary benefits. The state workers' compensation program, through a special fund or uninsured fund, will incur the costs of providing coverage to the employee but will bring a civil or criminal action against the employer for repayment and penalties. In several states, failure to provide the appropriate workers' compensation coverage can permit the individual employee to bring a legal action in addition to the legal action by the state workers' compensation agency. Often the employer is stripped of all defenses.

Given the paperwork requirements of most workers' compensation systems, managers can incur liability for failing to file the appropriate forms in a timely manner. In most states, failing to file the appropriate forms in a timely manner can carry an interest penalty. Additionally, EMS professionals should be aware that it is the employee's right to file a workers' compensation claim and it is often the employer's responsibility to file the appropriate form(s) with the agency or party. Liability can be assumed by the EMS professional for refusing to file the form or failing to file the form with the agency to initiate benefits. In most states, civil and criminal penalties can be imposed for such actions and additional penalties such as loss of self-insurance status can also be imposed on the employer.[2]

EMS professionals may be confronted with situations where it is believed that the injury or illness is not work related. EMS professionals often assume liability by playing judge and jury when the claim is being filed and inappropriately denying or delaying payment of benefits to the employee. In most states, civil and criminal penalties can be imposed for such actions and other penalties, such as loss of self-insurance status, can additionally be imposed on the employer. The EMS professional should become knowledgeable in the proper method through which to appropriately petition for the denial of a non-work-related claim through the proscribed adjudication process.[3]

In all states, an employee who files a workers' compensation claim possesses the right not to be harassed, coerced, discharged, or discriminated against for *filing* or pursuing the claim. Any such discrimination against an employee usually carries civil penalties from the workers' compensation agency and often separate civil action is permitted by the employee against the employer. In these civil actions, injunctive relief, monetary damages, and attorney fees are often awarded.

In most states, employees who file fraudulent workers' compensation claims are subject to both civil and criminal sanctions. The employer bears the burden of proving the fraudulent claim and can often request an investigation be conducted by the workers' compensation agency. Additionally, in some states, employees who intentionally fail to wear personal protective equipment or to follow safety rules can have their workers' compensation benefits reduced by a set percentage, and conversely, an employer who does not comply with the OSHA or other state safety and health regulations, causing the injury or illness, can be assessed an additional percentage of workers' compensation benefits over and above the proscribed level.[4] EMS professionals should also be aware that in a number of states, failure by the employer to comply with the OSHA or state plan safety and health regulations that directly or indirectly results in the injury or death of an employee can result in the employee or his or her family recovering workers' compensation benefits and being permitted to evade the exclusivity of workers' compensation to bring a civil action against the employer for additional damages. With the burden of attempting to disprove that an injury or illness was incurred on the job, managers are often placed in the position of an investigator or as the individual responsible for securing outside investigation services to attempt to gather the necessary information to deny a workers' compensation claim. The areas of potential liability with regards to surveillance, polygraph testing, drug testing, and other methods through which evidence can be secured is substantial. Prior to embarking on any type of evidence gathering that may directly or indirectly invade the injured individual's privacy, the EMS professional should seek legal counsel to identify the potential laws such as common law trespass, invasion of privacy, federal and state polygraph laws, alcohol and controlled substance-testing perameters, and other applicable laws. Potential sanctions for violations of these laws usually take the form of a civil action against the employer and individual involved, but criminal penalties can also be imposed for such actions as criminal trespass.

The above are but a few of the areas of potential liability for an EMS professional in the area of workers' compensation. EMS professionals should be aware that workers' compensation is an administrative system and any deviation from the proscribed procedures that may directly or indirectly affect the injured employees workers' compensation benefits is a potential mine field for liability. The assessment of criminal sanctions in the area of workers' compensation is infrequent and is usually reserved for egregious type situations. Assessment of civil penalties by the workers' compensation commission or agency, however, for mismanagement of a workers' compensation claim is far too frequent and the potential of legal action by the injured employee inside and outside of the workers' compensation system is a growing area of potential liability.

GENERAL GUIDELINES FOR EFFECTIVE MANAGEMENT OF WORKERS' COMPENSATION

EMS professionals responsible for the management of workers' compensation within the organization will find that an effective management system can control and minimize the costs related to this required administrative system while also maximizing the benefits to the injured or ill employee. Although the workers' compensation system is basically reactive in nature, EMS professionals should develop a proactive management system through which to effectively manage the workers' compensation claims once incurred within the organization. Below are basic guidelines to implement an effective workers' compensation management system:

1. Become completely familiar with the rules, regulations, and procedures of the workers' compensation system in your state. A mechanism should be initiated to keep the professional updated with all changes,

modifications, or deletions within the workers' compensation law or regulations. A copy of these laws and rules can normally be acquired from your state's workers' compensation agency at no cost. Additionally, the state bar association, universities, and law schools in many states have published texts and other publications to assist in the interpretation of the laws and rules.

2. A management system should be designed around the basic management principles of Planning, Organizing, Directing, and Controlling. Given the fact that most state workers' compensation programs are administrative in nature, appropriate *planning* can include, but is not limited to, such activities as acquiring the appropriate forms, developing status tracking mechanisms, establishing communication lines with the local medical community, and informing employees of their rights and responsibilities under the workers' compensation act. Organizing an effective workers' compensation system can include, but is not limited to, selection and training of personnel who will be responsible for completing the appropriate forms, coordination with insurance or self-insured administrators, acquisition of appropriate rehabilitation and evaluation services, and development of medical response mechanisms. The directing phase can include, but is not limited to, implementation of tracking mechanisms, on-site visitation by medical and legal communities, development of work-hardening programs, and installation of return-to-work programs. Controlling can include such activities as the establishment of an audit mechanism to evaluate case status and progress of the program, use of injured-worker home visitation, and acquisition of outside investigation services, among other activities.

3. Compliance with the workers' compensation rules and regulations must be of the highest priority at all times. Appropriate training and education of individuals working within the workers' compensation management system should be mandatory and appropriate supervision should be provided at all times.

4. First things must be first. When an employee incurs a work-related injury or illness, appropriate medical treatment should be quickly provided. In some states, the employee possesses the first choice of a physician while in other states the employer has this choice. The injured or ill employee should be provided the best possible care in the appropriate medical specialty or medical facility as soon as feasible. Improper care in the beginning can lead to a longer healing period and additional costs.

5. Employers often fool themselves by thinking that if employees are not told their rights under the state workers' compensation laws that there is less chance that an employee will file a claim. This is a falsehood. In most states, employees possess easy access to information regarding their rights under workers' compensation through the state workers' compensation agency, through their labor organization, or even through television commercials. A proactive approach that has proven to be successful

is for the manager or other representative of the employer to explain to the employee his or her rights and responsibilities under the workers' compensation laws of the state as soon as feasible following the injury. This method alleviates much of the doubt in the minds of the injured employee, begins or continues the bonds of trust, eliminates the need for outside parties being involved, and tends to improve the healing process.

6. The manager should maintain an open line of communication with the injured employee and attending physician. The open line of communication with the injured employee should be of a caring and informative nature and should never be used for coercion or harassment purposes. The open line of communication with the attending physician can provide the vital information regarding the status of the injured employee and any assistance the employer can provide to expedite the healing process.

7. Timely and accurate documentation of the injury or illness and appropriate filing of the forms to ensure payment of benefits are essential. Failure to provide the benefits in a timely manner as required under the state workers' compensation laws can lead the injured employee to seek outside legal assistance and cause a disruption in the healing process.

8. Appropriate, timely, and accurate information should be provided to the insurance carrier, organization team members, and others to ensure that the internal organization is fully knowledgeable regarding the claim. There is nothing worse than an injured employee receiving a notice of termination from personnel while laying in the hospital because personnel was not informed of the work-related injury and counted the employee absent from work.

9. As soon as medically feasible, the attending physician, insurance administrator, the injured employee, and the EMS professional can discuss a return to light or restricted work. A prudent manager may wish to use photographs or videotape of the particular restricted duty job, written job descriptions, and other techniques in order to ensure complete understanding of all parties of the restricted job duties and requirements. Once the injured employee is returned to restricted duty, the manager should ensure that the employee performs only the duties agreed upon and within the medical limitations proscribed by the attending physician. An effective return-to-work program can be one of the best tools in minimizing the largest cost factor with most injuries or illnesses, namely time-loss benefits.

10. In coordination with the injured employee and attending physician, a rehabilitation program or work-hardening program can be used to assist the injured employee to return to active work as soon as medically feasible. Rehabilitation or work-hardening programs can be used in conjunction with a return to work program.

11. Where applicable, appropriate investigative methods and services can be used to gather the necessary evidence to address fraudulent claims, deny non-work-related claims, or to address malingering or other situations.

12. A prudent manager should audit and evaluate the effectiveness of the workers' compensation management program on a periodic basis to ensure effectiveness. All injured or ill employees should be appropriately accounted for, the status of each meticulously monitored, and cost factors continuously evaluated. Appropriate adjustments should be made to correct all deficiencies and to ensure continuous improvement in the workers' compensation management system.

WHAT TO EXPECT IN A WORKERS' COMPENSATION HEARING

Within the framework of most workers' compensation systems, an arbitration system has been established to decide disputes in an informal and cost-effective manner. In most systems, the initial level of adjudication is a hearing before an administrative law judge, followed by an appeal stage before an appellate panel. Appeals from the appellate panel are normally to the commission or board. In some states, the final appeal stage lies with the commission or board, while in other states appeals to the state court system are allowed.

EMS professionals are often involved during the initial hearing phase before the administrative law judge. In some organizations, the EMS professional is responsible for the presentation of evidence at the hearing while in other organizations the EMS or safety professionals assist legal counsel in the preparation of the case. In either circumstance, it is important that the EMS professional be familiar with the rules and regulations of the individual state's workers' compensation system and the methods to prepare an effective case.

Workers' compensation hearings before an administrative law judge are often informal in comparison to a court of law. These hearings are often held in conference rooms in government buildings or even in hotel conference rooms. Most administrative law judges are granted wide discretion as to courtroom procedure, rules of evidence, and other procedural aspects of the hearing. Managers should be prepared for the administrative law judge to be actively involved in the hearing and to ask questions of the parties and witnesses.

In preparing for the hearing, the manager should know the time limitations proscribed by the administrative law judge. Often the parties are provided a limited time period to present each phase of their case. Additionally, appropriate preparation should be made regarding the recording, or lack thereof, of this hearing. There is great variation among jurisdictions as to whether this hearing is recorded and the type of recording method used by the administrative law judge.

In a hearing before an administrative law judge, a prudent manager should be prepared for the four major components of the hearing; namely the opening statement, presentation of testimony and evidence, cross-examination of opponent's witnesses, and a closing statement. Although

S.F. 1 (REV. FEBRUARY, 1991)
EMPLOYER'S FIRST REPORT
OF INJURY OR ILLNESS AND
SUPPLEMENTARY RECORD UNDER
THE OCCUPATIONAL SAFETY
AND HEALTH ACT

Department of Workers' Claims
WORKERS' COMPENSATION BOARD
1270 Louisville Road
Perimeter Park West, Building C
Frankfort, Kentucky 40601

IF THIS CASE WAS OSHA RECORDABLE, INDICATE REASON
FOR RECORDING AND GIVE OSHA CASE OR FILE NUMBER.

Reason for recording (e.g. "loss of consciousness")

OSHA Case or File Number (from your OSHA Form 200)

KRS 342.990 AUTHORIZES A FINE FOR EMPLOYER'S FAILURE TO SUBMIT THIS ORIGINAL REPORT WITHIN ONE WEEK OF KNOWLEDGE OF INJURY TO THE WORKERS' COMPENSATION BOARD. TO COMPLY WITH THIS LAW, EACH QUESTION SHALL BE ANSWERED COMPLETELY, ACCURATELY AND LEGIBLY. IMPROPERLY PREPARED REPORTS WILL BE REFUSED AND RETURNED. PLEASE USE TYPEWRITER OR PRINT IN INK. COMPLETE ALL QUESTIONS!

EMPLOYER

1. EMPLOYER'S NAME

EMPLOYER NUMBER

DO NOT WRITE IN THIS COLUMN

2. STREET OR ROAD

LOCATION AT WHICH EMPLOYEE WORKED

File No.

3. IF INDIVIDUAL OR PARTNERSHIP, NAME OF BUSINESS

4. CITY   COUNTY   STATE   ZIP

Employer No.

5. MAILING ADDRESS

6. AREA CODE TELEPHONE

7. UNEMPLOYMENT INSURANCE I.D. No.

U.I. No.

8. CITY   COUNTY   STATE   ZIP

9. NATURE OF BUSINESS (e.g. tree trimming, boot mfg.)

Industry

10. WORKERS'S COMPENSATION INSURANCE CARRIER (IF SELF-INSURED, CHECK HERE ☐)   POLICY NUMBER

11. SPECIFY PRODUCT OR SERVICE COMPRISING MAJORITY OF SALES (e.g. ski boots)

Soc. Sec. No.

EMPLOYEE

12. EMPLOYEE'S NAME   FIRST   MIDDLE   LAST

13. AREA CODE TELEPHONE (HOME)

14. SOCIAL SECURITY NO.

Age

15. EMPLOYEE'S HOME ADDRESS

16. SINGLE ☐   MALE ☐
MARRIED ☐   FEMALE ☐

17. DATE OF BIRTH

Sex

Marital Status

18. CITY   STATE   ZIP

19. DEPARTMENT IN WHICH REGULARLY EMPLOYED

Occupation

20. REGULAR OCCUPATION (JOB TITLE)

21. DEPARTMENT WHERE WORKING WHEN INJURY OCCURRED

Department

22. HOW LONG EMPLOYED BY YOU?   23. HOW LONG IN PRESENT JOB?

24. NUMBER OF HOURS WORKED
PER DAY   PER WK.

25. NUMBER OF DAYS WORKED
PER WK.

Months on Job

Shift

				Weekly Wage
				County of Injury
				Nature of Injury
				Body Part
				Accident Type
				Source of Injury
				Date Returned
				Time Present Job
				Extent of Disability
				Lost Workdays
				Injury Date
				Injury Hour
				Date of Disability
				Date of Report

26. EMPLOYEE'S WAGE RATE $ ____ or $ ____ HR. /WK. 27. COMMISSION OR PIECE WORK EARNINGS $ ____ IN ____ HRS. IN PAST 12 MO. 28. WEEKLY DOLLAR VALUE OF PAY IN KIND (LODGING, FOOD, ETC.) $

29. NO. OF DEPENDENTS (Please complete back of form)

30. PLACE OF ACCIDENT OR EXPOSURE (LOCATION, INCLUDING COUNTY)

31. DATE EMPLOYER NOTIFIED

32. ON EMPLOYER'S PREMISES? YES ☐ NO ☐

33. DATE OF OCCURENCE

34. TIME OF DAY

35. TIME WORKDAY BEGAN AND WOULD NORMALLY (A.M.) (P.M.) END FROM

36. HOW DID THE ACCIDENT OR EXPOSURE OCCUR? (Begin by telling what the employee was doing just before the accident or exposure? Be specific. If employee was using tools or equipment, or handling material, name them and tell what employee was doing with them.)

37. (Now describe fully the events which resulted in injury or illness. Tell what happened and how it happened. Specify how objects or substances were involved. Give full details of all factors which led or contributed to the accident or exposure)

38. WHAT THING DIRECTLY PRODUCED THIS INJURY OR ILLNESS? (Name objects struck against or struck by, vapor, poison, chemical, or radiation. If strain or hernia, the thing being lifted, pulled, pushed, etc. If injury resulted solely from bodily motion, the stretching, twisting, etc. which resulted in injury.)

39. DESCRIBE THE INJURY OR ILLNESS IN DETAIL AND INDICATE THE PART OF BODY AFFECTED. (e.g. amputation of right index finger at second joint, fracture of 2 ribs, lead poisoning, dermatitis of left hand, etc.)

40. NAME AND ADDRESS OF TREATING PHYSICIAN

41. NAME AND ADDRESS OF HOSPITAL

FATAL? YES ☐ NO ☐
IN PATIENT ☐
OUT PATIENT ☐

42. MEDICAL TREATMENT GIVEN (DESCRIBE)

IF RESTRICTIONS OF DUTY OR PERMANENT TRANSFER TO ANOTHER JOB, CHECK ☐

43. DATE STOPPED WORK BECAUSE OF THIS INJURY OR ILLNESS

44. DATE RETURNED TO WORK

45. NUMBER OF SCHEDULED WORK DAYS LOST TO DATE

46. WAS EMPLOYEE PAID FOR FULL DAY ON DATE OF INJURY? YES ☐ NO ☐

47. IF DEATH, GIVE NAME AND ADDRESS OF NEXT OF KIN

48. DATE OF DEATH

49. REPORT PREPARED BY

50. TITLE

51. DATE OF THIS REPORT

THE ACCIDENT OR EXPOSURE

EVERY QUESTION MUST BE ANSWERED AND FORM SIGNED

PERSONS ACTUALLY DEPENDENT ON INJURED EMPLOYEE, LIST YOUNGEST FIRST		
NAME	DATE OF BIRTH	RELATIONSHIP

<u>INSTRUCTIONS</u>

This form is designed for completion with a typewriter. Vertical spacing matches carriage advance of most typewriters. Horizontal spacing (4 steps) can be set up on tabulator.

<u>PLEASE USE TYPEWRITER OR COMPLETE LEGIBLY IN INK!</u>

<u>EMPLOYER</u>

1., 3., 5., 8. — Give the name and address exactly as it appears on your certificate of workers' compensation insurance. If you are an individual or a partner in business enter your name, or names of partners on line 1, and the name of your business enterprise on line 3. If a corporation, enter name of corporation on line 1 and leave line 3 blank.

2., 4. — Enter location of the establishment at which the employee was regularly employed at the time of the injury or illness.

6. — Enter telephone number at which person in charge of injury records can be reached.

7. — The employer number under which you pay unemployment insurance

166

9. — Classification of industry or business

10. — Name of company (not agent) carrying your workers' compensation insurance in Kentucky.

11. — The product or service which is responsible for the largest percentage of your gross sales.

EMPLOYEE

19., 21. — Use descriptive word or phrase which identifies the kind of work performed in the department.

23. — In present department and with present job title.

24., 25. — On the average over the most recent quarter.

27. — Earnings in dollars and hours worked (if known) in past 12 months.

28. — Include value of all materials or services (auto, utilities, etc.) furnished for private use of employee or his family.

THE ACCIDENT OR EXPOSURE

29. — Enter the number of dependents in space 29., then turn to back of form and fill in the ages and relationships of each person principally dependent on the employee at the time of injury.

31. — Date that employer first knew of the injury or illness.

33. — Date of injury if known, or date injury or illness was diagnosed.

35. — Employee's work shift on the day of the injury.

36.-39. — Follow instructions on front of form with care. Forms which are incompletely filled out will be returned for completion, and submission of a completed form will be required. The information from these questions is used to compile statistical information which is essential to the study of accidents and occupational hazards.

41. — Complete only if employee was taken to a hospital. Check "in patient" if employee was admitted to the hospital. Check "out patient" if he was treated in the emergency room, for example, and released without being admitted. In either case, give the name and address of the hospital.

42. — Indicate treatment given both at scene and at medical facility (if any).

45. — Use the OSHA criteria for counting lost work days.

many administrative law judges, in an effort to conserve time, expedite the opening and closing phases of the hearing, the EMS professional should be prepared to present a concise, complete, and accurate account of their case.

In opening statements, each party is normally afforded the opportunity to present its theory of the case. This is an opportunity to explain to the administrative law judge your theory of the case, outline the evidence to be presented to support your case, and to request a decision in your favor. Normally, the employee presents his or her case first followed by the employer.

Following the employee's opening statement, the employee is provided with an opportunity to call witnesses for direct examination and to present other documented evidence. In direct examination, open-ended questions are permitted but leading questions are usually not permitted. The rules of evidence are often relaxed in this hearing. Cross-examination of witnesses is always allowed. Additionally, the administrative law judge often questions the witnesses. After the employee has called all his or her witnesses, the employer is normally provided an opportunity to call witnesses in support of its position.

In cross-examination of the opponent's witnesses, leading questions (or "yes and no" questions) are normally permitted. A leading question is defined as "one which instructs the witness as to how to answer or puts into his mouth words to be echoed back."[5] The EMS professional should frame questions in a concise manner and "get to the point" of the examination as quickly as possible. Although this type of examination is intended to unearth discrepancies, bias, and lack of credibility in the witness's testimony, the EMS professional should bear in mind the issues in dispute and not permit this examination to evolve into a character assassination or personal attack.

Written documentation, diagrams, photographs, videotape, and other evidence are normally presented to the administrative law judge for review and acceptance into evidence. This type of evidence can be provided at the end of the opening statement (but prior to witness testimony) or can be provided in conjunction with witness testimony. Both parties are provided time to examine the evidence or be provided a copy of the documents.

In most states, the administrative law judge will not render an immediate decision in the case. The administrative law judge will conclude the hearing at the end of closing statements and provide a written decision to the parties via mail. Appeals from the written decision normally must be filed within a relatively short period from the receipt of the written decision (commonly 30 days).

Preparation is the key to success in a workers' compensation administrative hearing. EMS professionals should develop their theory of the case, assemble all necessary evidence and witnesses to support their theory, maintain an objective viewpoint, and prepare a file or manual containing all information and evidence prior to the hearing. Presentations in opening and closing statements should be concise and to the point, and information and evidence should always be at your fingertips for immediate location. Above all, always be professional during the hearing.

CHAPTER 8

Employment Torts

A countryman between two lawyers is like a fish between two cats.
—Benjamin Franklin

In law, nothing is certain but the expense.
—Samuel Butler

This chapter addresses other collateral legal considerations that may affect emergency service organizations primarily focused on the relationship between the emergency service employee and the organization. With the deterioration of the at will employment doctrine by Congress and the courts, the new technologies emerging daily, and the dwindling number of unionized shops, emergency service organizations face the potential of increased litigation under new and novel theories in areas that were not even fathomed by emergency service organizations twenty years ago.

WORKPLACE PRIVACY ISSUES

A general outline for the various forms of workplace privacy issues can be found in Restatement (Second) of Torts Section 652A(2) (1977). In employment-based invasion of privacy actions, the allegations usually center upon one of the following:

1. Access to personal information in the possession of the employer;

2. Unreasonable collection of information by an employer;

3. Retaliation by an employer for an employee's refusal to provide it with personal information;

4. Unreasonable means used by an employer to collect information;

5. Personnel decisions based upon a person's off-duty activity;

6. Unwarranted disclosure of personal information about an employee by an employer; or

7. Employer insults and affronts to the dignity of an individual.[1]

The issue of workplace privacy is a growing concern. There has been an apparent increase in incidents of people staging accidents to bilk insurance companies, sales scams with special emphasis on targeting elderly citizens and/or poorly educated individuals, acts of embezzlement, theft of valuable and confidential information, résumé fraud to secure a job or promotion, and theft by employees. An NBC Nightly News report (May 21, 1996) indicated that a survey showed one-third of all employees steal from their employers, and in the United States alone, an estimated $4 billion is lost from fraud and abuse.

EMS organizations are faced daily with decisions about the honesty and reliability of employees who seek to occupy or already enjoy positions of trust. Thus, many public and private sector employers have resorted to various investigative techniques in both the pre- and posthiring stages of employment. These include personal surveillance, security cameras, monitoring calls, as well as background investigations. A relatively new concern is the rapid increase and use of technology. E-mail and facsimile (fax) transmissions are also causing numerous problems and concerns for employers.

What legal issues may a dismissed employee maintain in tort against an employer for invasion of privacy? Basically, there are four accepted variations of the tort of invasion of privacy. These are:

1. Intrusion upon seclusion,

2. Appropriation of name or likeness,

3. Publicity given to private life, and

4. Publicity placing a person in false light.[2]

A traditional invasion of privacy action probably would not be brought for the dismissal of an employee itself but for other acts connected with the dismissal. The appropriation of name or likeness is unlikely to be involved in the dismissal situation and the false light variant is difficult to distinguish from defamation. Accordingly, a dismissed employee is most likely to benefit from the intrusion and publicity given due to private life variance.

INTRUSION UPON SECLUSION

The intrusion upon seclusion issue consists of an intentional interference with the plaintiff's private affairs in a manner "that would be highly offensive to a reasonable man;"[3] it does not depend on any publicity given to the information collected about the plaintiff. Most of the cases accepting the intrusion variant of the privacy tort have involved intrusion into a physical area with respect to which the plaintiff had a reasonable expectation of privacy. It's as simple as going through the desk or locker of employees who believe they have a personal right of privacy in these places. In several circumstances, the courts have agreed.

Most privacy cases have involved the acquisition of information. Thus, if an emergency service employee was dismissed for reasons related to his private life, and the employee could prove that the employer had in some way unreasonably investigated his private life, a claim could be made. For example, wire tapping has been held to constitute an invasion of privacy. Information acquired in polygraph examinations similarly may constitute invasion of privacy, depending upon the subjects inquired into.

In the employment context, intrusion into seclusion may involve an employer's testing of employees, gathering of medical information, obtaining credit records, electronic surveillance, and obtaining background information on an employee's suitability for employment. Many other issues involving workplace investigations also address this subject. Complaints of sexual harassment require employers to investigate the allegations. Growing concerns involving workers' compensation and whether injuries are bona fide may require an investigation or surveillance or both. In addition, investigations may be required when employees complain of other discriminatory acts at the hands of their supervisors.

Surveillance of employees in plain view at the workplace as part of a work-related investigation is a permissible practice.[4] However, this does not permit the employer to spy on employees while they are in the bathroom or other private settings. There is absolutely no employer protection to place surveillance cameras, one-way mirrors, or other forms of surveillance in bathrooms or other private settings.[5]

Courts have been inclined to grant employers latitude with respect to home surveillance if done as part of a claims investigation. However, there is an increased likelihood that surveillance of an employee's non-work-related activities may be deemed by a court or jury to cross the line of acceptable activities. The key is the intrusiveness of the activity. As long as the surveillance is conducted on public property and does not interfere with the daily activities of the individuals being monitored, most courts provide latitude to the surveillance.

The underlying facts in *May* involved an investigation of an employee who claimed a work-related injury. The employer was informed that the employee, Mr. May, was engaged in outside work while assigned to light duty. The employer hired an investigation service to determine the truth of the allegations. A videotape of Mr. May's activities was taken from a van in a public road. Neighbors were interviewed and Mrs. May was followed on several occasions. The Mays were unaware of the surveillance until the videotape was played during a workers' compensation proceeding.

The court stated that:

> [I]t is not uncommon for defendants and employers to investigate personal injury and workers' compensation claims. Because of the public interest in exposing fraudulent claims, a plaintiff or claimant must expect that a reasonable investigation will be made after a claim is filed. It is only when an investigation is conducted in a vicious or malicious manner not really limited and designated to obtain

information needed for the defense of a legal claim or deliberately calculated to frighten or torment that the courts will not countenance it.[6]

APPROPRIATION OF NAME OR LIKENESS

One who appropriates to his or her own use or benefit the name or likeness of another is subject to liability to the other for invasion of his privacy.[7] This tort reserves to the employee, the exclusive use of his or her name or photograph, usually for commercial gain.

This could be an important area for emergency service organizations who may utilize a photograph or name of an employee in advertisements for donations, marketing plans, or even photographs while performing rescue services.

PUBLICITY GIVEN TO PRIVATE LIFE

Under this third category, publicity given to private life, one can be subject to liability for invasion of privacy when the matter publicized is of the kind that would be highly offensive to a reasonable person and is not of legitimate concern to the public.[8] This tort of public exposure of private facts typically involves disclosure of private facts without the consent of the employee. In the context of employment, it may involve attempts to gain background information about an employer applicant, or disclosure of medical information. Unlike defamation (i.e., libel or slander), truth is not a defense. The disclosure of private facts is generally made to a wide audience. Republication of a private fact already known by the employee to fellow employees does not generally provide a cause of action. However, if an employer communicated to a larger number of people private information about the employee in connection with the employee's dismissal, a claim might be established under this theory.[9]

In *Bratt v. International Business Machines Corp.*, the court, applying Massachusetts law, held that the disclosure of information obtained when an employee used IBM's open door internal grievance policy was not an invasion of privacy because the information disclosed was not "intimate" or "highly personal."[10] The court affirmed summary judgment for the employer on this allegation. It held that disclosure of mental problems to supervisors was not an invasion of privacy because they had a legitimate need to know. It reversed summary judgment respecting disclosure of psychiatric problems by the company doctor to supervisors. It held that the expectation of privacy was much greater with respect to information disclosed in the doctor-patient setting, particularly when company policy reinforced the employee's expectation that such communication would not be divulged. The court noted that the privacy interest of the employee might be outweighed by the legitimate interest of the employer. A balancing test should be employed by the fact finder.[11]

PUBLICITY PLACING A PERSON IN FALSE LIGHT

This claim involves both inaccurate portrayals of private facts, and accurate portrayals where disclosure would be highly objectionable to the ordinary person. Such a claim generally has been difficult to maintain.[12] The key defense is whether the plaintiff has truly been placed in a "false light."

OTHER PRIVACY ISSUES

Sexual privacy is another topic encompassing a variety of employment-related issues such as dating and marriage between employees, dating and sexual relationships with outsiders such as employees in competing companies or customers, extramarital relationships, sexual orientation, and even dress codes. In general, the courts have granted employees wide latitude in adopting policies addressing these issues.

Generally, employees can be discharged on the basis of martial status. There are few states that provide statutory protection regarding marital status and it is nonexistent under federal law. Obviously, an emergency service organization cannot use this as a protected basis for discrimination or in retaliation for an employee exercising his or her rights as recognized under public policy. However, antinepotism policies have generally been upheld.

The theory behind spouses not working together is that it prevents conflict in the workplace, that is, complaints of favoritism by co-workers, interference with workplace productivity, and so on. Employers generally prevail in these types of claims.[13] In addition, many employers have policies forbidding dating among employees, especially between employees and supervisors. Discipline including termination has been upheld by the courts for violations of these policies, even in the face of invasion of privacy suits.[14]

Privacy claims have also failed where employees were fired after continuing friendships with former company officers or employees.[15] Most states, excluding California, have sided with employers when employees are discharged for dating or marrying a competitor's employee.

E-MAIL

A fairly new issue that presents itself to most employers is e-mail and the potential for an invasion of privacy claim. Many employees assume their e-mail is private and cannot be accessed by anyone else. When a company then reads their e-mail—either as part of an investigation or for some other reason—the employee might sue for invasion of privacy.

As of this date, the author knows of no such successful suit, but a growing number of employees are bringing such lawsuits for invasion of privacy. Even so, they can become expensive for companies to fight even if they win, and an e-mail policy may go a long way toward preventing the suits from being brought in the first place.

Examples of some of the cases where employees brought suit include the following:

- An employee sued after being fired for sending an e-mail in which he said he wanted to "kill the back-stabbing bastards" who managed the sales department.[16]

- Two employees at Nissan Motor Corporation were fired for sending e-mail that was critical of the manager.[17]

- A California employee after she discovered that employees' e-mail was being monitored.[18]

Even though these cases were brought under state law and dismissed, companies could soon face a rash of suits under a federal statute, the Electronic Communication Privacy Act of 1986.[19] This Act prohibits the intentional interception or disclosure of wire, oral, or electronic communications. It does not apply if the interception is made by "the person or entity providing a wire or electronic communication service," so it would probably allow a company to read messages on its own internal e-mail system.

However, as a growing number of company e-mail systems are linked to the Internet, it's not clear whether the exception would apply in such a case. The Act does allow e-mail to be monitored if one of the parties to the e-mail has consented to the monitoring. Therefore, it would be important for companies who want to monitor their employees' e-mail to protect themselves by getting employees to sign-off on the monitoring in advance. With regard to sexual orientation, while not a protected class under federal law, it is conceivable that the employer inquiries of this nature which lead to an employee's termination may become a basis for both an invasion of privacy claim and an ADA claim.[20]

Dress and grooming policies have also been generally upheld in favor of employers. The key issue is that employers have a right to ensure a "proper" public image and customers and co-workers should not be put off by how a co-worker is dressed. There have been a number of cases regarding sex discrimination on this issue but invasion of privacy has generally not been upheld in these types of cases.

PRIVACY—DRUG TESTING

Another major issue regarding invasion of privacy concerns substance abuse and drug and alcohol testing. Obviously, it is undisputed that employers have a number of legitimate work-related reasons for wanting and needing to know if employees are using illegal drugs, alcohol, or other potentially harmful substances. The reasons include having a good public corporate image, reducing medical costs, loss of productivity, and possible theft incidental to supporting such a habit.

Generally, U.S. constitutional restrictions against drug testing apply only to public sector employees, as the requisite "state action" is not present for private employers. However, in the future, constitutional claims may increasingly be asserted against private sector employers in industry subject to government-imposed drug testing requirements.[21]

Under the Fourth Amendment of the U.S. Constitution, courts have found that urinalysis infringes upon one's reasonable expectation of privacy, and thereby constitutes a search and seizure within the meaning of the Fourth Amendment. The courts then balance the competing interest of the individual's right to privacy against the government's rights to investigate misconduct. In the case of *National Treasury Employee's Union*, the U.S. Supreme Court applied a reasonableness requirement of the Fourth Amendment and approved tests performed on employees seeking promotion into highly sensitive areas of the U.S. Custom Service.[22] The courts found the reasonableness standard met because of three criteria.

1. Advanced notice was provided to the employees.

2. Elaborate chain of custody and quality control procedures were employed.

3. Individuals were given the opportunity to resubmit positive test to a lab of their own choosing.

In another case, where railroad labor organizations filed suit to enjoin regulations promulgated by the Federal Railroad Administrations, which govern drug and alcohol testing of railroad employees, the Supreme Court found:

1. The Fourth Amendment was applicable to drug and alcohol testing; however,

2. Due to the compelling government interests served by the regulations, which outweighed the employees privacy concerns, the drug and alcohol tests mandated or authorized by the regulations were reasonable under the Fourth Amendment even though there was no requirement of a warrant or a reasonable suspicion that any particular employee might be impaired; thus,

3. Suspicionless post-accident testing of trained crews pursuant to a 1985 Federal Railroad Administration Regulation is valid.[23]

Some states and at least one municipality have enacted laws that place limits on drug testing in employment. Generally, the issues include reasonable suspicion that an employee is under the influence, chain of custody issues, and guarantees of privacy. In *Wilkinson*, a California Appellate Court held that the state constitutional right to privacy applied to private sector employees, but that the drug testing program did not violate that right because the program was reasonable and the employer had an interest in a drug and alcohol free workplace.[24]

Federal statutes have been enacted such as the Omnibus Transportation Employee Testing Act of 1991[25] and the Drug Free Workplace Act of

1988.[26] Obviously, the public has the right to be secure in the knowledge that individuals employed in industry such as aviation, railroads, and trucking are not human time bombs waiting to go off as they fly an airplane, operate a train, or drive down the interstate in a heavy tractor trailer.

Drug testing must be done as quickly as possible and as accurately as possible. There are testing requirements set forth in the mandatory guidelines for Federal Drug Testing Programs, 53 Fed. Reg. 11, 1979 (April 11, 1988) and these should be followed to the letter. Employers should find a company with a well established reputation for such testing and set up procedures with guidelines from experts in the field to avoid or minimize liability.

In a tort claim premised upon invasion of privacy for drug testing courts have centered their inquiry into whether there has been an unreasonable intrusion into an employee's seclusion. Factors include:

1. the type of job the employee performs;

2. whether objective evidence of probable cause exists to believe an employee is under the influence;

3. the methods used to conduct the testing (i.e., does a person watch an employee provide a urine specimen or does the person wait outside the bathroom door).[27]

However, at least the 6th Circuit has ruled the right of privacy not to be implicated if the employer has a bona fide right to investigate.[28]

DEFAMATION

As emergency service professionals are increasingly involved in issues such as drug testing, the potential for defamation actions is increasing. Defamation occurs when an untrue statement is communicated to a third party that tends to harm the reputation of another so as to lower him in the estimation on the community or to deter third persons from dealing with him. As stated by the Kentucky Supreme Court in McCall, defamation is a statement or communication to the third person that tends to:

1. bring a person into public hatred, contempt, or ridicule;

2. cause him to be shunned or avoided; or

3. injure to him in his business or occupation.[29]

The prima facie elements of defamation needed in most jurisdictions are:

1. the statement is false and defamatory;

2. about the plaintiff;

3. which is published;

4. which publication is due to negligent or reckless fault of the defendant;

5. which publication was not privileged; and

6. which publication causes injury to reputation.[30]

Publication is an important element of defamation. The publication must be shown to have been done either negligently or intentionally. Unless, the employee's communication to the third party was privileged, no actual malice must be proven. In another case, *Hay*,[31] a hotel manager informed his entire staff that they were suspects following a robbery where evidence indicated the crime was an "inside job." Because the accusation was made before the entire group, the statement was considered published. The hotel manager then subjected the entire staff to polygraph examinations.

In some circumstances, publication of the allegedly defamatory statement may encompass more than oral or written statements communicated to a third person. Some courts recognize that "acts" can constitute publication of a defamatory statement. In a Pennsylvania case, the court refused to grant summary judgment because an issue remained as to whether defamatory meanings could be inferred from an employer's actions in terminating the employee, such as packing up the employee's belongings and changing the locks on the office door.[32]

Another important aspect is the nature of the words used, which have a bearing on the damages in a defamation case. Words that are harmful by themselves are considered defamatory per se. Injury may be presumed if defamation per se is involved. Most causes of action based on defamation in the employment relationship concern statements impugning the character of the individual or his abilities as an employee.

In *O'Brien v. Papagino's of America*, a jury found that the employer statement that the plaintiff was terminated for drug use was not completely true. The jury also found that the employer had a retaliatory motive as well. It awarded the plaintiff damages for both defamation and wrongful termination.[33]

Truth is an absolute defense in a defamation action even where the plaintiff asserts that the alleged defamatory statements were inspired by malice and the alleged defamation is per se defamatory.[34]

Probably the most common affirmative defense asserted in defamation claims arising from the employment relationship is qualified privilege. The publication is qualified when circumstances exist that cast on the defendant the duty to communicate to certain other parties information concerning the plaintiff. For example, managers within the corporation may disclose to other managers rumors or comments made about employees that are defamatory. However, due to the potential for harm within the workplace setting, courts have found qualified privilege in these situations. If the publication is qualified, the presumption of malice is lost and must be proven by the plaintiff.

WORKPLACE NEGLIGENCE

NEGLIGENT HIRING

One of the newest tort theories being developed is that of negligent hiring. This theory has its foundations as an exception to the fellow servant rule and operates to find liability against the employer where an employee is improperly hired and ultimately causes injury to another employee. The general rule under the fellow servant doctrine is that the employer would be exempt from liability because of the negligence, carelessness, or intentional misconduct of a fellow employee. However, the courts in at least twenty-eight states and the District of Columbia have recognized exceptions to this general rule under the theory of negligent hiring.[35]

The foundation for the theory of negligent hiring can be traced back to the case of *Whalen*.[36] In this case, the Illinois Supreme Court found that an employer had a duty to exercise reasonable and ordinary care in the employment and selection of careful and skillful co-employees.[37] In recognition of this exception, the tort of negligent hiring has been expanded significantly by the courts to find that an employer may be liable for the injurious acts of an employee if these acts were within the scope of the employment.[38] This theory was expanded even further when courts began finding the employer liable even when the employee's acts were outside the scope of the workplace or the employment setting.[39] In the early cases, the theory of negligent hiring developed into what we would today call negligent security. Many of the cases dealt with maintenance personnel or rental property managers with access to individuals' dwellings through master keys and other means.[40] In these cases, the court generally found that where the owner or employer knew that the duties of the job required these individuals to go into the personal residence of the individuals, the employer possessed a duty to use reasonable care in selecting an employee reasonably fit to perform these duties.[41] In more recent cases, the doctrine of negligent hiring has been significantly expanded to cover a wide variety of areas. For example, employers have been found liable in cases where they have employed truck drivers with known felony backgrounds who ultimately assaulted individuals, cases involving sexual harassment charges, and situations where off-duty management personnel assaulted others. The basis for the vast majority of these cases involved the employer's failure to properly screen and evaluate the individual before offering employment.[42]

In the area of workplace violence, the recent case of *Yunker v. Honeywell, Inc.* [496 N.W. 2d 419 (Minn. App. 1993)] appears to be one of the first to address this issue. In this case, the Minnesota Court of Appeals reversed the lower court's finding that Honeywell, Inc., as a matter of law, did not breach its duty in hiring and supervising an employee who shot and killed a co-worker off of the employer's premises. In reversing the summary judgment ruling for the employer, the court not only applied a negligence theory but also made a distinction between the negligent hiring theory and negligent retention theory.

In this case, an individual worked at Honeywell from 1977 to his conviction and imprisonment for the strangulation death of a co-worker in 1979. On his release from prison, the employee reapplied and was rehired as a custodian by Honeywell in 1984. In addition, the individual befriended a female co-worker assigned to his maintenance crew. The female employee later severed the relationship and stopped spending time with the individual and requested a transfer from the particular Honeywell facility.

The individual began to harass and threaten the female employee both at work and at her home. On July 1, 1988, the female employee found a death threat scratched on her locker door at work. The individual did not report to work after that date and Honeywell accepted his formal resignation on July 11, 1988. On July 19, 1988, the individual killed the female co-worker in her driveway at close range with a shotgun. The individual was convicted of first degree murder and sentenced to life imprisonment.

The estate of the female employee brought a wrongful death action against Honeywell based on the theories of negligent hiring, negligent retention, and negligent supervision of a dangerous employee. The district court dismissed the negligent supervision theory because it derives from the respondeat superior doctrine, which the court recognized relied on the connection to the employer's premises or chattels.[43] The court additionally found negligent hiring as predicted upon the negligence of the employer in placing a person with known propensities, or propensities that should have been discovered by reasonable investigation in an employment position and that it should have known the hired individual posed a threat of injury to others.[44] The court went further in distinguishing the doctrine based on the scope of the employer's responsibility associated with the particular job. In this case, the individual was a custodian, which did not expose him to the general public and required only limited interaction with fellow employees.

The appeals court, in upholding the summary judgment for Honeywell, stated that: "To reverse the district court's determination on duty as it relates to hiring would extend *Ponticas* and essentially hold that ex-felons are inherently dangerous and that any harmful act they commit against persons encountered through employment would automatically be considered foreseeable. Such a rule would deter employers from hiring workers with criminal record and offend our civilized concept that society must make reasonable effort to rehabilitate those who have erred so that they can be assimilated into the community."[45]

Additionally, the court made the distinction between negligent hiring and negligent retention as theories of recovery. The court noted that negligent hiring focuses on the adequacy of the employer's preemployment investigation of the employee's background. The court found that there was a record of evidence of a number of episodes in which the individual's postimprisonment employment at Honeywell demonstrated propensity for abuse and violence toward fellow employees including sexual harassment of females and threats to kill a co-worker during an angry confrontation after a minor car accident. The *Yunker* case exemplifies the general trend in the

U.S. Courts to permit theories of recovery for victims of workplace violence incidents. Employers should be cautious and take the appropriate steps in the hiring and screening phases to possibly avoid this potential area of legal liabilities. The trend to permit recovery under the theory of negligent hiring appears to be expanding in the courts and employers can no longer rely upon the doctrine of the fellow servant rule to protect them in this area.

NEGLIGENT RETENTION

Closely allied with the tort theory of negligent hiring is that of negligent retention. In general terms, the theory of negligent retention involves an employer who possesses the knowledge that an employee has a propensity toward violence in the workplace but who permits the employee to retain his or her employment status despite this knowledge. In *Yunker v. Honeywell, Inc.*,[46] set forth above, the Minnesota Court of Appeals defined negligent retention as focused "on when the employer was on notice that an employee posed a threat and failed to take steps to insure the safety of third parties."[47]

Looking at the general theory of negligence, four basic elements are required to establish a prima facie case: duty, breach, causation, and damage. Under the negligent retention theory, the *duty* would be created when the employer possessed knowledge of an individual with a propensity toward workplace violence, the *breach* would apply when the employer failed to act or react to this knowledge, the *causation* would attach when the individual with a propensity actually assaulted or otherwise harmed fellow employees, and the *damages* would stem from this causation. The pivotal issue in most negligent retention cases involves whether the employer possessed knowledge of the propensity of the individual. In actuality, this is a catch-22 situation for many employers. If the employer did not properly screen the individual prior to hiring and the individual performed a workplace violence incident, the negligent hiring theory would apply. If, in the event the employer did not acquire the knowledge during the hiring phase and permitted the employee to continue to work and later acquired information regarding the propensity and failed to react, the theory of negligent retention would apply.

Prudent emergency service organizations should take the appropriate steps to properly screen and evaluate employees during the preemployment phase of the operation in order to avoid the possibility of liability in the area of negligent hiring. Once an individual is employed, the employer appears to possess an affirmative duty to take appropriate steps to safeguard employees in the workplace once the employer possesses knowledge as to the employee's propensity toward workplace violence. In essence, the employer must react once the knowledge is acquired in order to safeguard other employees in the workplace from the particular individual's propensity toward violence.

The theory of negligent retention possesses one of the greatest areas of potential legal liability for emergency service organizations. Given the interaction with the public, the requirements and stress of the job, as well as the outside activities of employees, there is a substantial probability that an employee could be involved in an action that places the employer on notice of a potential problem. If the emergency service organization does not address or chooses to ignore the problem and subsequently the employee detrimentally affects co-workers or the public, the potential for liability under this theory is possible.

NEGLIGENT SUPERVISION

The theory of negligent supervision has been gaining strength in various courts in the United States. Under this theory, the employer may assume liability where a management person fails to properly supervise an employee who ultimately inflicts harm on fellow employees or co-workers. In the negligent supervision cases, the proximate cause issues are the primary focus in most cases.

In the case of *St. Paul Fire and Marine Insurance v. Knight*,[48] the issue of negligent supervision, as well as negligent hiring and negligent retention, was brought before the court. In this public sector case, a claim was made that an adolescent stress center had improperly hired, supervised, and retained an employee who sexually assaulted a young patient. The particular incident occurred off premises and the party knew that the meeting with the ex-supervisor was not part of the center's "after care" program. The court reversed the lower court, holding that there was no evidence that the employer should have known of its employee's sexual activities and that the incident did not arise out of the employment since the employer possessed specific policies prohibiting contact with former patients.

This novel theory of negligent supervision is gaining ground in the courts. The general rule is that the employer has an affirmative duty to supervise its employees in the workplace. Where an employer fails to properly supervise or take appropriate actions that could ultimately lead to some negative behavior, such as sexual harassment or workplace violence, the potential of liability exists. This theory, in most circumstances, is applied in combination with the negligent hiring and negligent retention theories.

NEGLIGENT TRAINING

The theory of negligent training involves the employer's failure to provide necessary or appropriate training or to provide proper or wrong information within the training function. This theory has limited application and is primarily focused on the specific facts of the situation; it may be applicable in situations where an employer failed to provide the necessary training or where the training was improper. For example, an employer possesses an affirmative duty to train individuals going into confined space areas under the OSHA standards. The employer fails to provide this training in violation of the OSHA standard. The employee enters the confined space area and becomes injured. The only remaining issue is that of damages. Although this particular scenario would probably be covered under workers' compensation, several states have permitted tort recovery outside of workers' compensation when the accident was caused by the willful negligence of the employer.

The theory of negligent training has also surfaced in the public sector in dealing with firearm safety for police officers, workplace safety, medical training for EMTs, and other areas. The principal elements in a negligent training action would involve the employer's duty to provide appropriate training to employees. Prudent emergency service organizations should pay special attention to situations in which an affirmative duty is created, such as is covered by the EMT laws, paramedic laws, OSH Act, EPA, or other laws, where mandatory training is required by law. Employers should also evaluate any special relationships that may have been created by this requirement or law.

NEGLIGENT SECURITY

The theory of negligent security is often invoked in areas where the employer possessed an affirmative duty to safeguard employees or the general public. The duty is created for the employer normally through applicable laws or through knowledge due to past incidents. The pivotal issues in a negligent security case normally involve whether a duty was created and whether that duty was breached rather than issues of causation and damages.

As an example, an emergency service organization has a large employee parking lot where employees are required to park their vehicles. The employee parking area has substandard lighting and the organization possesses knowledge of several attempted assaults in the parking area. A female employee, working the late shift, leaves the facility and walks to her vehicle where she is sexually assaulted. In this example, the organization possessed knowledge of past assaults and the issue is whether this knowledge created a duty to safeguard this employee in the parking area. Was this duty breached when the organization failed to provide adequate lighting or security for the female employee leaving the plant? Was the failure to provide adequate security or lighting the cause of the sexual assault? The only remaining issue would be the extent of the damages and whether the particular workers' compensation statute applied to the parking lot areas.

Another area where the theory of negligent security may be applicable is the issue of domestic violence filtering into the workplace. Does the emergency service organization possess an affirmative duty to safeguard employees from the potential of outside violence from family members or significant others? Knowledge of the problem and a reasonable duty to protect appear to be the key issues. As a general rule, employers possessing knowledge of past incidents or being cognizant of the potential risks should safeguard employees from hazards created by outside forces. Although emergency service organizations do not want to invade the privacy in domestic relations situations, the potential risk to the employee and co-workers may precipitate the need for additional security in the workplace. With the issue of ex-employees, again the employer should be cognizant of the potential risk of ex-employees returning to the workplace.

WORKPLACE VIOLENCE

Workplace violence has fast become the leading cause of work-related deaths in the United States and is opening an expanding area of potential liability against employers who failed to safeguard their workers. According to the statistics from the National Institute of Occupational Safety and Health (NIOSH), over 750 workplace killings a year were reported in the 1980s.[49] Additionally, according to the National Safe Workplace Institute, there were approximately 110,000 incidents of workplace violence in the United States in 1992.[50] A common misconception is that incidents of violence are a fairly new phenomena, however, incidents of workplace violence have been happening for a substantial period of time; the primary reason for the emphasis in this area now is their increased frequency and severity.

According to the U.S. Bureau of Labor Statistics, there were 1,063 homicides on the job in 1993 and of these 59 were killed by co-workers or by disgruntled ex-employees.[51] This report also noted that there were 22,396 violent physical acts that occurred on the job in 1993 and approximately 6% of these incidents were committed by present or former co-workers. In addition to the incidents of workplace violence among and between employees and ex-employees, incidents of other individuals entering the workplace, such as disgruntled spouses, have also drastically increased. Another concern to consider within the realm of workplace violence is the incidents of sabotage and violence directed at the company by outside organizations. Examples of such incidents would be the World Trade Center bombing and the bombing of the Federal Building in Oklahoma City.

Incidents of workplace violence have been highly publicized. The most visible organization with a substantial number of workplace violence incidents is the U.S. Postal Service, which recorded some 500 cases of workplace violence toward supervisors in an eighteen-month period in 1992 and 1993.[52] The U.S. Postal Service also recorded 200 incidents of violence from supervisors toward employees.[53] Below are just a few of the other highly publicized incidents that resulted in injury or death to individuals.

- The shooting spree at the Chuck E. Cheese restaurant in Denver in which a kitchen worker killed four employees and wounded a fifth.

- The ex-employee of the Fireman's Fund Insurance Company who killed three individuals, wounded two others, and killed himself in Tampa, Florida.

- The 1986 Edmond, Oklahoma shooting where a letter carrier killed fourteen and wounded six others.

- The disgruntled postal worker in Dearborn, Michigan who shot another employee in May 1993.

- The former postal worker who killed four employees and injured another in the Montclair, New Jersey post office.

So what exactly is workplace violence? Generally, workplace violence is defined as "physical assaults, threatening behavior, or verbal abuse occurring in the work setting."[54] Although incidents of threatening behavior, such as bomb threats or threats of revenge, are not statistically available, there is a substantial likelihood that these types of incidents are also on the upswing.

Many private sector companies and fire and emergency service organizations in the United States have taken steps to safeguard their employees in the workplace through a myriad of security measures, policy changes, and other methods. The potential legal liabilities in this particular area have drastically increased for employers. In most circumstances, the employer would be responsible for any costs incurred by the employee through the individual state workers' compensation system. Now, however, new and novel theories such as negligent retention, negligent hiring, negligent training, as well as the potential of governmental monetary fines, such as OSHA, have emerged to increase the potential risk.

Most experts concede that there are no magic answers when it comes to addressing problems in the area of work-related violence. Given the fact that the potential of violence exists on a daily basis and the method in which the violence can be precipitated can come from a wide variety of areas, the intangibles indicate that workplace violence is a very complicated issue. Is this a new issue? Absolutely not. Incidents of workplace violence have been occurring since the Industrial Revolution began in the United States. The frequency (the number of incidents) and the severity of these types of workplace incidents have substantially increased. This fact may correlate with a variety of reasons including, but not limited to, the increased violence in our society, the availability of weapons, the downsizing of the workplace, the management style, and numerous other reasons. Additionally, when you consider the different types of workplaces in America and the variety of management approaches, there is no one simple answer to this multifaceted question.

The Occupational Safety and Health Administration has provided guidelines for specific industries such as the retail industry and health care operations.[55] Many employers have taken proactive steps to develop a general strategy for protecting their employees and thus reducing the potential legal risks and providing ancillary efficacy benefits to employees and management. In addition to the proactive strategy, many employers have developed a reactive plan and implemented stringent employee screening and monitoring processes to identify and address potential incidents of workplace violence in order to minimize potential risks.

In most circumstances, employers are better able to combat the potential risk of workplace violence when the threat is initiated by an employee rather than an ex-employee or outside individual. Researchers have provided a general profile of individuals with a propensity toward workplace violence that includes such examples as employees with depression, suicidal threats, poor health, and other traits. Incidents precipitated by ex-employees, spouses of employees, and individuals outside the organization are substantially harder for the employer to address due to the lack of control element in the workplace.

As an emergency service organization attempts to address the potential risks of workplace violence and the correlating legal risks and costs, the organization must be very cautious not to trample upon the individuals' rights and freedoms. As organizations develop and implement more stringent activities and programs to curtail or minimize the potential risks of workplace violence, they must be extremely cautious to avoid creating additional legal risks through their actions. Privacy laws, acquisition of information laws, and discrimination laws provide avenues of potential redress in this area.

Private sector companies as well as fire and emergency service organizations now walk a legal tightrope because of the expanding emphasis on workplace violence. To a great extent, this area of law is still expanding and emergency service organizations should attempt to maintain an approach that provides the maximum protection to employees while not affecting employees privacy rights or other individual rights. This is a difficult endeavor but one that is becoming a necessity in the American workplace.

CHAPTER 9

Employment Discrimination

About money and sex it is impossible to be truthful ever; one's ego is too involved.
—Malcolm Muggeridge

Silence is the unbearable repartee.
—G.K. Chesterton

This chapter first introduces and discusses in general Title VII of the Civil Rights Act of 1964, as amended by the Civil Rights Act of 1991 and other intervening acts, as well as the Age Discrimination and Employment Act. Emergency Medical Service organizations should be aware that discrimination actions are one of the major areas of litigation against EMS organizations.

BRIEF HISTORY OF TITLE VII—THE CIVIL RIGHTS ACT OF 1964

Many EMS professionals have heard of the "at-will" employment doctrine, which has been the foundation of employment law in the United States for many years. The at-will doctrine stands for the proposition that an employment contract that is not for a fixed term is terminable by the employer at any time and for any or no reason at all. Over the years there have been many exceptions developed to erode this general doctrine but The Civil Rights Act of 1964 was one of the first.

Title VII of the Civil Rights Act of 1964 is only one part of this major piece of federal legislation. In fact, it is the 7th "title" or major section of the statute. It is now commonly called Title VII.

Title VII imposes a ban on private employers from discrimination on the basis of race, color, sex, national origin, or religion. It does not, as many people believe, prohibit discrimination on the basis of age. The prohibition of age discrimination is relatively new and became law with the passage of the Age Discrimination in Employment Act (ADEA) in 1967.

Title VII and the ADEA take much the same approach in that they both impose a direct ban on discriminatory employment practices such as hiring, firing, promotion, retaliation, and on categorization alone, for example racial or age lines.

TITLE VII OF THE CIVIL RIGHTS ACT OF 1964

Title VII of the Civil Rights Act of 1964 prohibits employers, employment agencies, and labor organizations from discriminating on the basis of race, color, sex, pregnancy, religion, or national origin. It also prohibits retaliation against employees or individuals who exercise their rights under the Act.

COVERAGE

An employer is subject to Title VII if it has 15 employees on the payroll on each working day of at least 20 weeks in the current or preceding calendar year. Employment agencies and labor organizations also are covered by Title VII.

A labor organization is defined under the act as any organization or its agent "engaged in an industry affecting commerce" in which employees participate and which exists for the purpose of dealing with employers concerning grievances, labor disputes, wages, rates of pay, hours, or other terms or conditions of employment. That definition also can include any conference, general committee, joint or system board, or joint council that is subordinate to a national or international labor organization.

A labor organization is engaged in an industry affecting commerce if it either maintains or operates a hiring hall or hiring office as defined at 42 U.S.C. 2000e(e), or the number of members of the labor organization is 15 or more and the labor organization:

- is the certified representative of employees under the National Labor Relations Act or the Railway Labor Act;

- is the national, international, or local labor organization recognized or acting as the representative of employees of an employer or employers engaged in an industry affecting commerce;

- has chartered a local labor organization or subsidiary body that is representing or actively seeking to represent employees of the employers;

- has been chartered by a labor organization representing or actively seeking to represent employees as the local or subordinate body through which such employees can enjoy membership or become affiliated with such labor organization; or

- is a conference, general committee, joint or system board, or joint council subordinate to a national or international labor organization.

UNLAWFUL PRACTICES

Title VII prohibits employers from discriminating against any worker or job applicant on the basis of race, color, sex, pregnancy, religion, or national origin. This means that employers cannot use any of these factors to:

- fail or refuse to hire an individual;

- discharge or discipline a worker;

- discriminate against employees in terms of their compensation, working conditions, or privileges of employment;

- limit, segregate, or classify employees or job applicants in any way that tends to deprive them of individual or employment opportunities or that adversely affects their status as employees;

- limit or restrict admission to any program that provides apprenticeship or other training, including on-the-job training;

- indicate a preference in advertisements related to employment or training opportunities; or

- engage in any employment practice that has a "disparate impact" on a protected class, unless the employer can demonstrate that the "challenged practice is job related for the position in question and consistent with business necessity."

UNIONS

Where a union acts as an employer it cannot violate any of the prohibitions imposed on employers generally. Where a union is acting in its union capacity rather than as an employer, it cannot use race, color, sex, religion, or national origin to:

- exclude or expel from membership or otherwise discriminate against an individual;

- limit, segregate, or classify members or applicants or fail or refuse to refer an individual for employment in any way that would deprive, or tend to deprive, the member of employment opportunities or otherwise adversely affect his/her status as an employee or as an applicant for employment;

- cause or attempt to cause an employer to discriminate against an individual; or

- operate or join with employers in the operations of an apprenticeship training or retraining program in which discrimination is practiced.

Unions also have a duty to challenge discriminatory practices of employers with which they bargain.

EXCEPTIONS

Some actions that differentiate between workers are permitted under Title VII. For example, it is not unlawful to:

- pay different wages or provide different terms or privileges of employment to workers if such actions are based on a bona fide merit, seniority, or other system designed to measure quantity or quality of production;

- take religion, sex, or national origin—but not race—into account in making employment decisions about jobs in which these factors are legitimate job qualifications; or

- base an employment decision on the results of professionally developed ability tests that are not designed, intended, or used to discriminate.

ENFORCEMENT

Employees or job applicants who believe that they have been discriminated against can file a Title VII charge with the Equal Employment Opportunity Commission. A charge must be filed within 180 days after the alleged unlawful employment practice occurred. Before processing a charge, EEOC must notify the employer of the allegations and give state and local fair employment agencies at least 60 days to resolve it. EEOC investigates the charge after the state or local agency has acted or 60 days have elapsed. During investigations, EEOC can require employers to provide relevant records or evidence.

If the investigation reveals no evidence of discrimination, EEOC issues a letter of determination stating that there is no reasonable cause to believe that discrimination occurred. If EEOC finds support for the discrimination charge, it must try to resolve the dispute informally through conciliation proceedings. If this effort fails, the commission can file suit against the employer in a U.S. district court.

The act allows employees and job applicants who have Title VII complaints to bring suit, directly in a U.S. district court after their charges have been on file with EEOC for 180 days and the commission has not dismissed them. Complainants also retain their private right to sue for 90 days after receiving a no cause determination by EEOC.

REMEDIES

When a court finds that discrimination has occurred, it can order the employer to:

- stop engaging in the unlawful employment practices;

- undertake affirmative action;

- delete improper entries from the victims' personnel records;

- provide other equitable relief; and

- increase the wages or salaries of discrimination victims and pay them back wages with interest. An employer's back-pay obligation can cover up to two years from the date the charge was filed with EEOC. Such pay can be reduced by any amounts the victim earned during that period.

In addition, the 1991 Civil Rights Act now allows courts to award compensatory and punitive damages. However, punitive damages are limited to cases in which the discrimination was committed with malice or reckless indifference to the individual's rights.

REPORTS AND RECORDKEEPING

Title VII requires employers to file reports as well as keep certain records.

Reports

—Employers with 100 or more workers are required to file annual EEO-1 reports with EEOC.

Records

—Title VII requires employers to keep certain records, including all personnel and employment records that relate to applications, hiring, promotions, transfers, layoffs, terminations, pay rates, and other compensation terms, and selections for training or apprenticeship programs. Employers also must keep all personnel records related to a discrimination charge until its final disposition.

Labor Organizations

—Also must file reports and maintain certain records under Title VII.

Every labor organization subject to Title VII must file a biennial EEO-3 report with EEOC on or before December 31. Such reports and the records necessary to the completion of the report must be kept for one year from the due date of the report.

Notices—42 U.S.C. § 2000e-10; 29 C.F.R. § 1601.30

All employers are required to post an official EEO notice stating that equal employment is the law and that individuals should contact EEOC if they feel their employer has discriminated against them. Employers can obtain the poster from EEOC.

CIVIL RIGHTS ACT OF 1991

IN GENERAL

The Civil Rights Act of 1991 contains a number of provisions that broaden or clarify existing civil rights laws. In brief, the Act:

- prohibits all racial discrimination in the making and enforcement of contracts;

- provides for damages and jury trials in cases of intentional employment discrimination;

- shifts the burden of proof to employers in cases of disparate impact;

- clarifies that any discrimination practice is unlawful, even if other lawful factors motivated the action;

- prohibits certain consent order challenges;

- extends discrimination protection to U.S. citizens working abroad for American companies;

- prohibits discrimination in employment testing;

- requires the Equal Employment Opportunity Commission to establish a Technical Assistance Training Institute and conduct educational and out-reach activities;

- expands the right to challenge discriminatory seniority systems;

- provides for the same interest against the federal government for delay in payments of awards that is provided in cases involving private employers;

- increases the time for filing a Title VII suit against the federal government from 30 days to 90 days after receipt of a notice of right to sue;

- authorizes the awarding of expert witness fees;

- establishes a "Glass Ceiling Commission" to study and make recommendations on eliminating barriers to the advancement of women and minorities;

- extends coverage of the major civil rights laws to Senate employees and presidential appointees; and

- extends coverage of Title VII to employees of the House of Representatives.

CIVIL RIGHTS LAW AFFECTED

The 1991 act broadens and clarifies coverage of existing civil rights laws. Most of the act's provisions apply directly to Title VII of the Civil Rights Act of 1964, but four other laws also are affected. The changes to these laws are described below.

Title VII of the Civil Rights Act of 1964

The 1991 Act amended Title VII by:

- requiring employers to demonstrate that a challenged practice is job re-lated and consistent with business necessity;

- extending employees the right to challenge seniority systems when adop-ted, when they are actually harmed by the application of a system;

- prohibiting consent decree challenges by certain individuals after court approval;

- clarifying that any discriminatory practice is unlawful, even if lawful factors also motivated the action;

- including expert witness fees in recoverable attorneys' fees;

- extending protection from discrimination to U.S. citizens employed abroad by American companies; and

- prohibiting the adjusting of test scores, use of different cut-off scores, or altering of the results of employment-related tests on the basis of race, color, religion, sex, or national origin.

The Civil Rights Act of 1866

The 1991 act clarified that the 1866 law prohibited not only racial bias that occurs in the hiring process and in promotions, but also on-the-job harassment, and other posthiring conduct.

The 1991 act also expanded the categories of intentional bias victims who can obtain compensatory and punitive damages. Previously, only victims of intentional racial and ethnic bias could receive compensatory and punitive damages. The 1991 act extends such coverage to victims of intentional sex, religious, and disability discrimination under Title VII, ADA, and the Rehabilitation Act.

In intentional discrimination cases, compensatory damages can be recovered from private employers, state and local governments, or the federal government. However, punitive damages can be sought only from private employers, and the complainant must demonstrate that the employer engaged in the discriminatory practice "with malice or with reckless indifference."

Further, most compensatory and all punitive damages are capped according to the size of an employer's work force in each of 20 or more weeks in the current or proceeding year. Damages cannot exceed:

- $50,000 for employers with more than 14 and fewer than 101 employees;

- $100,000 for employers with more than 100 and fewer than 201 employees;

- $200,000 for employers with more than 200 and fewer than 501 employees; and

- $300,000 for employers with more than 500 employees.

Backpay, interest on backpay, or other relief authorized under 42 U.S.C. Section 2000e-5(g) is not included in compensatory damages, and caps do not apply to past pecuniary losses such as medical bills.

An individual seeking compensatory or punitive damages can demand a jury trial, but courts are prohibited from informing the jury about cap limitations.

No compensatory or punitive damages can be awarded in reasonable accommodation cases where the employer demonstrates that it has made a good faith effort to reasonably accommodate the person with the disability.

Attorneys' Fees Awards Act

The 1991 act amended ADA by extending protection from disability discrimination to U.S. citizens employed by American companies.

Age Discrimination in Employment Act

The 1991 Act deleted a provision in ADEA that allowed the running of the limitations period for filing suit to be suspended up to one year while EEOC attempted to resolve the charge. A new provision was added that requires EEOC to notify complainants when a charge is dismissed or otherwise terminated. Suit then must be filed within 90 day of receipt of that notice.

AGE DISCRIMINATION IN EMPLOYMENT ACT

IN GENERAL

The Age Discrimination in Employment Act prohibits employers from discrimination against workers or job applicants who are 40 years of age or older and prohibits retaliation by employers against employees for exercising their rights under the act. The act also prohibits discrimination by unions.

COVERAGE

ADEA applies to employers with 20 or more employees; labor organizations with 25 or more employees; labor organizations with 25 or more members engaged in an industry affecting commerce; employment agencies that serve at least one covered employer; and federal, state, and local governments.

UNLAWFUL PRACTICES

Employers cannot use the age of a worker or job applicant who is 40 years of age or older to:

• discharge or fail or refuse to hire an individual;

- discriminate with respect to compensation or terms or conditions of employment; or
- limit, segregate, or classify employees in any way that would deprive them of employment opportunities, or adversely affect their employment status.

ADEA also bars employers from advertising any employment preference that discriminates against individuals who are 40 years of age or older, reducing the wages of any employee to comply with the act, or discriminating in favor of younger individuals within the 40-and-older age group.

Unions are prohibited from expelling or excluding persons from membership on the basis of age. A union can be held jointly liable with an employer if a contract provision of a collective bargaining agreement violates ADEA.

ADEA EXCEPTIONS

Employers do not violate ADEA in cases in which they can show that:

- the employment decision being challenged was made on the basis of a factor other than age;
- age is a bona fide occupational qualification (BFOQ) for the position in question;
- the terms of a bona fide seniority system were used in making the employment decision; or
- they had good cause to fire or discipline the individual, if the complaint involves discharging or disciplining a person 40 years of age or older.

The act also allows employers to require executives or top policymakers to retire upon reaching a certain age if the employees are at least 65 years old, they have been in their current position for at least two years, and they are immediately entitled to annual retirement benefits of at least $44,000.

ENFORCEMENT

Individuals who believe they have been discriminated against on the basis of age must file charges with the Equal Employment Opportunity Commission within 180 days of the alleged violation, or 300 days in cases first filed with a state agency. EEOC can file suit only after it has made a good-faith effort to resolve the charge through conciliation.

Employees or applicants can file a private lawsuit in federal court 60 days after they file a charge with EEOC. However, if EEOC files an ADEA action on behalf of employees or applicants, they lose the right to file their own ADEA actions in federal court, but retain their right to file suit in a state court. If EEOC does not file suit, it must notify the employee or applicant and indicate whether the charge was "dismissed" or otherwise "terminated."

Although the charging party does not need a "right-to-sue" notice from EEOC before filing a private action in a federal court, it must file any private action withing 90 days of receiving the EEOC's notice of dismissal or termination.

REMEDIES

Courts are authorized by ADEA to grant "such legal or equitable relief as may be appropriate," including:

- ordering the employer to stop engaging in the unlawful employment practices;

- requiring the employer to undertake affirmative action;

- awarding front pay for future earnings lost as a result of the discrimination;

- increasing the wages or salaries of discrimination victims and paying them back wages with interest; and

- expunging improper entries in victims' personnel records.

In cases involving a willful violation of ADEA, the court also is allowed to award victims up to twice the amount of back wages due.

RECORDS

ADEA requires covered employers to keep:

- all payroll or other records that contain each employee's name, address, date of birth, occupation, pay rate, and earnings for three years;

- all personnel records that relate to recruitment, hiring, promotion, demotion, transfer, layoff, recall, training, and overtime policies for at least one year from the date of any personnel action; and

- benefit plans and written seniority or merit-rating systems for at least one year beyond the date they are terminated.

NOTICES

Covered employers must display a poster—available from EEOC—that describes ADEA requirements.

THEORIES OF EMPLOYMENT DISCRIMINATION

Current legal theorist's believe that most if not all employment discrimination issues today can be organized into four basis categories. In order of historical perspective, they are *(1) disparate treatment, (2) policies or practices that perpetuate the effects of past discrimination, (3) policies and practices that cause an adverse impact on a protected group, and (4) failure to make "reasonable accommodation"* in situations where disability or religious practices are concerned.[1]

With these four basis theories in mind, the participant can better understand the basic elements of discrimination law proof. Therefore, under Title VII, it is an unlawful employment practice to discriminate against a person:

1. by a *respondent* (recognized under Title VII as an employer, employment agency, or labor organization);

2. *on a basis* recognized under Title VII (race, color, religion, sex, national origin, or reprisal);

3. *on an issue* recognized under Title VII (for example: hiring; discharge; compensation; terms; conditions or privileges of employment; limitation, segregation, or classification of employees or applicants; exclusion or explusion from membership; and retaliation);

4. *with a causal connection* between the basis and the issue.

Thus, to establish disparate treatment discrimination under Title VII, a plaintiff might show that an employer (the respondent) discharged (the issue) the plaintiff because of (the causal connection) his or her race (the basis).

Generally, it is the causal connection that is most difficult to prove. By using one of the four theories set forth above, the plaintiff attempts to provide the causal connection to prove his or her case of discrimination.

FIRST THEORY OF EMPLOYMENT
DISCRIMINATION—DISPARATE TREATMENT

The theory of disparate treatment as employment discrimination is basically "different" treatment. Under Title VII of the Civil Rights Act of 1964, disparate treatment is unlawful when it is based upon race, color, sex, religion, or national origin. Under the Age Discrimination in Employment Act (ADEA) disparate treatment is unlawful when based upon age. Under the Americans with Disabilities Act (ADA) disparate treatment is unlawful when based upon disability.

Generally, the disparate treatment theory is the most easily understood type of discrimination. The employer simply treats some people less favorably than others because of their race, color, religion, sex, national origin, age, or disability. Proof of discriminatory motive is critical in disparate treatment cases. This can be done with direct evidence or inferred in situations where there is proof of differences in treatment.

In any individual disparate treatment case, the central question is whether the defendant's actions were motivated by discriminatory intent. The plaintiff may prove the defendant's discriminatory intent by either direct or circumstantial evidence. For example, direct evidence exists when a plaintiff offers a memorandum written by the company president stating that he did not hire the plaintiff because she was black. Circumstantial evidence, on the other hand, does not directly prove a fact of consequence to the determination of an action. Rather, it permits the fact finder to infer existence of such a fact. In the above example, if the plaintiff offers records showing that no black has ever been hired by the company, even though many apparently qualified blacks have applied, those records provide circumstantial evidence that permits the judge or jury to infer that the decision not to hire the plaintiff was motivated by discriminatory intent.

As stated above, in most cases, plaintiffs lacked direct evidence of discriminatory intent and must prove discrimination indirectly by inference. The allocation of proof in such cases has been set forth by the U.S. Supreme Court in *McDonnell Douglas Corp. v. Green*, *Texas Department of Community Affairs v. Burdine*, and *St. Mary's Honor Center v. Hicks*. These cases indicate that disparate treatment cases follow the following general format and allegation of proof:

1. The plaintiff must first establish a prima facie case of discrimination;

2. The employer must respond with a legitimate, nondiscriminatory reason for its actions; and

3. In order to prevail the plaintiff must establish that the employer's articulated legitimate, nondiscriminatory reason was a pretext to mask unlawful discrimination.

While not the only method of proving disparate treatment, this legal analysis has been applied to cases alleging disparate treatment in hiring, discharge, discipline, promotion, transfer, demotion, retaliation, and other issues. This analytical framework has also been applied in cases brought under 42 U.S.C. Section 1981, the ADEA, the Rehabilitation Act, and the Employee Retirement Income Security Act (ERISA).

The Prima Facie Case

As stated above, the plaintiff must first establish a prima facie case. The elements of a prima facie case of disparate treatment are:

1. membership in a protected group;

2. application and/or qualification for a job that the employee was seeking or employed in;

3. rejection for the position or some adverse action taken by the employer; and

4. the employer's continued solicitation of applicants with qualifications equal to the plaintiff's and/or some other form of damages.

These elements are flexible and must be tailored on a case-by-case basis to differing factual circumstances. The Supreme Court stated in *McDonnell Douglas* that this analytical framework was never intended to be rigid, mechanized, or ritualistic. Rather, it is merely a sensible way to evaluate the evidence in light of common experience as it bears on the critical question of discrimination. Thus, plaintiffs may be permitted, in some circumstances, to use different kinds of circumstantial evidence to establish a prima facie case.

SECOND THEORY OF EMPLOYMENT DISCRIMINATION—DISPARATE IMPACT

The essence of disparate treatment, as described above, is "intentional discrimination." By contrast, the theory of disparate impact holds that an employer is liable for discrimination when a *policy or practice, which on its face is neutral to a protected category or class,* even in the absence of a showing of discriminatory intent, *has an adverse impact on a protected group.* Put another way, an adverse or disparate impact is the consequence of an employment practice or decision-making process that is neutral in its treatment of different groups on its face but that in fact affects one group more harshly than another group when it is actually applied. Thus, while disparate treatment focuses on discriminatory "intent," disparate impact focuses on discriminatory "*results.*"

To prevail on a disparate impact claim, the employee or candidate must first prove what is called a prima facie case of disparate impact based upon [protected class]. To establish a prima facie case, the candidate or employee must prove the following elements by a preponderance of the evidence:

1. there is an imbalance in the employer's work force—that is, there is an exclusion or mistreatment of disproportionate numbers of a protected group;

2. the candidate or employee (plaintiff) is a member of that protected group; and

3. there is a cause-and-effect relationship between the imbalance in the employer's work force and employment practices that seem to be impartial.

It should be noted that the candidate or employee is not required to identify a particular or specific practice or element of a decision-making process that caused the disparate impact if the practices or elements cannot be separated for analysis.

THIRD THEORY OF EMPLOYMENT DISCRIMINATION—FAILING TO MAKE REASONABLE ACCOMMODATION

This theory of employment discrimination is based upon the *failure to make a "reasonable accommodation,"* where that is required, to a qualified individual with a disability under the Americans with Disabilities Act of 1990 or to the religious observations and practices of an employee or applicant. A full discussion of reasonable accommodation under the ADA is discussed in Chapter 3.

As set forth in Title VII, *"religion"* is an unlawful basis for discrimination, similar to sex or race. However, religion is treated differently in that, in some cases, employers are required to treat religion issues differently and, in fact, may be required to offer preferential treatment, that is, "reasonable accommodation," to candidates or employees based upon religious considerations. For example, an employer may fail to make a reasonable accommodation when it discharges an employee whose religion prevents him or her from working on the Sabbath (a Sabbatarian). The reasonable accommodation may be, in the absence of any legitimate undue hardship on the employer, adjusting the employee's schedule to allow him or her to work alternative days in order to avoid working the Sabbath.

Title VII, as originally enacted, did not impose the duty to accommodate with respect to religion. It was the EEOC that first articulated this obligation upon employers, as set out in its regulations. The purpose behind the EEOC regulatory requirement was to attempt to mitigate the impact of facially neutral policies on employees with sincere convictions about Sabbath work or other religious issues that affected their ability to work.

Later, in 1970, the 6th Circuit Court of Appeals cast doubt on these regulations in the case of *Dewey vs. Reynolds Metals Company*, which was affirmed by the U. S. Supreme Court. In 1972, Congress responded by amending Title VII by establishing an affirmative duty "to reasonably accommodate" (Public Law No. 92-261).

There has been great concern over this amendment because the First Amendment of the U.S. Constitution states that "Congress shall make no law respecting an establishment of religion, or prohibiting the free exercise thereof. . . ." It was then argued that this amendment to Title VII, requiring reasonable accommodation, effectively accorded preferential treatment to those professing certain religious beliefs and practices. Therefore, it was argued that this amendment was a law "respecting an establishment of religious beliefs and practices," and thus was a violation of the First Amendment.

In 1985, the U.S. Supreme Court, in *Estate of Thornton vs. Clador, Inc.*, held that a Connecticut statute requiring an employer to provide employees with an absolute and unqualified right not to work on their chosen Sabbath day had the primary effect of advancing a particular religious practice and therefore violated the Establishment Clause of the First Amendment. However, *Clador* was not dispositive of the Title VII accommodation issue. As

Justice O'Conner pointed out in her concurring opinion:

> Title VII calls for reasonable rather than absolute accommodation and extends that requirement to all religious beliefs and practices rather than protecting only the Sabbath observance. I believe an objective observer would perceive it as an antidiscrimination law rather than an endorsement of religion or a particular religious practice.

Elements of Proof

In a failure to accommodate case, the plaintiff's prima facie case is composed of three elements:

1. a bona fide belief

2. notice to the employer, and

3. adverse employment action (such as discharge) of the plaintiff.

The burden would then shift to the defendant (employer) to prove that it attempted to accommodate the plaintiff's religious beliefs but was unable to accommodate without an undue hardship. Under this analysis, most cases have turned upon the issue of whether the requested accommodation was "reasonable" or would cause an "undue hardship."

FOURTH THEORY OF EMPLOYMENT DISCRIMINATION—PERPETUATION OF PAST DISCRIMINATION

This theory of employment discrimination revolves around *policies or practices that perpetuate in the present the effects of past discrimination*. Title VII provides that it shall not be an unlawful employment practice for an employer to apply different standards of compensation, or different terms, conditions, or privileges of employment pursuant to a bona fide seniority or merit system provided that such differences are not the result of an intention to discriminate because of race, color, religion, sex, or national origin.

This theory of employment discrimination *generally involves* issues involved in *seniority and transfer rights*. The use of seniority for the allegation of benefits in the workplace is deeply rooted in American industrial relations. Seniority often is used to determine who is promoted and who is laid off, and it commonly affects entitlement to benefits ranging from the length of vacations to the amount of an employee's pension.

It should be noted that even before the enactment of Title VII, the U.S. Supreme Court emphasized the "overriding importance" of seniority rights in the nation's economy. There are two general purposes for which seniority is used in the workplace. "*Competitive seniority*" is employed to allocate entitlement to scarce benefits among competing employees, while "*benefit seniority*" is used to compute noncompetitive benefits that are dependent upon or increase with the length of employment. Seniority can be measured in a number of ways. It may include length of time with the employer, in a particular plant, in a department, in a job, or in a line of progression. Furthermore, different measures of seniority may be used by the same employer for different purposes, such as company-wide seniority for calculation of benefits and bargaining-unit seniority for bidding, layoffs, and recall rights.

After the enactment of Title VII, seniority systems were used by some employers, and some unions, as a means of preventing minority individuals from advancing to more desirable and higher-paying jobs. For example, some employers discriminated against protected groups by assigning them to relatively inferior employment. These companies had facially neutral seniority systems that restricted transfer, such as departmental rather than plant-wide seniority systems. As such, skilled jobs would be grouped in the same department and unskilled jobs would be included in a separate department. This meant that long service members of a protected group who had established substantial seniority rights in a low-paying, unskilled department would lose those departmental seniority rights or protections should they transfer to the skilled, higher-paying, more desirable department. They would forever be disadvantaged relative to more recently hired majority group members with respect to competition for jobs and protections against layoffs.

TITLE VII—STATUTORY PROVISIONS

Title VII provides in part:

> Notwithstanding any other provision of this Title, it shall not be an un-lawful employment practice for an employer to apply different standards of compensation, or different terms, conditions, or privileges of employment pursuant to a bonafide seniority or merit system ... provided that such differences are not the result of an intention to discriminate because of race, color, religion, sex, or national origin ... Section 703(h) of Title VII—Civil Rights Act of 1964. (42 U.S.C. §2000e–2(h)].

THE SUBSEQUENT EFFECT OF TITLE VII

In the years immediately following the enactment of Title VII, many challenges were raised to the legality of these seniority systems. Plaintiffs argued that even if a seniority system was neutral on its face, it was unlawful if it perpetuated the effects of past discriminatory hiring, promotion, and transfer practices and policies. Employers, and often the unions with whom the seniority systems were negotiated, responded that Title VII was intended to immunize facially neutral seniority systems, regardless of their impact on the ability of minorities to advance in the workplace.

Initially, the lower courts agreed with the argument that facially neutral seniority systems could be challenged as continuing the effects of past discrimination. In one case, the court held that a facially neutral seniority and transfer system constituted present discrimination and violated Title VII if it contained members of a previously discriminated-against protected group in the inferior possessions where they originally had been placed. Although the original discriminatory job assignments predated Title VII and therefore were not actionable, the court concluded that "Congress did not intend to freeze an entire generation of Negro employees into discriminatory patterns that existed before the Act" (*Querels v. Phillip Morris, Inc.*). The remedy in *Querels* was that all African-Americans hired before a particular date who were tracked into the generally lower-paying department would be allowed to transfer and fill vacancies in the departments with more opportunities for better paying jobs, taking with them full employment seniority.

THE BONA FIDE SENIORITY SYSTEM DEFENSE

In its landmark decision of *Teamsters v. United States*, the U.S. Supreme Court held that in the absence of a showing of specific discriminatory intent, Title VII provides a defense even where adverse impact results. Thus a bona fide seniority system is lawful, even where the employer engaged in preact discriminatory hiring and promotion practices, and even though the seniority system perpetuated into the present the effects of preact discrimination.

In *Teamsters*, the United States sued a trucking company and the Teamsters Union, alleging a pattern or practice of racial discrimination in hiring, transfer, and promotion. The company and the union allegedly locked minorities into the less-desirable city driver jobs and prevented them from obtaining the better paying line driver positions.

For purposes of bidding, protection from layoff, and recall, bargaining unit seniority was controlling. The practical effect of this was that employees who transferred to the line driver positions forfeited all the seniority they had accumulated in the separate city driver bargaining unit. The lower courts found that although both white and African-American employees were adversely affected by this policy, there was a disproportionate impact on minorities who earlier had been refused line driver positions as a result of discriminatory hiring practices. The seniority system was found to carry into the present the effects of this earlier discrimination and was thus deemed to be a continuing violation of Title VII.

The Supreme Court reversed this decision. It stated that a facially neutral seniority system that perpetuated past discrimination would be actionable under the adverse impact doctrine. The court concluded, however, that both literal language of Section 703(h) and its legislative history revealed Congress's intent to shield seniority systems from precisely such challenges. In particular, the court focused on Title VII's congressional sponsor's efforts to address the fears of the legislation's opponents that well-established seniority rights would be disturbed as a result of Title VII's passage.

The court's *Teamsters* decision specifically addressed applicability of Section 703(h) only where the underlying discriminatory conduct occurred prior to the effective date of Title VII. Thus, of even greater significance in the long run was the Supreme Court's decision in *United Airlines, Inc. v. Evans*.

In *Evans*, the plaintiff had been forced to resign as a result of the employer's "no marriage" rule for female flight attendants. Even though that rule subsequently had been found to violate Title VII, when the plaintiff was rehired she was given no credit for her prior service, as dictated by the company seniority system. She contended that the seniority system perpetuated the effects of the earlier discrimination.

The Supreme Court held that a seniority system does not independently violate Title VII simply because it perpetuates the effects of prior discriminatory acts, even if those acts occurred after the effective date of Title VII. Furthermore, a plaintiff must file a timely charge of discrimination after the alleged act of discrimination. Acts that are not the subject of a timely charge are, in the Court's words, "the legal equivalent of a discriminatory act which occurred before the statute was passed" and are not actionable even though the seniority system perpetuates their effects into the present. Otherwise, the Court concluded, plaintiffs could substitute a claim for seniority credit for almost every claim that is barred by limitations.

Thus, these cases effectively foreclose Title VII challenges to seniority systems under the adverse impact doctrine.

Challenges to the Seniority Systems after the *Teamsters* Decision

Cases after the *Teamsters* decision have focused on whether (1) the system under attack is a seniority system at all, and (2) if so, whether it is a "bonafide" seniority system. Thus, due to the broad immunity enjoyed by seniority systems under Section 703(h), some plaintiffs have attempted to avoid its application by arguing that the employment practice under challenge is not a seniority system at all. Therefore, the courts have had to resolve the issue of what constitutes a seniority system. Title VII does not define the term nor is any comprehensive definition set forth in the legislative history.

The Supreme Court has given fairly vague definitions of what kind of systems are true seniority systems within the meaning of Section 703(h). The Court did state that a "seniority system" is a scheme that alone or in tandem with non-"seniority" criteria allots to employees ever improving employment rights and benefits as their relative links of pertinent employment increase. Unlike other methods of allocating employment benefits and opportunities, such as subjective evaluations or educational requirements, the principal feature of any and every "seniority system" is that preferential treatment is dispensed on the basis of some measure of time served in employment (*California Brewers, Assoc. v. Bryant*).

BONA FIDE SENIORITY SYSTEM

As stated above, even if an employment practice qualifies as a seniority system, it also must be bona fide, that is, it must not be adopted or operated with a discriminatory intent in order to enjoy the protection of Section 703(h).

Thus, the burden of proof falls on plaintiffs to prove that a seniority system is not bona fide if they wish to attack the effects of discrimination.

The Fifth Circuit Court of Appeals has stated that it considers the "totality of the circumstances" surrounding the development and maintenance of a seniority system to determine whether it is bona fide. It also identified four particular factors that make up the core of that inquiry. These include:

1. whether the seniority system operates to discourage all employees equally from transferring between seniority units;

2. whether the seniority units are the in same or separate bargaining units (if the latter, whether the instruction is rational and in conformance with industry practice);

3. whether the seniority system had its genesis and racial discrimination;

4. whether the system was negotiated and has been maintained free from any illegal purpose.

It has also been stated that this four-factor test is only a guideline and is not meant to be an exhaustive list of all the factors that a court might or should consider in making a finding of discriminatory intent.

THE EMPLOYMENT DISCRIMINATION CASE

PROOF OF DISCRIMINATION

As stated above, the employment candidate or employee who becomes a plaintiff must first set forth a prima facie case to pursue an employment discrimination case. The burden then shifts to the employer to rebut the plaintiff's prima facie case. The following outlines the steps and required proof in an employment discrimination case.

THE EMPLOYERS' BURDEN OF PRODUCING EVIDENCE

If the plaintiff's prima facie case is not challenged by the employer then the employee should win her or his employment discrimination case. However, in reality, the plaintiff's prima facie case rarely stands unrebutted. Once the plaintiff creates an inference of discrimination by setting forth a prima facie case, the burden shifts to the employer to articulate a legitimate non-discriminatory reason for the adverse action in order to rebut the inference of discrimination. This is done through the introduction of admissible evidence. The employer's burden at this point is only one of coming forward with this evidence. The ultimate burden of persuasion remains with the plaintiff.

Common reasons set forth by employers to rebut an inference of discrimination include, among others, lesser comparative qualifications, inability to get along with supervisors or fellow employees, misconduct, business justification such as the need to eliminate positions, insubordination, inferior test scores, poor performance, the need to comply with rules set forth in union collective-bargaining agreements, and greater familiarity with the favored employee's work.

PLAINTIFF'S PROOF OF PRETEXT

If the defendant, generally an employer, successfully presents evidence of a legitimate nondiscriminatory reason for the adverse action, the plaintiff may still prevail by proving that the proffered justification was a pretext for discrimination. At this stage, the plaintiff's burden of showing pretext emerges with the ultimate burden of persuading the court that the plaintiff had been a victim of intentional discrimination.

As stated, the burden of persuasion, with respect to pretext, remains with the plaintiff. While a satisfactorily evidentiary explanation by the employer destroys the legally mandatory inference of discrimination arising from the plaintiff's prima facie case, the evidence and inferences that properly can be drawn from the evidence presented during the plaintiff's prima facie case may be considered in determining whether the defendant's explanation is pretextual.

In *St. Mary's Honor Center v. Hicks*, the Supreme Court addressed the issue of proof in disparate treatment cases. The plaintiff in *Hicks* was an African-American shift commander in a State Correctional Institution. He established a prima facie case of demotion and discharge because of his race. The employer sustained its burden of production by introducing evidence of two legitimate nondiscriminatory reasons for taking these actions. These were the severity and number of rule violations committed by Mr. Hicks. The plaintiff then proved that these alleged reasons were factually false and thus not the real reasons for his demotion and discharge. However, the District Court concluded that the plaintiff failed to carry his ultimate burden by proving that his race was the real reason for his demotion and discharge. Although the plaintiff had proven the existence of a crusade to terminate him, he had not proven that the crusade was racially rather than personally motivated.

The Eighth Circuit Court of Appeals reversed the District Court's decision, holding that once the plaintiff proved that all of the employer's proffered reasons for the adverse action were false, that the plaintiff was then entitled to judgment as a matter of law. The Eighth Circuit reasoned that the employer, having been caught in a lie, was in no better a position than if it had remained silent and never produced evidence of any legitimate nondiscriminatory reason. The U.S. Supreme Court reversed the Eighth Circuit on a 5 to 4 vote. The Supreme Court stated that the Eighth Circuit had erred in holding that a judgment should automatically be entered for a plaintiff when pretext is proven. Instead, the Supreme Court stated that when the employer meets its burden of production, the presumption of discrimination created by the plaintiff's prima facie case simply drops out of the picture and the case then proceeds to the ultimate question: Whether the plaintiff has proven that the defendant intentionally discriminated against him because of his race.

It should be noted that in addition to producing evidence of falsity of the employer's stated pretextual reason, there are three categories of evidence that can be used to prove pretext; these include:

1. direct evidence of discrimination, such as discriminatory statements or admissions;

2. comparative evidence; and

3. statistics.

Direct evidence may take the form of statements by managers demonstrating bias. For example, racially offensive comments by company executives, comments about a person's age, and the need to eliminate "old fogies" and other such comments referring to persons in protected classifications support direct evidence issues.

In comparative evidence, the plaintiff generally shows pretext for discrimination with evidence that similarly situated employees outside of the plaintiff's protected group received favorable treatment or did not receive the same adverse treatment. In addition, the plaintiff may also attempt to prove pretext by showing that the employer's treatment of the plaintiff departed from its normal policies or practices, thereby suggesting an inference of disparate treatment of similarly situated persons.

In these cases the plaintiff has the burden of showing that the facts support discrimination. Employers on the other hand generally respond by contending that the plaintiff's situation to other employees was not in fact similarly situated. In addition, employers may also offer evidence that they treated similarly situated individuals outside of the plaintiff's protected group the same as members of the plaintiff's protected group.

Statistics, although admissible, are rarely determinative in individual disparate treatment cases. Thus, good statistics will not immunize an employer against claims of individual and disparate treatment and bad statistics alone will not suffice to prove pretext in individual disparate treatment cases. The general usefulness of statistics in these cases depends primarily upon their relevance to the specific decision affecting the individual plaintiff and particular decision maker, rather than employer decisions that affect members of the plaintiff's protected class in general. One other important consideration for employers outlining their proof is the "same decision maker" line of cases. In these cases, the employer points out that the supervisor or manager who approved the adverse action was the same supervisor who, sometime earlier, had approved the plaintiff's hiring or promotion. The argument then is, for example, that the decision maker who knowingly hired a person in a protected category would be unlikely to discriminate against the same individual, particularly within a relative short period of time. This approach has been well established in age cases and other courts have applied it in other contexts as well.

However, this approach should be used with caution. For example, even though an employer may be willing to hire women in entry level jobs, it does not mean that employer may not discriminate against them in promotions to preserve a glass ceiling.

SEXUAL HARASSMENT—A FORM OF SEX DISCRIMINATION

Sexual harassment is basically a form of discrimination prohibited by Title VII of the Civil Rights Act of 1964 as sex discrimination. Under the traditional Title VII framework, an action by an employer against an employee is unlawful only if the action involves a decision to hire, fire, or impose a condition of employment because of the statutory "basis," that is, race, color, sex, religion, or national origin. Thus, Title VII forbids harassment by which one, some, or all persons of one's sex suffers significantly unfavorable employment conditions as a result of acts or omissions of the employer, under circumstances that permit the conclusion that the injury would not have been sustained if the victim's sex had been different.

There are two legal theories supporting claims of sexual harassment as sex discrimination. The first is quid pro quo harassment and the second is hostile environment harassment.

QUID PRO QUO HARASSMENT

In essence, quid pro quo harassment is such that an individual has been forced to choose between suffering and economic detriment (i.e. economic harm or damages) and submitting to sexual demands. It is basically a "put out or get out" demand that makes employment benefits contingent upon sexual cooperation. In contrast, hostile environment harassment is such that the individual has been required to endure a work environment that, while not necessarily causing direct economic harm, causes psychological or emotional harm or otherwise unreasonably interferes with the individual's job performance.

The quid pro quo theory is generally stated when someone, generally a manager or supervisor, relies upon his or her apparent or actual authority to extort sexual consideration from an employee. Quid pro quo harassment occurs whenever a supervisor conditions the granting of an economic or other job benefit upon the receipt of sexual favors from a subordinate, or punishes that subordinate for refusing to comply.

The Equal Employment Opportunity Commission (EEOC) guidelines identify basic varieties of quid pro quo harassment:

> Unwelcome sexual advances, request for sexual favors, and other verbal or physical conduct of a sexual nature constitutes sexual harassment when (1) submission to such conduct is made either explicitly or implicitly a term or condition of an individual's employment, bracket or (2) submission to or rejection of such conduct by an individual is used as a basis for employment decisions affecting such individual . . . .

In quid pro quo cases, the length of time between the sexual favors and the job detriment may be either explicit or implicit. The connection between the rejection of a sexual advance and a later adverse job action may either be close in time or later. The later action is often the result of a soured romance or termination of the relationship.

In order for an employee to sustain a case of quid pro quo harassment, he or she must set forth a "prima facie case." This is the minimum claim an employee must prove to survive a motion to dismiss or motion for summary judgment. In quid pro quo harassment, the prima facie case elements are as follows:

1. Membership in a protected group (for example, employee is female while supervisor is male);

2. Unwelcome sexual advances;

3. An adverse employment action;

4. The Causal Connection—that the sexual advances were due to the complainant's sex and that the complainant's reaction to the sexual advance affected a tangible aspect of the complainant's term, condition, or privilege of employment; and

5. Employer responsibility.

Each of these elements of a prima facie case will be addressed below.

1. *Membership in a Protected Class*
The first element, membership in a protected class, requires only a simple statement of gender. This element will be present in every sexual harassment case. Currently, claims of same-sex sexual harassment are headed toward the U.S. Supreme Court for review and decision. The Federal Court of Appeals is split on whether same-sex sexual harassment is a protected class.

2. *Unwelcome Sexual Advances*
This element of the prima facie case is in two parts. First, there must be a sexual advance and it must be unwelcome to the employee. The EEOC Guidelines describe sexual harassment as involving "unwelcome sexual advances, request for sexual favors, and other verbal or physical conduct of a sexual nature." In the typical quid pro quo case, the sexual nature of the request is plain. A supervisor demands that an employee provides sexual favors to obtain or retain job benefits. Generally, the employee would testify at trial as to the nature of the request and its unwelcomeness.

The unwelcome requirement of quid pro quo harassment does not require complete and outright rejection. Possible responses might include:

1. Outright rejection

2. Initial rejection and later acceptance

3. Initial acceptance followed by later rejection

4. Ambiguous conduct

5. Course submission

6. Unwelcome acceptance.

The U.S. Supreme Court, has suggested that deciding whether sexual advances were unwelcome requires the use of an objective standard rather than consideration of the employee's subjective feelings. Other courts have taken this a step further and stated that the objective standard to be used is that of a "reasonable woman."

3. *The Adverse Employment Action*

A quid pro quo case ordinarily requires proof of economic harm. In many cases, the employee shows that she suffered some tangible job detriment to a term condition or privilege of employment. This detriment may be termination, denial of a promotion or pay increase, denial of training, or failure to rehire after a layoff. Courts have generally rejection quid pro quo claims in the absence of a clear economic loss. The EEOC has stated that in coercion cases, a violation occurs even though the employee has suffered no tangible job detriment but rather has received the job benefit or avoided the job detriment that was involved in the sexual bargain.

4. *The Causal Connection*

The causal connection in quid pro quo cases has two prongs. The first is that because of the complainant's sex she was subjected to a sexual advance. The second is that because of her reaction to the sexual advance she was subjected to (or avoided) a tangible job detriment. The problem then becomes whether the employee can show the link between the harassment and the adverse action. In most cases, to establish this causal link, the employee must show that the alleged harasser was involved in the decision that caused the job detriment; if so, she will likely prove this element of her case.

5. *Employer Responsibility*

In general, courts have found employers automatically liable for the actions of their supervisory personnel in quid pro quo cases. The discriminatory act is imputed to the employer without regard to whether it knew or should have known of the discrimination or granted the actual authority to discriminate. Quid pro quo harassment may be perpetrated only by the employer or by someone who has the power to grant or deny the job benefit in question. If the supervisor lacks this authority to make or influence employment decisions, quid pro quo harassment is generally not possible.

HOSTILE ENVIRONMENT HARASSMENT

A "hostile work environment" exists, for purposes of Title VII of the Civil Rights Act of 1964, when the workplace is permeated with discriminatory intimidation, ridicule, and insult that is sufficiently severe or pervasive as to alter the conditions of the victim's employment and create an abusive working environment. This theory has been most recently set forth in the U.S. Supreme Court case of *Harris v. Forklift Systems*.

The plaintiff has alleged that he or she has been forced into a hostile work environment because of sexual harassment. To prevail on such a theory, the plaintiff does not need to demonstrate that any substantial job benefits either were conditioned on submitting to hostile sexual conduct or were denied because of refusing to give in to that conduct. Rather, to establish a claim of hostile environment sexual harassment the plaintiff must prove by a preponderance of the evidence that the workplace was permeated with discriminatory intimidation, ridicule, and insult that are sufficiently severe or pervasive to alter the conditions of the plaintiff's employment and create an abusive working environment.

In evaluating hostile environment sexual harassment claims, a jury must consider the following factors:

1. the total physical environment of the plaintiff's work area;

2. the degree and type of obscenity that filled the environment of the workplace, both before and after the plaintiff arrived;

3. the reasonable expectations of the plaintiff upon;

4. the nature of the unwelcome sexual acts or words;

5. the frequency of the offensive encounters;

6. the severity of the conduct;

7. the context in which the sexual harassment occurred;

8. whether the conduct was unwelcome;

9. the effect on the plaintiff's psychological well-being;

10. whether the conduct was physically threatening;

11. whether it was merely an offensive utterance; and

12. whether it unreasonably interfered with the plaintiff's work performance.

As noted above, the harassment must be unwelcome and hostile. In determining whether the conduct was unwelcome, you should consider all the evidence and base your decision on it. In determining whether the conduct is hostile, the harassment must be sufficiently severe or extensive to alter the conditions of the plaintiff's employment and to create an abusive work environment.

The more severe the conduct, the less extensive it must be for you to find that it is hostile. In determining whether conduct is hostile, you should consider whether:

1. the conduct was verbal, physical, or both,

2. the conduct occurred one time or repeatedly,

3. the conduct was plainly offensive,

4. the alleged harasser was a co-worker or supervisor,

5. others joined in the harassment, and

6. the harassment was directed at more than one person.

TAKING PREVENTIVE ACTION

The best way for an EMS organization to minimize the incidence and impact of sexual harassment is to have a positive program designed to discourage harassment and to take prompt corrective action when any incident occurs. The EEOC Guidelines generally prescribe methods to prevent sexual harassment.

> An employer should take all steps necessary to prevent sexual harassment from occurring, such as affirmatively raising the subject, expressing strong disapproval, developing appropriate sanctions, informing employees of their right to raise and how to raise the issues of harassment under Title VII, and developing methods to sensitize all concerned.

A well designed sexual harassment program will have the following components:

1. A written policy directed specifically against sexual harassment that defines what unlawful harassment is and states that sexual harassment will not be tolerated;

2. A complaint procedure calculated to encourage victims of harassment to come forward;

3. Effective methods of communicating the policy to all employees;

4. Training and education programs to sensitize supervisors and employees to sexual harassment concerns;

5. A prompt and thorough investigation of every complaint;

6. Prompt corrective action, including appropriate sanctions if it is determined that unlawful harassment has occurred; and

7. An assessment of supervisory support of the company's sexual harassment program and regular auditing to ensure that the program is understood and effectively implemented.

Strong preventive and remedial action by an EMS organization will not only assist in defending a claim of unlawful harassment and avoid or minimize the employer's liability, it may diminish the incidence of harassment. The greater the extent to which employees are aware of their rights and are confident of potential disciplinary measures for transgressors, the less likely it is that sexual harassment will occur.

Employers must "take all steps necessary to prevent sexual harassment." The importance of adopting, publicizing, and enforcing a written sexual harassment policy, separate from general antidiscrimination policies, was emphasized by the Supreme Court in *Meritor Savings Bank v. Vinson*.

There are certain minimum elements to include in a sexual harassment policy. First, the policy language should make clear that sexual harassment will not be tolerated. The policy should state that offenders will be subject to discipline up to and including discharge. Second, because employees and supervisors may be confused about what constitutes sexual harassment, the policy should define it and provide examples of sexually harassing conduct, to ensure that employees do not misinterpret offensive sexual conduct as harmless teasing or practical joking. Third, the policy statement should require that supervisors and employees promptly report any sexually harassing conduct that they experience or witness, while ensuring all employees that no one will be retaliated against for any honest report.

Every sexual harassment program should include an internal grievance procedure. Employees who believe they have been the victims of sexual harassment must be able to report their complaints to management and have them investigated.

The complaint procedure should designate a specific department or position to handle sexual harassment complaints. The designated persons should be trained to follow an effective investigative procedure and should be authorized by top management to make the necessary inquiries.

The complaint procedure should allow complainants to file complaints with at least one easily accessible person who is outside the chain of command. A policy that gives the supervisor the exclusive responsibility for receiving reports and correcting the harassment will "necessarily discourage reporting and diminish an employee's faith in the system" when the supervisor is the alleged harasser.

The written complaint procedure should include a clause informing employees that they have a right to complain without fear of retaliation. The company must ensure that complainants are not treated as "troublemakers."

The sexual harassment policy should be made known to each employee, either independently or with the distribution of other employee materials, such as an employee handbook.

Many harassers do not believe that they are sexually harassing others. Training programs are also an effective means of demonstrating the company's commitment to eradicating sexual harassment. These programs inform supervisors in detailed terms of the kinds of conduct that may be viewed as sexual harassment.

The sexual harassment policy should ensure that the employer will promptly and thoroughly investigate complaints of sexual harassment. Whenever possible, claims of sexual harassment should be reduced to writing and signed by the complainant.

The sexual harassment policy should call for prompt corrective action if harassment is found. It is also important for employers to follow up on individual cases to ensure that the corrective action is having the desired effect.

Supervisory commitment to eradicating sexual harassment in the workplace is an essential element of any successful program. Supervisors should know that their work performance is evaluated, in part, on their enforcement of the employer's sexual harassment policy and program.

Employee surveys or workplace audits can measure the workplace atmosphere and create a more positive environment. The results may be used for training programs to clarify any misunderstandings concerning the definition of sexual harassment and the employer's policies and procedures on the subject.

Title VII does not outlaw all sexual relationships in the workplace or prohibit all types of sexual favoritism. Title VII does forbid unwelcome sexual conduct that is made a condition of obtaining or retaining a job benefit, or that is so severe or pervasive as to render the work environment hostile.

Many employers attempt to protect themselves by simply banning social relationships between supervisors and employees. With an antifraternization policy in place, an employer need not inquire deeply into the nature of ongoing relationships between supervisors and subordinates. Antifraternization rules may also prevent sex discrimination and hostile environment claims by third party employees not involved in the intracompany sexual relationship who believe that the employee who submits to sexual conduct with the supervisor receives more favorable treatment. Antifraternization rules raise special problems of their own.

A variation of an antinepotism policy, the "no-spouse" policy, may be adopted to combat co-worker complaints of unfair favoritism based on spousal relationships. As long as policies against hiring or continuing the employment of employee spouses are applied equally to male and female employees, and do not have an adverse impact on women, they are lawful under Title VII. Employers must take care to research the governing state law before implementing antinepotism policies.

Concerns about sexual harassment may also influence an employer's dress code policy. Dress standards are generally not prohibited under Title VII. Employers can implement different standards for each sex, if the standards are not based on offensive or demeaning sex stereotypes.

EQUAL EMPLOYMENT OPPORTUNITY COMMISSION (EEOC) PROCEDURES
FILING THE CHARGE

The Equal Employment Opportunity Commission's (EEOC) administrative process begins with the filing of the charge of discrimination by the complaining person. This charge must be in writing and under oath or affirmation. A person does not have to go an EEOC office to file a charge. If the aggrieved person provides sufficient information over the phone, the local EEOC office will draft the charge and mail it to the person for his or her signature. A charge is normally adequate and initiated when the EEOC issues a written statement sufficiently precise to identify the parties and to describe generally the action or practice complained of. In states with work-sharing agreements with the EEOC, filing with the state agency handling fair employment practices is deemed filing with the EEOC. The procedure by which an EEOC investigator works with an aggrieved individual to file a charge is termed the *intake process*. It should be noted that the EEOC has endorsed the use of testers—persons who pose as job applicants for the purpose of gathering information or evidence of discrimination, and testers have also been used in sexual harassment cases.

The next step is for the aggrieved individual to complete a questionnaire identifying the parties, describing the circumstances of the alleged harassment, and identifying any witnesses and any other victims. The EEOC investigator then meets with the complainant to discuss the allegations. The EEOC investigator will review the information provided to ensure that the charge states a valid claim under the statute and that the EEOC has jurisdiction. This review will include a determination that the person or entity charged (the "respondent") is covered by Title VII. An employer is covered if it employs 15 or more employees for 20 or more calendar weeks in the current or preceding year.

DETERMINATION OF TIMELINESS

The EEOC investigator then reviews the timeliness of the charge. A charge must be filed within 180 days of the alleged discrimination, or within 300 days in a state with a fair employment practices statute that prohibits discrimination.

1. Equitable Tolling

In some cases, equitable circumstances can excuse the late filing of a charge. If so, the time period for filing is deemed tolled for the duration of the special circumstances. In one case, tolling was allowed where the complainant has suffered severe psychological problems as a result of sexual harassment that affected her ability to file a charge.

2. Continued Violations

The theory of continuing violation applies to a pattern of unlawful conduct that continues over a period of time. It does not excuse a late filing as there still must be actual conduct within the charge-filing period. That is, the plaintiff must show that one incident of harassment occurred within the 180-day period. Where the harassing conduct is part of a pattern that began outside of the charge-filing period and continues into that period, however, some courts hold that the charge must lawfully include the entire history of harassment.

The Fifth Circuit Court of Appeals has described some of the factors that help identify whether the continuing violation theory applies. These include:

1. The Subject Matter—Do the alleged acts involve the same type of discrimination, tending to connect them in a continuing violation?

2. Frequency—Are the alleged acts recurring or more in the nature of an isolated work assignment or employment decision?

3. Degree of Permanence—Does the act have the degree of permanence that should trigger an employee's awareness that the continued existence of the adverse consequences of the act is to be expected without being dependent on a continuing intent to discriminate?

EEOC'S INTAKE PROCESS

If the investigator believes that there are jurisdictional problems, the investigator will try to counsel the complainant not to file a charge. The complainant, however, has a statutory right to file, and if the complainant insists, a charge will be taken.

The investigator then drafts the formal charge from the information given by the complainant. The charge contains the names and addresses of the parties, the date of the alleged discrimination, and a short statement of the discrimination alleged.

After the charge is signed by the complainant, it will be reviewed to determine if any expedited processing is required. Title VII authorizes the EEOC to seek preliminary relief in a U.S. District Court. Charges that allege continuing sexual harassment are potential candidates for an expedited investigation and for an application for a temporary restraining order and preliminary injunction from the Court. For this reason, in most district offices of the EEOC, an EEOC attorney will review incoming charges.

THE INVESTIGATION

The formal EEOC investigation begins with the service of the Charge of Discrimination. Title VII requires that a respondent be provided with Notice (within 10 days) that a charge has been filed. In the usual case, service of the charge will be accompanied by a request that the respondent provide a *position statement* setting forth its response to the allegations of the charge. Like an answer to a court complaint, the position statement, in conjunction with the charge, will define what is at issue and, therefore, what needs to be investigated.

Obviously, the position statement is vital to the respondent's defense of a discrimination charge. It should be thoroughly prepared and persuasive. It can substantially assist the respondent's case in defending its position. If the response is inaccurate or overstated, it may be counterproductive to the respondent's position.

Once the respondent's position statement has been submitted to the EEOC, it is extremely difficult for the respondent to change the theory of defense without compromising its credibility. If the EEOC finds reasonable cause to believe that discrimination has occurred, the EEOC may then attempt to conciliate a settlement between the parties. If conciliation fails, the position statement is included in material submitted to the general counsel and EEOC Commissioners to determine whether to litigate the matter or provide a right to sue notice to the party. It is also made available to the complainant.

The position statement should offer a narrative of the facts. It should set forth and describe the respondent's policies with regard to the type of discrimination alleged. Any steps taken by the respondent under its (hopefully) lawful policy should be described with respect to the complainant's allegations.

Obviously, it is helpful to support all major factual statements with attached documents and affidavits. Credibility is a critical factor in most employment discrimination cases. A respondent can increase its chances of prevailing if it can demonstrate that one or more of the complainant's assertions conflict with or are inconsistent with objective credible facts.

Request for Information

Following receipt of the respondent's position statement, the investigator will frequently send the respondent a written request for information. This request for information is similar to an interrogatory or a request for production of documents in civil litigation. Examples of the information typically sought include:

1. Identification of previous complaints of discrimination of the type alleged by the complainant;

2. A copy of any existing policy on discrimination, including the procedure by which an employee may complain;

3. A description of how employees are informed of the policy;

4. A description of management training on employment discrimination; and

5. The personnel files of the charging party, the person(s) alleged to have discriminated against the charging party (if any), and other employees who have complained of the type of discrimination alleged.

Witness Interviews

Testimony in the form of affidavits is critical to any employment discrimination investigation. The testimony of the complainant will be taken at intake. Witnesses identified by the complainant may be interviewed as soon as they can be located. The respondent's witnesses are typically interviewed at the work site.

To avoid any undo influence by the parties, the EEOC investigator is instructed to interview witnesses under conditions that ensure privacy. While the respondent's attorney has a right to attend the interview of management officials, the investigator will seek to conduct interviews of nonmanagement employees in private. EEOC's investigators are instructed to question the charging party and any persons alleged with discrimination in detail. Supervisory and managerial employees as well as co-workers will be asked about their knowledge of the alleged harassment.

If the employer fails to respond to a request for information, or refuses to allow the investigator to interview necessary witnesses, the EEOC has the right to issue administrative subpoenas that are judicially enforceable.

Resolution of the Charge

When an EEOC investigator has obtained sufficient evidence and information to make a determination whether the charge has merit, the investigator may conduct a predetermination interview with the parties. During this interview, the investigator will review the evidence obtained, inform the party of the proposed determination, and invite the submission of additional evidence.

Thereafter, the EEOC will issue its determination. The Act directs that the EEOC determine whether there is *reasonable cause* to believe the charge is true. Thus, if the EEOC determines that the charge has merit then it will state that it has found "cause" in its findings. A determination that the charge is without merit is termed a "no cause" finding. Under the Federal Rules of Evidence, determinations of cause or no cause are generally admissible at trial as factual findings of a public agency. That is, a plaintiff would have a right at trial to introduce an EEOC probable cause determination.

If the EEOC finds cause, Title VII requires that the agency attempt to resolve the matter informally by conciliation. Conciliation of a charge of discrimination would typically include instituting an appropriate policy, providing relief to the complainant and any other victims, and disciplining any persons involved in the discrimination. If conciliation is not successful, the EEOC may file an enforcement action in Federal District Court, or advise the charging parties of their right to file a private suit within 90 days. This Notice is generally called a "Notice of Right to Sue."

In summation, prudent EMS organizations may wish to consider proactive measures to eliminate or minimize the chances of discrimination in the workplace. Preparation and immediate reaction when a situation arises can assist in preventing a costly legal contest that not only can result in potential monetary losses but also efficacy losses for the EMS organization. Preparation and appropriate training of personnel can prevent discrimination in your workplace.

Example
XYZ Corporation
Sexual Harassment Policy

SEXUAL HARASSMENT IS STRICTLY PROHIBITED AT XYZ

Sexual harassment is a form of employee misconduct that undermines the integrity of the employment relationship. All employees must be allowed to work in an environment free from unsolicited and unwelcome sexual overtures. Sexual harassment does not refer to occasional compliments. It refers to behavior that is not welcome, that is personally offensive, that debilitates morale, and therefore interferes with the effectiveness of its victims and their co-workers.

Sexual harassment is a prohibited practice when it results in discrimination for or against an employee on the basis of conduct not related to work performance. Specifically, no supervisor shall threaten or insinuate, either explicitly or implicitly, that an employee's refusal to submit to sexual advances will adversely affect the employee's employment, evaluation, wages, advancement, or any other condition of employment or career development.

Other sexual harassing conduct in the workplace, whether committed by supervisors or nonsupervisory personnel, is also prohibited. This includes repeated, offensive sexual flirtations, advances, propositions; continual or repeated verbal abuse of a sexual nature; graphic verbal commentaries about an individual's body; sexually degrading words used to describe an individual; horseplay of a sexual nature; and the display in the workplace of sexually suggestive objects or pictures. Same-sex harassment is also strictly prohibited.

Any employee who believes he or she has been the subject of sexual harassment must report the alleged act either orally or in writing to his or her supervisor or higher level manager, a Human Resources representative, or the President of XYZ. *All complaints will be investigated immediately*. Supervisors should discuss any concerns with an employee who feels he or she is the victim of discrimination. If possible, the complaint should be resolved at that time. All actions taken to resolve complaints through internal reviews will be conducted in the strictest of confidence.

An employee need not bring his or her complaint initially before a supervisor who may be engaged in the harassment. In this type of situation, employees immediately notify and submit their complaint to a higher level manager, the human resources department, or to the President of XYZ.

Employees have the right to file charges directly with a federal, state, or local government agency. Any supervisor who receives a copy of a discrimination complaint from any governmental agency shall immediately notify the Human Resources department and the office of the President of XYZ.

Sexual harassment is illegal under both state and federal law. In some cases, it may be susceptible to prosecution under the criminal sexual conduct law. Sexual harassment is a serious violation of XYZ's policy, and will not be condoned or permitted. Any employee who has been found by XYZ, after appropriate investigation, to have sexually harassed another employee will be subject to appropriate sanctions. Depending on the severity of the circumstances, this may range from a written warning up to termination.

Correspondence should be sent to the Human Resources Manager, XYZ Corporation, xxx Schumann Road, Hightown, Kentucky 99999, or to the President's office (same address as above). Telephone calls may be made in strict confidence to the Human Resources Manager at (000) 999-9999.

CHAPTER 10

Governmental Agency Compliance

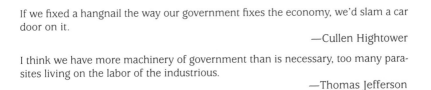

If we fixed a hangnail the way our government fixes the economy, we'd slam a car door on it.

—Cullen Hightower

I think we have more machinery of government than is necessary, too many parasites living on the labor of the industrious.

—Thomas Jefferson

EMS professionals often possess direct responsibility or oversight authority when their organization interacts with governmental agencies. It is vitally important that you thoroughly understand the scope and magnitude of this important responsibility. Normally, the primary governmental agencies that most public and private sector EMS professionals are responsible to include the federal or state agencies responsible for workplace safety and health, the federal or state agencies responsible for environmental protection, and the federal or state agencies responsible for the enforcement of labor and employment laws. It is vital that EMS organizations be familiar with the various federal, state, and local agencies that possess jurisdiction over various components of their operation, and ensure compliance with all regulations.

THE FEDERAL OCCUPATIONAL SAFETY AND HEALTH ACT OF 1970

Before the Federal Occupational Safety and Health Act (hereinafter referred to as the OSH Act) of 1970 was enacted, safety and health compliance was limited to specific industry safety and health laws and laws that governed federal contractors. It was during this period prior to the enactment of the OSH Act that Congress gradually began to regulate safety and health in the American workplace through such laws as the Walsh-Healey Public Contracts Act of 1936, the Labor Management Relations Act (Taft-Hartley Act) of 1947, the Coal Mine Safety Act of 1952, and the McNamara-O'Hara Public Service Contract Act of 1965.

With the passage of the controversial OSH Act in 1970, federal and state governmental agencies became actively involved in managing health and safety in the private sector workplace. Employers were placed on notice that unsafe and unhealthful conditions or acts would no longer be permitted to endanger the health, and often the lives, of American workers. In many circles, the Occupational Safety and Health Administration, hereinafter referred to as OSHA, became synonymous with the "safety police," and employers were often forced, under penalty of law, to address safety and health issues in their workplaces.

Today, the OSH Act itself is virtually unchanged from its 1970 roots and the basic methods for enforcement, standards' development, and promulgation, as well as adjudication, are virtually unchanged. OSHA has, however, added many new standards in the past 30 years based primarily on the research conducted by the National Institute for Occupational Safety and Health (NIOSH) and recommendations from labor and industry. Moreover, the Occupational Safety and Health Review Commission (OSHRC) has been very active in resolving many disputed issues and clarifying the law as it stands.

There is trend within Congress, industry, and labor that in order to achieve the ultimate goal of reducing workplace injuries, illnesses, and fatalities, additional revisions are needed to the OSH Act and the structure of OSHA. Change is likely to be forthcoming, but it will be based upon the learning from past mistakes and on the resolution of issues in order to achieve our ultimate goal of a safe and healthful workplace for all.

Throughout the history of the United States, the potential for the American worker to be injured or killed on the job was a brutal reality. Many disasters, such as that at Gauley Bridge, West Virginia,[1] fueled the call for laws and regulations to protect the American worker. As early as the 1920s, many states recognized the safety and health needs of the industrial worker and began to enact workers' compensation and industrial safety laws. The first significant federal legislation was the Walsh-Healey Public Contracts Act of 1936, which limited working hours and the use of child and convict labor. This law also required that contracts entered into by any federal agency for over $10,000 contain the stipulation that the contractor would not permit conditions that were unsanitary, hazardous, or dangerous to employees' health or safety.

In the 1940s, the federally enacted Labor Management Relations Act (Taft-Hartley Act) provided workers with the right to walk off a job if it was "abnormally dangerous." Additionally, in 1947, President Harry S. Truman created the first Presidential Conference on Industrial Safety.

In the 1950s and 1960s, the federal government continued to enact specialized safety and health laws to address particular circumstances. The Coal Mine Safety Act of 1952, the Maritime Safety Act, the McNamara-O'Hara Public Service Contract Act (protecting employees of contractors performing maintenance work for federal agencies), and the National Foundation on the Arts and Humanities Act (requiring recipients of federal grants to maintain safe and healthful working conditions) were all passed during this time.

The federal government's first significant step in developing extensive coverage for workplace safety and health was passage of the Metal and Nonmetallic Mine Safety Act of 1966. Following passage of this Act, President Lyndon B. Johnson, in 1968, called for the first comprehensive occupational safety and health program as part of his Great Society program. Although this proposed plan never made it to a vote in Congress, the seed was planted for future legislation.

In 1970, fueled by the new interest in workplace health and safety, Congress pushed for more comprehensive laws to regulate the conditions of the American workplace. To this end, the OSH Act of 1970 was enacted. The overriding purpose and intent of the OSH Act were "to assure so far as possible every working man and woman in the Nation safe and healthful working conditions and to preserve our human resources."[2]

The OSH Act covers virtually every American workplace that employs one or more employees and engages in a business that in any way affects interstate commerce.[3] The OSH Act covers employment in every state, the District of Columbia, Puerto Rico, Guam, the Virgin Islands, American Samoa, and the Trust Territory of the Pacific Islands.[4] The OSH Act does not, however, cover employees in situations where other state or federal agencies have jurisdiction that requires the agencies to prescribe or enforce their own safety and health regulations.[5] Additionally, the OSH Act exempts residential owners who employ people for ordinary domestic tasks, such as cooking, cleaning, and child care.[6] It also does not cover federal,[7] state, and local governments[8] or Native American reservations.[9]

The OSH Act does require that every employer engaged in interstate commerce furnish employees "a place of employment ... free from recognized hazards that are causing, or are likely to cause, death or serious harm."[10] To help employers create and maintain safe working environments and to enforce laws and regulations that ensure safe and healthful work environments, Congress provided for the creation of the Occupational Safety and Health Administration (OSHA), to be a new agency under the direction of the Department of Labor.

Today, OSHA is one of the most widely known and powerful enforcement agencies. It has been granted broad regulatory powers to promulgate regulations and standards, investigate and inspect, issue citations, and propose penalties for safety violations in the workplace.

The OSH Act also established an independent agency to review OSHA citations and decisions, the Occupational Safety and Health Review Commission (OSHRC). The OSHRC is a quasi-judicial and independent administrative agency composed of three commissioners appointed by the president who serve staggered six-year terms. The OSHRC has the power to issue orders, uphold, vacate, or modify OSHA citations and penalties, and direct other appropriate relief and penalties.

The educational arm of the OSH Act is the National Institute for Occupational Safety and Health (NIOSH), which was created as a specialized educational agency of the existing National Institutes of Health. NIOSH conducts occupational safety and health research and develops criteria for new

OSHA standards. NIOSH can conduct workplace inspections, issue subpoenas, and question employees and employers, but it does not have the power to issue citations or penalties.

STATE SAFETY PLANS

As permitted under the OSH Act, OSHA encourages individual states to take responsibility for OSHA administration and enforcement within their own respective boundaries. Each state possesses the ability to request and be granted the right to adopt state safety and health regulations and enforcement mechanisms.[11] For a state plan to be put into effect, the state must first develop and submit its proposed program to the Secretary of Labor for review and approval. The Secretary must certify that the state plan's standards are "at least as effective" as the federal standards and that the state will devote adequate resources to administering and enforcing standards.[12]

In most state plans, the state agency has developed more stringent safety and health standards than OSHA[13] and has usually developed more stringent enforcement schemes.[14] The Secretary of Labor has no statutory authority to reject a state plan if the proposed standards or enforcement scheme are more strict than the OSHA standards but can reject the state plan if the standards are below the minimum limits set under OSHA standards.[15] These states are known as "state plan" states and territories.[16] (As of 1991 there were 21 states and two territories with approved and functional state plan programs.[17]) Employers in state plan states and territories must comply with their state's regulations; federal OSHA plays virtually no role in direct enforcement.

OSHA does, however, possess an approval and oversight role with regards to state plan programs. OSHA must approve all state plan proposals prior to enactment and OSHA maintains oversight authority to "pull the ticket" of any/all state plan programs at any time they are not achieving the identified prerequisites. Enforcement of this oversight authority was recently observed following the fire resulting in several workplace fatalities at the Imperial Foods facility in Hamlet, North Carolina. Following this incident, federal OSHA assumed jurisdiction and control over the state plan program in North Carolina and made significant modifications to this program before returning the program to state control.

HR Professionals need to ask the following questions when determining jurisdiction under the OSH Act:

1. Am I a covered employer under the OSH Act?

2. If I am a covered employer, what regulations must I follow to ensure compliance?

The answer to the first question is "yes" for every class of private sector employer. Any employer in the United States that employs one or more persons and is engaged in a business that in any way affects interstate commerce is within the scope of the federal OSH Act.[18] The phrase "interstate commerce" has been broadly construed by the U.S. Supreme Court, which has stated that interstate commerce "goes well beyond persons who are themselves engaged in interstate or foreign commerce."[19] In essence, anything that crosses state lines, whether a person or goods and services, places the employer in interstate commerce. Although there are exceptions to this general statement,[20] "interstate commerce" generally has been "liberally construed to effectuate the congressional purpose" of the OSH Act.[21]

Upon finding that it is covered by the OSH Act, an employer must distinguish between a state plan jurisdiction and federal OSH Act jurisdiction. If its facilities or operations are located within a state plan state, an employer must comply with the regulations of its state. HR professionals should contact their state department of labor to acquire the pertinent regulations and standards. If facilities or operations are located in a federal OSHA state, the applicable standards and regulations can be acquired from any area OSHA office or can be found in the Code of Federal Regulations.[22]

A common jurisdictional mistake occurs when an employer operates multiple facilities in different locations.[23] EMS professionals should ascertain which state or federal agency has jurisdiction over the particular facility or operations and which regulations and standards apply.

PROMULGATION OF OSHA STANDARDS

The OSH Act requires that a covered employer comply with specific occupational safety and health standards and all rules, regulations, and orders issued pursuant to the OSH Act that apply to the workplace.[24] The OSH Act also requires that all standards be based on research, demonstration, experimentation, or other appropriate information.[25] The Secretary of Labor is authorized under the Act to "promulgate, modify, or revoke any occupational safety and health standard,"[26] and the OSH Act describes the procedures that the Secretary must follow when establishing new occupational safety and health standards.[27]

The OSH Act authorizes three ways to promulgate new standards. From 1970 to 1973, the Secretary of Labor was authorized in Section 6(a) of the Act[28] to adopt national consensus standards and establish federal safety and health standards without following lengthy rulemaking procedures. Many of the early OSHA standards were adapted mainly from other areas of regulation, such as the National Electric Code and American National Standards Institute (ANSI) guidelines. However, this promulgation method is no longer in effect.

The usual method of issuing, modifying, or revoking a new or existing OSHA standard is set out in Section 6(b) of the OSH Act and is known as informal rulemaking. It requires notice to interested parties, through subscription in the *Federal Register* of the proposed regulation and standard, and provides an opportunity for comment in a nonadversarial administrative hearing.[29] The proposed standard can also be advertised through magazine articles and other publications, thus informing interested parties of the proposed standard and regulation. This method differs from the requirements of most other administrative agencies that follow the Administrative Procedure Act[30] in that the OSH Act provides interested persons an opportunity to request a public hearing with oral testimony. It also requires the Secretary of Labor to publish in the *Federal Register* a notice of the time and place of such hearings.

Although not required under the OSH Act, the Secretary of Labor has directed, by regulation, that OSHA follow a more rigorous procedure for comment and hearing than other administrative agencies.[31] Upon notice and request for a hearing, OSHA must provide a hearing examiner in order to listen to any oral testimony offered. All oral testimony is preserved in a verbatim transcript. Interested persons are provided an opportunity to cross-examine OSHA representatives or others on critical issues. The Secretary must state the reasons for the action to be taken on the proposed standard, and the statement must be supported by substantial evidence in the record as a whole.

The Secretary of Labor has the authority not to permit oral hearings and to call for written comment only. Within 60 days after the period for written comment or oral hearings has expired, the Secretary must decide whether to adopt, modify, or revoke the standard in question. The Secretary can also decide not to adopt a new standard. The Secretary must then publish a statement of the reasons for any decision in the *Federal Register*. OSHA regulations further mandate that the Secretary provide a supplemental statement of significant issues in the decision. Safety and health professionals should be aware that the standard as adopted and published in the *Federal Register* may be different from the proposed standard. The Secretary is not required to reopen hearings when the adopted standard is a "logical outgrowth" of the proposed standard.[32]

The final method for promulgating new standards, and the one most infrequently used, is the emergency temporary standard permitted under Section 6(c).[33] The Secretary of Labor may establish a standard immediately, if it is determined that employees are subject to grave danger from exposure to substances or agents known to be toxic or physically harmful and that an emergency standard would protect the employees from the danger. An emergency temporary standard becomes effective on publication in the *Federal Register* and may remain in effect for six months. During this six-month period, the Secretary must adopt a new permanent standard or abandon the emergency standard.

Only the Secretary of Labor can establish new OSHA standards. Recommendations or requests for an OSHA standard can come from any interested person or organization, including employees, employers, labor unions, environmental groups, and others.[34] When the Secretary receives a petition to adopt a new standard or to modify or revoke an existing standard, he or she usually forwards the request to NIOSH and the National Advisory Committee on Occupational Safety and Health (NACOSH)[35] or the Secretary may use a private organization such as the American National Standards Institute (ANSI) for advice and review.

THE GENERAL DUTY CLAUSE

The OSH Act requires that an employer must maintain a place of employment free from recognized hazards that are causing or are likely to cause death or serious physical harm, even if there is no specific OSHA standard addressing the circumstances. Under Section 5(a)(1), known as the "general duty clause," an employer may be cited for a violation of the OSH Act if the condition causes harm or is likely to cause harm to employees, even if OSHA has not promulgated a standard specifically addressing the particular hazard. The general duty clause is a catch-all standard encompassing all potential hazards that have not been specifically addressed in the OSHA standards. For example, if a company is cited for an ergonomic hazard and there is no ergonomic standard to apply, the hazard will be cited under the general duty clause.

Prudent EMS professionals should take a proactive approach in maintaining their competency in this expanding area of OSHA regulations. As noted previously, the first notice of any new OSHA standard, modification of an existing standard, revocation of a standard, or emergency standard must be published in the *Federal Register*. EMS professionals can use the *Federal Register*, or professional publications that monitor OSHA standards, to track the progress of proposed standards. With this information, EMS professionals can provide testimony to OSHA when necessary, prepare their organizations for acquiring resources and personnel necessary to achieve compliance, and get a head start on developing compliance programs to meet requirements in a timely manner.

CIVIL (MONETARY) PENALTIES

The OSH Act provides for a wide range of penalties, from a simple notice with no fine to criminal prosecution. The Omnibus Budget Reconciliation Act of 1990 multiplied maximum penalties sevenfold. Violations are categorized and penalties may be assessed as outlined in Table 10.1:

TABLE 10.1
Violation and Penalty Schedule

Penalty	Old penalty schedule (in dollars)	New penalty schedule (1990) (in dollars)
De minimis notice	0	0
Nonserious	0–1,000	0–7,000
Serious	0–1,000	0–7,000
Repeat	0–10,000	0–70,000
Willful	0–10,000	25,000 minimum 70,000 maximum
Failure to abate notice	0–1,000 per day	0–7,000 per day
New posting penalty		0–7,000

Each alleged violation is categorized and the appropriate fine issued by the OSHA area director. It should be noted that each citation is separate and may carry with it a monetary fine. The gravity of the violation is the primary factor in determining penalties.[36] In assessing the gravity of a violation, the compliance officer or area director must consider (1) the severity of the injury or illness that *could* result and (2) the probability that an injury or illness *could* occur as a result of the violation.[37] Specific penalty assessment tables assist the area director or compliance officer in determining the appropriate fine for the violation.[38]

After selecting the appropriate penalty table, the area director or other official determines the degree of probability that the injury or illness will occur by considering:

1. the number of employees exposed;

2. the frequency and duration of the exposure;

3. the proximity of employees to the point of danger;

4. factors such as the speed of the operation that require work under stress; and

5. other factors that might significantly affect the degree of probability of an accident.[39]

OSHA has defined a serious violation as "an infraction in which there is a substantial probability that death or serious harm could result ... unless the employer did not or could not with the exercise of reasonable diligence, know of the presence of the violation."[40] Section 17(b) of the OSH Act requires that a penalty of up to $7,000 be assessed for every serious violation cited by the compliance officer.[41] In assembly line enterprises and manufacturing facilities with duplicate operations, if one process is cited as possessing a serious violation, it is possible that each of the duplicate processes or machines may be cited for the same violation. Thus, if a serious violation is found in one machine and there are many other identical machines in the enterprise, a very large monetary fine for a single serious violation is possible.[42]

Currently the greatest monetary liabilities are for "repeat violations," "willful violations," and "failure to abate" cited violations. A *repeat* violation is a second citation for a violation that was cited previously by a compliance officer. OSHA maintains records of all violations and must check for repeat violations after each inspection. A *willful* violation is the employer's purposeful or negligent failure to correct a known deficiency. This type of violation, in addition to carrying a large monetary fine, exposes the employer to a charge of an "egregious" violation and the potential for criminal sanctions under the OSH Act or state criminal statutes if an employee is injured or killed as a direct result of the willful violation. *Failure to abate* a cited violation has the greatest cumulative monetary liability of all. OSHA may assess a penalty of up to $1,000 per day per violation for each day in which a cited violation is not brought into compliance.

In assessing monetary penalties, the area or regional director must consider the good faith of the employer, the gravity of the violation, the employer's past history of compliance, and the size of the employer. OSHA has stated the use of its egregious case policy, which has seldom been invoked in recent years.[43] Under the egregious violation policy, when violations are determined to be conspicuous, penalties are cited for each violation, rather than combining the violations into a single, smaller penalty.

In addition to the potential civil or monetary penalties that could be assessed, OSHA regulations may be used as evidence in negligence, product liability, workers' compensation, and other actions involving employee safety and health issues.[44] OSHA standards and regulations are the baseline requirements for safety and health that must be met, not only to achieve compliance with the OSHA regulations, but also to safeguard an organization against other potential civil actions.

TYPES OF VIOLATIONS

The OSHA monetary penalty structure is classified according to the type and gravity of the particular violation. Violations of OSHA standards or the general duty clause are categorized as "de minimis,"[45] "other" (nonserious),[46] "serious,"[47] "repeat,"[48] and "willful."[49] Monetary penalties assessed by the Secretary vary according to the degree of the violation. Penalties range from no monetary penalty to 10 times the imposed penalty for repeat or willful violations.[50] Additionally, the Secretary may refer willful violations to the U.S. Department of Justice for imposition of criminal sanctions.[51]

DE MINIMIS VIOLATIONS

When a violation of an OSHA standard does not immediately or directly relate to safety or health, OSHA either does not issue a citation or issues a "de minimis" citation. Section 9 of the OSH Act provides that "[the] Secretary may prescribe procedures for the issuance of a notice in lieu of a citation with respect to de minimis violations which have no direct or immediate relationship to safety or health."[52] A de minimis notice does not constitute a citation and no fine is imposed. Additionally, there usually is no abatement period, and thus there can be no violation for failure to abate.

The *OSHA Compliance Field Operations Manual* (OSHA Manual)[53] provides two examples of when de minimis notices are generally appropriate:

1. "in situations involving standards containing physical specificity wherein a slight deviation would not have an immediate or direct relationship to safety or health,"[54] and

2. "where the height of letters on an exit sign is not in strict conformity with the size requirements of the standard."[55]

OSHA has found de minimis violations in cases where employees, as well as the safety records, are persuasive in exemplifying that no injuries or lost time have been incurred.[56] Additionally, in order for OSHA to conserve valuable resources to produce a greater impact on safety and health in the workplace, it is highly likely that the Secretary will encourage use of the de minimis notice in marginal cases and even in other situations where the possibility of injury is remote and the potential for injuries would be minimal.

OTHER OR NONSERIOUS VIOLATIONS

"Other" or nonserious violations are issued where a violation could lead to an accident or occupational illness, but the probability that it would cause death or serious physical harm is minimal. Such a violation, however, does possess a direct or immediate relationship to the safety and health of workers.[57] Potential penalties for this type of violation range from no fine up to $7,000 per violation.[58]

In distinguishing between a serious and a nonserious violation, the OSHRC has stated that "a non-serious violation is one in which there is a direct and immediate relationship between the violative condition and occupational safety and health but no such relationship that a resultant injury or illness *is death or serious physical harm.*"[59]

The *OSHA Manual* provides guidance and examples for issuing nonserious violations. It states that:

> an example of non-serious violation is the lack of guardrail at a height from which a fall would more probably result in only a mild sprain or cut or abrasion; i.e., something less than serious harm.[60]
>
> A citation for serious violation may be issued or a group of individual violations (which) taken by themselves would be nonserious, but together would be serious in the sense that in combination they present a substantial probability of injury resulting in death or serious physical harm to employees.[61]
>
> A number of nonserious violations (which) are present in the same piece of equipment which, considered in relation to each other, affect the overall gravity of possible injury resulting from an accident involving the combined violations ... may be grouped in a manner similar to that indicated in the preceding paragraph, although the resulting citation will be for a non-serious violation.[62]

The difference between a serious and a nonserious violation hinges on subjectively determining the probability of injury or illness that might result from the violation. Administrative decisions have usually turned on the particular facts of the situation. The OSHRC has reduced serious citations to nonserious violations when the employer was able to show that the probability of an accident, and the probability of a serious injury or death, was minimal.[63]

SERIOUS VIOLATIONS

Section 17(k) of the OSH Act defines a serious violation as one where:

there is a substantial probability that death or serious physical harm could result from a condition which exists, or from one or more practices, means, methods, operations or processes which have been adopted or are in use, in such place of employment unless the employer did not, and could not with exercise of reasonable diligence, know of the presence of the violation.[64]

Section 17(b) of the Act provides that a civil penalty of up to $7,000 *must* be assessed for serious violations, whereas for nonserious violations civil penalties *may* be assessed.[65] The amount of the penalty is determined by considering (1) the gravity of the violation, (2) the size of the employer, (3) the good faith of the employer, and (4) the employer's history of previous violations.[66]

To prove that a violation is within the serious category, OSHA must only show a substantial probability that a foreseeable accident would result in serious physical harm or death. Thus, contrary to common belief, OSHA does not need to show that a violation would create a high probability that an accident would result. Because substantial physical harm is the distinguishing factor between a serious and a nonserious violation, OSHA has defined "serious physical harm" as "permanent, prolonged, or temporary impairment of the body in which part of the body is made functionally useless or is substantially reduced in efficiency on or off the job." Additionally, an occupational illness is defined as "illness that could shorten life or significantly reduce physical or mental efficiency by inhibiting the normal function of a part of the body."[67]

After determining that a hazardous condition exists and that employees are exposed or potentially exposed to the hazard, the *OSHA Manual* instructs compliance officers to use a four-step approach to determine whether the violation is serious.

1. Determine the type of accident or health hazard exposure that the violated standard is designed to prevent in relation to the hazardous condition identified.

2. Determine the type of injury or illness that it is reasonably predictable could result from the type of accident or health hazard exposure identified in step 1.

3. Determine that the type of injury or illness identified in step 2 includes death or a form of serious physical harm.

4. Determine that the employer knew or with the exercise of reasonable diligence could have known of the presence of the hazardous condition.[68]

The *OSHA Manual* provides examples of serious injuries, including amputations, fractures, deep cuts involving extensive suturing, disabling burns, and concussions. Examples of serious illnesses include cancer, silicosis, asbestosis, poisoning, and hearing and visual impairment.[69]

EMS professionals should be aware that OSHA is not required to show that the employer actually knew that the cited condition violated safety or health standards. The employer can be charged with constructive knowledge of the OSHA standards. OSHA also does not have to show that the employer could reasonably foresee that an accident would happen, although it does have the burden of proving that the possibility of an accident was not totally unforeseeable. OSHA does need to prove, however, that the employer knew or should have known of the hazardous condition and that it knew there was a substantial likelihood that serious harm or death would result from an accident.[70] If the Secretary cannot prove that the cited violation meets the criteria for a serious violation, the violation may be cited in one of the lesser categories.

WILLFUL VIOLATIONS

The most severe monetary penalties under the OSHA penalty structure are for willful violations. A "willful" violation can result in penalties of up to $70,000 per violation, with a minimum required penalty of $5,000. Although the term "willful" is not defined in OSHA regulations, courts generally have defined a willful violation as "an act voluntarily with either an intentional disregard of, or plain indifference to, the Act's requirements."[71] Further, the OSHRC defines a willful violation as "action taken knowledgeably by one subject to the statutory provisions of the OSH Act in disregard of the action's legality. No showing of malicious intent is necessary. A conscious, intentional, deliberate, voluntary decision is properly described as willful."[72]

There is little distinction between civil and criminal willful violations other than the due process requirements for a criminal violation and the fact that a violation of the general duty clause cannot be used as the basis for a criminal willful violation. The distinction is usually based on the factual circumstances and the fact that a criminal willful violation results from a willful violation that caused an employee death.

According to the OSHA Manual, the compliance officer "can assume that an employer has knowledge of any OSHA violation condition of which its supervisor has knowledge; he can also presume that, if the compliance officer was able to discover a violative condition, the employer could have discovered the same condition through the exercise of reasonable diligence."[73]

Courts and the OSHRC have agreed on three basic elements of proof that OSHA must show for a willful violation. OSHA must show that the employer (1) knew or should have known that a violation existed, (2) voluntarily chose not to comply with the OSH Act to remove the violative condition, and (3) made the choice not to comply with intentional disregard of the OSH Act's requirements or plain indifference to them properly characterized as reckless. Courts and the OSHRC have affirmed findings of willful violations in many circumstances, ranging from deliberate disregard of known safety requirements[74] through fall protection equipment not being provided.[75] Other examples of willful violations include cases where safety equipment was ordered but employees were permitted to continue work until the equipment arrived,[76] inexperienced and untrained employees were permitted to perform a hazardous job,[77] or where an employer failed to correct a situation that had been previously cited as a violation.

REPEAT AND FAILURE TO ABATE VIOLATIONS

"Repeat" and "failure to abate" violations are often quite similar and confusing to EMS professionals. When, upon reinspection by OSHA, a violation of a previously cited standard is found but the violation does not involve the same machinery, equipment, process, or location, this would constitute a repeat violation. If, upon reinspection by OSHA, a violation of a previously cited standard is found but evidence indicates that the violation continued uncorrected since the original inspection, this would constitute a failure to abate violation.[78]

The most costly civil penalty under the OSH Act is for repeat violations. The OSH Act authorizes a penalty of up to $70,000 per violation but permits a maximum penalty of 10 times the maximum authorized for the first instance of the violation. Repeat violations can also be grouped within the willful category (i.e., a willful repeat violation) to acquire maximum civil penalties.

In certain cases, where an employer has more than one fixed establishment and citations have been issued, the *OSHA Manual* states,

> the purpose for considering whether a violation is repeated, citations issued to employers having fixed establishments (e.g., factories, terminals, stores) will be limited to the cited establishment.... For employers engaged in businesses having no fixed establishments, repeated violations will be alleged based upon prior violations occurring anywhere within the same Area Office Jurisdiction.[79]

When a previous citation has been contested but a final OSHRC order has not yet been received, a second violation is usually cited as a repeat violation. The *OSHA Manual* instructs the compliance officer to notify the assistant regional director and to indicate on the citation that the violation is contested.[80] If the first citation never becomes a final OSHRC order (i.e., the citation is vacated or otherwise dismissed), the second citation for the repeat violation will be removed automatically.[81]

As noted previously, a failure to abate violation occurs when, upon reinspection, the compliance officer finds that the employer has failed to take necessary corrective action and thus the violation continues uncorrected. The penalty for a failure to abate violation can be up to $7,000 per day to a maximum of $70,000. EMS professionals should also be aware that citations for repeat violations, failure to abate violations, or willful repeat violations can be issued for violations of the general duty clause. The *OSHA Manual* instructs compliance officers that citations under the general duty clause are restricted to serious violations or to willful or repeat violations that are of a serious nature.[82]

FAILURE TO POST VIOLATION NOTICES

A new penalty category, the failure to post violation notices, carries a penalty of up to $7,000 for each violation. A failure to post violation occurs when an employer fails to post notices required by the OSHA standards, including the OSHA poster, a copy of the year-end summary of the OSHA 200 form, a copy of OSHA citations when received, and copies of other pleadings and notices.

CRIMINAL LIABILITY AND PENALTIES

The OSH Act provides for criminal penalties in four circumstances.[83] In the first, anyone inside or outside of the Department of Labor or OSHA who gives advance notice of an inspection, without authority from the Secretary, may be fined up to $1,000, imprisoned for up to six months, or both. Second, any employer or person who intentionally falsifies statements or OSHA records that must be prepared, maintained, or submitted under the OSH Act, if found guilty, may be fined up to $10,000, imprisoned for up to six months, or both. Third, any person responsible for a violation of an OSHA standard, rule, order, or regulation that causes the death of an employee may, upon conviction, be fined up to $10,000, imprisoned for up to six months, or both. If convicted for a second violation, punishment may be a fine of up to $20,000, imprisonment for up to one year, or both.[84] Finally, if an individual is convicted of forcibly resisting or assaulting a compliance officer or other Department of Labor personnel, a fine of $5,000, three years in prison, or both can be imposed. Any person convicted of killing a compliance officer or other OSHA or Department of Labor personnel acting in his or her official capacity may be sentenced to prison for any term of years or life.

OSHA does not have authority to impose criminal penalties directly, instead, it refers cases for possible criminal prosecution to the U.S. Department of Justice. Criminal penalties must be based on violation of a specific OSHA standard; they may not be based on a violation of the general duty clause. Criminal prosecutions are conducted like any other criminal trial, with the same rules of evidence, burden of proof, and rights of the accused. A corporation may be criminally liable for the acts of its agents or employees.[85] The statute of limitations for possible criminal violations of the OSH Act, as for other federal noncapital crimes, is five years.[86]

Under federal criminal law, criminal charges may range from murder to manslaughter to conspiracy. Several charges may be brought against an employer for various separate violations under one federal indictment.

The OSH Act provides for criminal penalties of up to $10,000 and/or imprisonment for up to six months. A repeated willful violation causing an employee death can double the criminal sanction to a maximum of $20,000 and/or one year of imprisonment. Given the increased use of criminal sanctions by OSHA in recent years, personnel managers should advise their employers of the potential for these sanctions being used when the safety and health of employees are disregarded or put on the back burner.

Criminal liability for a willful OSHA violation can attach to an individual or a corporation. In addition corporations may be held criminally liable for the actions of their agents or officials.[87] EMS professionals, safety managers, and other corporate officials may also be subject to criminal liability under a theory of aiding and abetting the criminal violation in their official capacity with the corporation.[88]

EMS professionals should also be aware that an employer could face two prosecutions for the same OSHA violation without the protection of double jeopardy. The OSHRC can bring an action for a civil willful violation using the monetary penalty structure described previously and the case then may be referred to the Justice Department for criminal prosecution of the same violation.[89]

Prosecution of willful criminal violations by the Justice Department has been rare in comparison to the number of inspections performed and violations cited by OSHA on a yearly basis. However, the use of criminal sanctions has increased substantially in the last few years. With adverse publicity being generated as a result of workplace accidents and deaths[90] and Congress emphasizing reform, a decrease in criminal prosecutions is unlikely.

The law regarding criminal prosecution of willful OSH Act violations is still emerging. Although few cases have actually gone to trial, in most situations the mere threat of criminal prosecution has encouraged employers to settle cases with assurances that criminal prosecution would be dismissed. Many state plan states are using criminal sanctions permitted under their state OSH regulations more frequently.[91] State prosecutors have also allowed use of state criminal codes for workplace deaths.[92]

EMS professionals should exercise extreme caution when faced with an on-the-job fatality. The potential for criminal sanctions and criminal prosecution is substantial if a willful violation of a specific OSHA standard is directly involved in the death. The OSHA investigation may be conducted from a criminal perspective in order to gather and secure the appropriate evidence to later pursue criminal sanctions.[93] A prudent HR professional facing a workplace fatality investigation should address the OSHA investigation with legal counsel present and reserve all rights guaranteed under the U.S. Constitution.[94] Obviously, under no circumstances should an HR professional condone or attempt to conceal facts or evidence as this constitutes a cover-up.

RIGHTS AND RESPONSIBILITIES UNDER THE OSH ACT—THE OSHA INSPECTION

OSHA performs all enforcement functions under the OSH Act. Under Section 8(a) of the Act, OSHA compliance officers have the right to enter any workplace of a covered employer without delay, to inspect and investigate a workplace during regular hours and at other reasonable times, and to obtain an inspection warrant if access to a facility or operation is denied.[95] Upon arrival at an inspection site, the compliance officer is required to present his or her credentials to the owner or designated representative of the employer before starting the inspection. The employer representative and an employee and/or union representative may accompany the compliance officer on the inspection. Compliance officers can question the employer and employees and inspect required records, such as the OSHA Form 200, which records injuries and illnesses.[96] Most compliance officers cannot issue on-the-spot citations, they only have authority to document potential hazards and report or confer with the OSHA area director before issuing a citation.

A compliance officer or any other employee of OSHA is not required to provide advance notice of the inspection under penalty of law.[97] The OSHA area director is, however, permitted to provide notice under the following circumstances:

1. In cases of apparent imminent danger, to enable the employer to eliminate the danger as quickly as possible;

2. When the inspection can most effectively be conducted after regular business hours or where special preparations are necessary;

3. To ensure the presence of employee and employer representatives or appropriate personnel needed to aid in inspections; or

4. When the area director determines that advance notice would enhance the probability of an effective and thorough inspection.[98]

Compliance officers can also take samples, obtain photographs, and gather other evidence related to the inspection. Additionally, compliance officers, can use other "reasonable investigative techniques," including personal sampling equipment, dosimeters, air sampling badges, and other equipment.[99] Compliance officers must, however, take reasonable precautions when using photographic or sampling equipment to avoid creating hazardous conditions (i.e., a spark-producing camera flash in a flammable area) or disclosing a trade secret.[100]

An OSHA inspection has four basic components: (1) the opening conference, (2) the walk-through inspection, (3) the closing conference, and (4) the issuance of citations, if necessary. In the opening conference, the compliance officer may explain the purpose and type of inspection to be conducted, request records to be evaluated, question the employer, ask for appropriate representatives to accompany him or her during the walk-through inspection, and ask additional questions or request more information. The compliance officer may, but is not required to, provide the employer with copies of the applicable laws and regulations governing procedures and health and safety standards. The opening conference is usually brief and informal; its primary purpose is to establish the scope and purpose of the walk-through inspection.

After the opening conference and review of appropriate records, the compliance officer, usually accompanied by a representative of the employer and a representative of the employees, conducts a physical inspection of the facility or worksite.[101] The general purpose of this walk-through inspection is to determine whether the facility or worksite complies with OSHA standards. The compliance officer must identify potential safety and health hazards in the workplace, if any, and document them to support issuance of citations.[102]

The compliance officer uses various forms to document potential safety and health hazards observed during the inspection. The most commonly used form is the OSHA-1 Inspection Report where the compliance officer records information gathered during the opening conference and walk-through inspection.[103]

Two additional forms are usually attached to the OSHA Inspection Report. The OSHA-1A form, known as the narrative, is used to record information gathered during the walk-through inspection; names and addresses of employees, management officials, and employee representatives accompanying the compliance officer on the inspection; and other information. A separate worksheet, known as OSHA-1B, is used by the compliance officer to document each condition that he or she believes could be an OSHA violation. One OSHA-1B worksheet is completed for each potential violation noted by the compliance officer.

When the walk-through inspection is completed, the compliance officer usually conducts an informal meeting with the employer or the employer's representative to "informally advise (the employer) of any apparent safety or health violations disclosed by the inspection."[104] The compliance officer informs the employer of the potential hazards observed and indicates the applicable section of the standards allegedly violated, advises that citations may be issued, and informs the employer or representative of the appeal process and rights.[105] Additionally, the compliance officer advises the employer that the OSH Act prohibits discrimination against employees or others for exercising their rights.[106]

In an unusual situation, the compliance officer may issue a citation(s) on the spot. When this occurs the compliance officer informs the employer of the abatement period, in addition to the other information provided at the closing conference. In most circumstances the compliance officer will leave the workplace and file a report with the area director who has authority, through the Secretary of Labor, to decide whether a citation should be issued, compute any penalties to be assessed, and set the abatement date for each alleged violation. The area director, under authority from the Secretary, must issue the citation with "reasonable promptness."[107] Citations must be issued in writing and must describe with particularity the violation alleged, including the relevant standard and regulation. There is a six-month statute of limitations and the citation must be issued or vacated within this time period. OSHA must serve notice of any citation and proposed penalty by certified mail, unless there is personal service, to an agent or officer of the employer.[108]

After the citation and notice of proposed penalty are issued, but before the notice of contest by the employer is filed, the employer may request an informal conference with the OSHA area director. The general purpose of the informal conference is to clarify the basis for the citation, modify abatement dates or proposed penalties, seek withdrawal of a cited item, or otherwise attempt to settle the case. This conference, as its name implies, is an informal meeting between the employer and OSHA. Employee representatives must have an opportunity to participate if they so request. EMS professionals should note that the request for an informal conference does not "stay" (delay) the 15-working-day period to file a notice of contest to challenge the citation.[109]

Under the OSH Act, an employer, employee, or authorized employee representative (including a labor organization) is given 15 working days from when the citation is issued to file a "notice of contest." If a notice of contest is not filed within 15 working days, the citation and proposed penalty become a final order of the Occupational Safety and Health Review Commission (OSHRC), and are not subject to review by any court or agency. If a timely notice of contest is filed in good faith, the abatement requirement is tolled (temporarily suspended or delayed) and a hearing is scheduled. The employer also has the right to file a petition for modification of the abatement period (PMA) if the employer is unable to comply with the abatement period provided in the citation. If OSHA contests the PMA, a hearing is scheduled to determine whether the abatement requirements should be modified.

When the notice of contest by the employer is filed, the Secretary must immediately forward the notice to the OSHRC, which then schedules a hearing before its administrative law judge (ALJ). The Secretary of Labor is labeled the "complainant," and the employer the "respondent." The ALJ may affirm, modify, or vacate the citation, any penalties, or the abatement date. Either party can appeal the ALJ's decision by filing a petition for discretionary review (PDR). Additionally, any member of the OSHRC may "direct review" any decision by an ALJ, in whole or in part, without a PDR. If a PDR is not filed and no member of the OSHRC directs a review, the decision of the ALJ becomes final in 30 days. Any party may appeal a final order of the OSHRC by filing a petition for review in the U.S. Court of Appeals for the circuit in which the violation is alleged to have occurred or in the U.S. Court of Appeals for the District of Columbia Circuit. This petition for review must be filed within 60 days from the date of the OSHRC's final order.

OSHA INSPECTION CHECKLIST

The following is a recommended checklist for EMS professionals in order to prepare for an OSHA inspection:

1. Assemble a team from the management group and identify specific responsibilities in writing for each team member. The team members should be given appropriate training and education. The team should include, but not be limited to, the following list.

   a) an OSHA inspection team coordinator,

   b) a document control individual,

    c) individuals to accompany the OSHA inspector,

    d) a media coordinator,

    e) an accident investigation team leader (where applicable),

    f) a notification person,

    g) a legal advisor (where applicable),

    h) a law enforcement coordinator (where applicable),

    i) a photographer, and

    j) an industrial hygienist.

2. Decide on and develop a company policy and procedures to provide guidance to the OSHA inspection team.

3. Prepare an OSHA inspection kit, including all equipment necessary to properly document all phases of the inspection. The kit should include equipment such as a camera (with extra film and batteries), a tape player (with extra batteries), a video camera, pads, pens, and other appropriate testing and sampling equipment (e.g., a noise level meter, an air sampling kit, etc.).

4. Prepare basic forms to be used by the inspection team members during and following the inspection.

5. When notified that an OSHA inspector has arrived, assemble the team members along with the inspection kit.

6. Identify the inspector. Check his or her credentials and determine the reason for and type of inspection to be conducted.

7. Confirm the reason for the inspection with the inspector (targeted, routine inspection, accident, or in response to a complaint).

    a) For a random or target inspection:

- Did the inspector check the OSHA 200 Form?

- Was a warrant required?

    b) For an employee complaint inspection:

- Did the inspector have a copy of the complaint? If so, obtain a copy.

- Do allegations in the complaint describe an OSHA violation?

- Was a warrant required?

- Was the inspection protested in writing?

    c) For an accident investigation inspection:

- How was OSHA notified of the accident?

- Was a warrant required?
- Was the inspection limited to the accident location?

d) If a warrant is presented:

- Were the terms of the warrant reviewed by local counsel?
- Did the inspector follow the terms of the warrant?
- Was a copy of the warrant acquired?
- Was the inspection protested in writing?

8. The opening conference

a) Who was present?

b) What was said?

c) Was the conference taped or otherwise documented?

9. Records

a) What records were requested by the inspector?

b) Did the document control coordinator number the photocopies of the documents provided to the inspector?

c) Did the document control coordinator maintain a list of all photocopies provided to the inspector?

10. Facility inspection

a) What areas of the facility were inspected?

b) What equipment was inspected?

c) Which employees were interviewed?

d) Who was the employee or union representative present during the inspection?

e) Were all the remarks made by the inspector documented?

f) Did the inspector take photographs?

g) Did a team member take similar photographs?[110]

There is no replacement for a well managed safety and health program. EMS professionals must ensure that their upper level management team realizes that they cannot get by on a shoestring safety program, as every aspect of the safety program is important, including preparing for an OSHA inspection. The preceding checklist was provided as an example of what can be done prior to an OSHA inspection. Please remember, OSHA inspectors are human too; treat them with respect and curtesy and they will generally be fair and even helpful. This is not to say you will not be cited for violations but you may avoid an inspector who is overzealous.

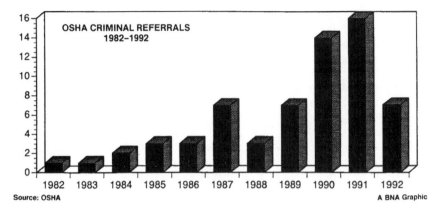

Figure 10.1: OSHA criminal referrals

EMPLOYER'S RIGHTS

EMPLOYER'S RIGHTS DURING AN OSHA INSPECTION

When a compliance officer or other Department of Labor representative enters a facility to perform an inspection, the employer has certain rights. It is entitled to know the purpose of the inspection, that is, whether it is based on an employee complaint or is a routine inspection. The employer also has the right to accompany the compliance officer during the inspection. This can be helpful or harmful; helpful in the sense that the employer can avoid certain areas, but harmful if a major violation is found and the employer in trying to explain, talks itself into more trouble and ends up with a higher fine and a more serious violation.

EMS professionals should know their rights under the OSH Act and U.S. Constitution. Because of the decision in *Marshall v. Barlow's, Inc.*,[111] three distinct avenues for addressing OSHA enforcement efforts have developed and can be efficiently used.

In *Barlow's*, the Supreme Court held that Section 8(a) of the OSH Act, which empowered OSHA compliance officers to search the work areas of any employment facility within the OSH Act's jurisdiction without a search warrant or other process, was unconstitutional.[112] The Court concluded that "the concerns expressed by the Secretary (of Labor) do not suffice to justify warrantless inspections under OSHA or vitiate the general constitutional requirement that for a search to be reasonable a warrant must be obtained."[113] This decision opened the door to the first avenue of approach—namely, requiring OSHA and state enforcement officers to acquire a warrant before entering a facility to conduct an inspection. This approach should be carefully evaluated with the help of legal counsel given the potential pitfalls and the possibility of sanctions against the employer for bad faith.

The second successful approach is limiting the scope and inspection techniques used by the OSHA or state inspection officer. This is normally an informal process where the personnel manager contacts the regional or area director before a voluntary compliance inspection and an agreement is reached on the specific area to be inspected,[114] or limitations are placed on photographing or videotaping to protect trade secrets.[115] If an agreement cannot be reached before the inspection, a court order may be acquired to protect the confidentiality of a trade secret.[116]

The third approach is to permit the warrantless compliance inspection of the facility.

EMS professionals should analyze their situation and facility and develop a policy and plan of action that advises subordinates on how to deal with OSHA and state compliance officers. This statement should include the policy's purpose; detailed steps to be followed when OSHA or state compliance officers attempt entry, during the inspection, at the closing conference, and after the inspection; and forms to assist the subordinate in this procedure. In addition, contingencies should be addressed for situations where a selected member of a team is on vacation or unavailable.

OSHA and most state plan programs offer free consultation services.[117] At the employer's request, OSHA or a State Plan Program can assist the employer with compliance and other issues. This voluntary program will not cite violations except under very limited and serious circumstances.

APPEAL RIGHTS AND PROCEDURES

Under Section 9(a) of the OSH Act, if the Secretary of Labor believes that an employer "has violated a requirement of Section 5 of the Act, of any standard, rule or order promulgated pursuant to Section 6 of this Act, or of any regulations prescribed pursuant to this Act, he shall within reasonable promptness issue a citation to the employer."[118] "Reasonable promptness" has been defined to mean within six months from the occurrence of a violation.[119]

Section 9(a) also requires that citations be in writing and "describe with particularity the nature of the violation, including a reference to the provision of the Act, standard, rule, regulation, or order alleged to have been violated."[120] The OSHRC has adopted a fair notice test that is satisfied if the employer is notified of the nature of the violation, the standard allegedly violated, and the location of the alleged violation.[121]

The OSH Act does not specifically provide for a method of service for citations. Section 10(a) authorizes service of notice of proposed penalties by certified mail, and in most instances the written citations are attached to the penalty notice.[122] Regarding the proper party to be served, the OSHRC has held that service is proper if it "is reasonably calculated to provide an employer with knowledge of the citation and notification of proposed penalty and an opportunity to determine whether to contest or abate."[123]

Under Section 10 of the Act, once a citation is issued, the employer, any employee, or any authorized union representative has 15 working days to file a notice of contest.[124] If the employer does not contest the violation, abatement date, or proposed penalty, the citation becomes final and not subject to review by any court or agency. If a timely notice of contest is filed in good faith, the abatement requirement is tolled and a hearing is scheduled. An employer may contest any part or all of the citation, proposed penalty, or abatement date. Employee contests are limited to the reasonableness of the proposed abatement date. Employees also have the right to elect party status after an employer has filed a notice of contest.

EMS professionals may also file a PMA if their organization cannot comply with any abatement that has become a final order. If the Secretary of Labor or an employer contests the PMA, a hearing is held to determine whether any abatement requirement, even if part of an uncontested citation, should be modified.[125]

The notice of contest does not have to be in any particular form and is sent to the area director who issued the citation. The area director must forward the notice to the OSHRC and the OSHRC must docket the case for hearing.

After pleading, discovery, and other preliminary matters, a hearing is scheduled before an ALJ. Witnesses testify and are cross-examined under oath, and a verbatim transcript is made. The Federal Rules of Evidence apply.[126]

Following closure of the hearing, parties may submit briefs to the ALJ. The ALJ's decision contains findings of fact and conclusions of law and affirms, vacates, or modifies the citation, proposed penalty, and abatement requirements. The ALJ's decision is filed with the OSHRC and may be directed for review by any OSHRC member *sua sponte* or in response to a party's petition for discretionary review. Failure to file a petition for discretionary review precludes subsequent judicial review.

The Secretary of Labor has the burden of proving the violation. The hearing is presided over by an ALJ and he or she renders a decision either affirming, modifying, or vacating the citation, penalty, or abatement date. The ALJ's decision then automatically goes before the OSHRC. The aggrieved party may file a petition requesting that the ALJ's decision be reviewed, but even without this discretionary review, any OSHRC member may direct a review of any part or all of the ALJ's decision. If, however, no member of the OSHRC directs a review within 30 days, the ALJ's decision is final. Through either review route, the OSHRC may reconsider the evidence and issue a new decision.

OSHRC review is, based on the factual determinations of the ALJ, and the ALJ's opinion is often afforded great weight. Briefs may be submitted to the OSHRC, but oral argument, although extremely rare, is also within the OSHRC's discretion.

In this administrative phase of the Act's citation adjudication process, the employer's good faith, the gravity of the violation, the employer's past history of compliance, and the employer's size are all considered in the penalty assessment. The area director can compromise, reduce, or remove a violation. Many citations can be compromised or reduced at this stage.

Although the OSHRC's rules mandate the filing of a complaint by the Secretary and an answer by the employer, pleadings are liberally construed and easily amended. Approximately 90 percent of the cases filed are resolved without a hearing, either through settlement, withdrawal of the citation by the Secretary, or withdrawal of the notice of contest by the employer.[127]

As permitted under Section 11(a) of the Act, any person adversely affected by the OSHRC's final order may file, within 60 days from the decision, a petition for review in the U.S. Court of Appeals for the circuit in which the alleged violation had occurred or in the U.S. Court of Appeals for the District of Columbia Circuit.[128] Under Section 11(b), the Secretary may seek review only in the circuit in which the alleged violation occurred or where the employer has its principal office.[129]

The courts apply the substantial evidence rule to factual determinations made by the OSHRC and its ALJs, but courts vary on the degree of deference afforded the OSHRC's interpretations of the statutes and standards. The burden of proof is on the Secretary of Labor at this hearing.[130] The rules of civil procedure, rules of evidence, and all other legal requirements apply, as with any trial before the federal court.

EMS professionals should be aware of their rights and responsibilities under the law. Although they should not fear inspections by OSHA, they should prepare for them to ensure that the legal rights of the employer are protected. In most circumstances, simple communication with the OSHA inspector or area director can correct most difficulties during an inspection. Once a citation is issued, the EMS professional should at least consider contesting the citation at the area director level in order to discuss reduction of monetary penalties. If an amicable solution cannot be reached at the regional level, personnel managers should be certain that the time limitations are met in order to preserve the right to appeal the decision. Meeting the specific time limitations set forth in the Act is of utmost importance. If the time limitation is permitted to lapse, the opportunity for appeal is lost.

SEARCH WARRANTS IN OSHA INSPECTIONS

OSHA's authority to conduct inspections and investigations is derived from Section 8(a) the OSH Act, which states:

> In order to carry out the purpose of this Act, the Secretary, upon presenting appropriate credentials to the owner, operator, or agent in charge is authorized to:
>
> (1) enter without delay and at reasonable times any factory, plant, establishment, construction site, or other area, workplace, or environment, where work is performed by an employee of an employer; and
>
> (2) to inspect and investigate during regular working hours and at other reasonable times, and within reasonable limits and in a reasonable manner, any such place of employment and all pertinent conditions, structures, machines, apparatus, devices, equipment, and materials therein, and to question privately any such employer, owner, operator, agent, or employee.[131]

In the vast majority of OSHA inspections no advance notice to the employer is provided. The decision in *Marshall v. Barlow's, Inc.* settled the issue regarding OSHA's ability to conduct warrantless inspections but opened the door to many related issues. *Barlow's* was not, however, the first case to address the requirement of administrative search warrants. In *Camara v. Municipal Court*[132] and *See v. City of Seattle*[133] (companion cases), the Supreme Court first required a search warrant for nonconsensual administrative inspections. These cases laid the foundation for the *Barlow's* decision and also specified and defined four exceptions to the warrant requirement in administrative inspections. The first three exceptions, namely the consent, plain view, and emergency inspection exceptions, were drawn directly from the law of search and seizure. The fourth, known as the *Colannade-Biswell* or licensing exception,[134] is the most controversial.

The Consent Exception

The usual exception to the search warrant requirement for OSHA used by the vast majority of employers is consent to the safety and health inspection. Valid consent by the employer waives the employer's Fourth Amendment rights and protection. In the administrative setting of an OSHA inspection, consent can be provided by the employer simply if it fails to object to the inspection.[135] This form of consent differs greatly from the criminal investigation requirement that the consent be knowing and voluntarily.[136] Additionally, OSHA compliance officers are not required to inform employers of their right to demand a warrant or even to ask for the employer's consent.[137]

Currently, employers must affirmatively exercise their right to require a search warrant before an inspection. OSHA has instructed compliance officers to answer employers' questions regarding search warrants in a straightforward manner, but they are not required to volunteer information or allowed to mislead, coerce, or threaten an employer.[138]

A major issue regarding the consent exception is whether the individual providing the consent has the authority to do so on behalf of the employer. Courts and the OSHRC have provided a broad interpretation to this question, permitting plant managers,[139] foremen,[140] and even senior employees to provide consent.[141] OSHA has also found that general contractors may provide consent to inspect a common worksite where other subcontractors are working.[142]

The Plain View Exception

A search warrant is not required for equipment, apparatus, and worksites that are in the plain view of the compliance officer or open to public view. For a compliance officer to issue a citation for a workplace hazard that is within the plain view exception, he or she must (1) be in a place or location where he or she possesses a right to be, and (2) observe (or smell, hear, or acquire through other senses) what is visible or held out to public view.[143]

The U.S. Supreme Court has set up a significant hurdle for challenging the plain view exception by limiting the right to challenge search and seizure claims to those individuals, companies, or other entities who have an actual and legitimate expectation of intrusion by a governmental action.[144] In the past, simply being the target of the OSHA inspection was usually sufficient for being able to complain of a search or seizure violation by OSHA. This interpretation, as applied to the plain view exception, would permit a compliance officer to observe and issue a citation for workplace violations from some distance off company property (such as from a adjacent hill or another building), and if the employer challenged the citation on grounds of search or seizure, the court would not permit the claim due to lack of standing. The plain view exception is often used when a compliance officer observes a violation in a public area, such as a trenching site located on a public street. Safety and health professionals should be aware of the areas surrounding the facility and operation that are open to public view and should keep the plain view exception in mind.

The Emergency Exception

The third exception to the search warrant requirement is an emergency situation. When there exists an urgent threat to human life and a delay in acquiring a search warrant may increase the hazard, or consent cannot be readily obtained from the employer because of the emergency situation, and the emergency need outweighs the individual's right to privacy, the compliance officer may enter the facility without acquiring a search warrant.

In these rare circumstances the compliance officer's duty to safeguard employees who are in imminent danger far outweighs the employer's right to privacy. There are no specific OSHA regulations defining what would constitute an emergency situation, but it is highly likely that a court would find that the emergency situation would require an extreme life-threatening situation likely to cause death or severe injury if the compliance officer did not intervene immediately.

The Colannade-Biswell Exception

The fourth and most controversial exception to the search warrant requirement is the *Colannade-Biswell* or licensure exception. Before the *Barlow's* decision in 1978, the Supreme Court held in *Colonnade Catering Corp. v. United States*[145] that warrantless nonconsensual searches of licensed liquor stores were permitted. Additionally, in *United States v. Biswell*,[146] the Court permitted nonconsensual warrantless searches of pawn shops under the Gun Control Act of 1968. The Court found that a business in a regulated industry, such as a liquor store or pawn shop, provided an implied waiver of its Fourth Amendment rights by engaging in these industries.[147]

From 1970 through 1978, several courts determined that the *Colannade-Biswell* exception applied to the OSH Act and OSHA compliance inspections,[148] whereas others found that the *Camara* and *See* decisions required OSHA to acquire a warrant.[149] The *Barlow's* decision settled the issue regarding OSHA's requirement to obtain a search warrant for routine compliance inspections, but it also opened the door to peripheral issues involving search warrant requirements.

MARSHALL V. BARLOW'S, INC. AND PROBABLE CAUSE

In basic terms, the *Barlow's*[150] decision reinstated the *Camara* and *See*[151] standards requiring that the probable cause standard be applied to OSHA and other administrative searches. Issues involving whether the *Barlow's* decision applies to nonroutine inspections and whether OSHA may acquire an ex parte warrant are still unresolved.[152] The Court in *Barlow's* did conclude, however, that the OSH Act authorized or intended to authorize issuance of search warrants and suggested that OSHA could amend its regulations to authorize issuance of ex parte search warrants.[153]

EMS professionals should be aware that the probable cause requirement for a search warrant is significantly different from the criminal probable cause standard. In *Barlow's*, the Court defined the administrative probable cause standard:

> A warrant showing that a specific business has been chosen for an OSHA search on the basis of a general administrative plan for the enforcement of the OSH Act derived from neutral sources such as, for example, dispersion of employees in various types of industries across a given area, and the desired frequency of searches in any of the lesser divisions of an area, would protect an employer's Fourth Amendment rights.[154]

Probable cause for an OSHA or other administrative search can be developed from any of three basic categories: (1) general information about the employer's industry, (2) general information about the individual employer, and (3) specific information about the employer's workplace. The general information regarding the employer's industry can be acquired by OSHA from many sources, including industry-by-industry data regarding workplace injuries and illnesses, days lost from work, and other data. General and specific information regarding the employer and workplace is usually acquired through employee complaints. Other sources of information include that acquired during past fatality or accident investigations, plain view observations by the compliance officer, and past history of citations.

When probable cause is shown and an administrative search warrant is issued, the permitted scope of the inspection is usually broad enough to encompass the entire operation. This is known as a wall-to-wall inspection.[155] Courts have generally permitted wall-to-wall inspections so that compliance officers, who normally are unfamiliar with the operation or facility under inspection, are given great latitude in meeting the intent and purposes of the OSH Act in locating and identifying workplace hazards.

Although employers now have a constitutional right to require a search warrant before an OSHA inspection, few have exercised this right.[156] OSHA inspections conducted under administrative search warrants continue to be rare; "approximately 97 to 99 percent of all employers voluntarily consent to inspection when the compliance officer knocks at the door." Most employers have found that it is fairly easy for OSHA to acquire an administrative search warrant, and creating an adversarial relationship with the compliance officer might do greater harm than good. Although most employers prefer to maintain good working relationships with compliance officers, some employers, due to individual circumstances, such as a belief that OSHA is harassing them, or because "impostors" have posed as OSHA inspectors soliciting bribes,[157] have exercised their constitutional right to require a search warrant before entry.[158]

CHALLENGING SEARCH WARRANT

In most circumstances, EMS professionals should carefully consider their option to require an OSHA compliance officer to obtain a search warrant. Many courts have sanctioned employers seeking a search warrant for contempt of court and other Rule 11 sanctions for frivolous actions, and the likelihood of successfully challenging an OSHA inspection warrant is minimal at best. The decision to require an administrative search warrant of OSHA should be extensively evaluated. Given the potential risks involved in requiring a search warrant, this decision should involve the board of directors, officers, and legal counsel of the organization.

If your employer chooses to require a search warrant, careful planning and preparation should take place before the actual inspection.

1. A policy statement or other directive should be distributed to other management team members informing them of the decision.

2. On-site personnel, who will be in charge when the compliance officer arrives at the scene, should be trained in all aspects of the preinspection and inspection processes and the potential risks involved.

3. All appropriate statements, forms, and other documents to be (a) provided to the compliance officer, (b) used for training the team members responsible for documenting the inspection and (c) used during the actual inspection by team members should be prepared in advance.

4. On-site team members should be provided with necessary equipment to document all aspects of the inspection (e.g., cameras, noise dosimeters) and must be properly trained to use, maintain, and calibrate the equipment and document test results.

In short, the management team responsible for performance of the company directive should be well prepared to address any and all issues or circumstances that may arise while the compliance officer is on-site.[159]

Four routes for challenging an administrative search warrant are normally available, depending on the court and the circumstances. An employer can (1) seek to enjoin issuance of the administrative warrant in federal district court, (2) refuse to permit the inspection after a warrant is issued and then move to quash the warrant or civil contempt proceedings brought by OSHA, (3) seek to enjoin enforcement of citations in federal district court after the inspection has taken place under protest, and (4) contest the validity of the warrant after the inspection has taken place before the OSHRC.[160]

Attempting to have the court enjoin OSHA from acquiring an ex parte warrant is normally difficult, given the fact that the employer seldom knows that the compliance officer is attempting to acquire such a warrant.[161] In 1980, OSHA reintroduced its regulation authorizing ex parte warrant applications.[162] Under this regulation, an employer's demand for a search warrant for a previous inspection is one of the factors that OSHA will consider in finding that an ex parte warrant is "desirable and necessary" for subsequent inspections even before seeking the employer's consent.[163] Refusal to admit a compliance inspector without a search warrant is only one of the situations where an ex parte warrant can be sought, and, conversely, OSHA has not always elected to pursue ex parte warrants in circumstances, such as the denial of entry, where grounds existed for pursuing such a warrant.

Defying the search warrant after the compliance officer has obtained it from the magistrate or court is potentially the most dangerous route for challenging a search warrant. As in *Barlow's*,[164] the employer may move the court to quash the search warrant or wait and defend a refusal to comply with the search warrant in civil contempt proceedings initiated by OSHA.[165] Although the Third Circuit in *Babcock & Wilcox Co. v. Marshall*[166] found that the federal court had authority to test the validity of a search warrant before an OSHA inspection, other courts have found that a motion to quash is not the proper method to challenge a warrant.[167] Selection of this route carries many other potential dangers. In addition to assessing other penalties, courts have found that some employers lacked good faith in defying the OSHA warrant and have placed those employers in civil contempt of court.[168]

The route for judicially challenging OSHA's enforcement authority is usually taken after the compliance officer completes the inspection under a search warrant. This option has not been successful as most courts have found that even if the inspection is completed under a search warrant and under protest, jurisdiction lies with the OSHRC and not the courts.[169] The leading case in this area is *In re Quality Products, Inc.*[170] Where the court found that the magistrate who issued the warrant had no authority to "stay and recall" the administrative search warrant and the court had no jurisdiction to consider the warrant's validity in a separate action while OSHA enforcement proceedings were pending (i.e., the employer would have to exhaust all administrative remedies with the OSHRC first).[171] In the few decisions that have permitted a motion to quash after an inspection, the motion to quash was treated as a motion to suppress the evidence obtained during the warrant required and under protest inspection.[172]

The most frequently used route for challenging a search warrant is challenging the validity of the warrant with the OSHRC after an inspection. The OSHRC does not have authority to question the validity of an administrative search warrant before an inspection,[173] but after the inspection takes place, it does have authority to rule on the constitutionality of an administrative search warrant obtained for the purpose of conducting an OSHA inspection. The employer must present any challenges to the administrative search warrant for review by the OSHRC.[174] The OSHRC's authority is consistent with the holding of several courts that the employer must exhaust all administrative remedies before seeking judicial relief.

EMS professionals may want to consider alternatives to requiring an administrative search warrant of OSHA. In many circumstances, understanding the scope of the inspection to be performed[175] or a simple telephone call to the regional director can solve most inspection concerns or conflicts.[176] Another alternative is the use of protective orders, which can modify the terms of the inspection, the time of the inspection, and other conditions to make the inspection more reasonable to the employer.

In short, requiring an administrative search warrant should be the last alternative considered when addressing an OSHA inspection situation. In most circumstances, the chances of prevailing or preventing the compliance officer from conducting an inspection of the worksite is minimal. In addition, the cost in management time, effort, legal fees, potential loss of goodwill in the community, or the creation of ill will with the local OSHA office generally outweighs the potential benefits of preventing an inevitable OSHA inspection.

EMPLOYEE RIGHTS—DISCRIMINATION PROTECTION UNDER THE OSH ACT

The OSH Act provides employees working for covered employers basic rights to file complaints with OSHA, to be protected against discrimination for reporting violations of the OSH Act, and even to refuse unsafe work without retaliation. In addition to the OSH Act, employees have additional protection under other federal laws, such as the National Labor Relations Act and state and local laws.

First, who is an employee afforded protection under the OSH Act? By regulation,[177] the Secretary of Labor has interpreted the term "person" as defined by Section 3(4) of the OSH Act, and the Section 11(c), "no person shall discharge or in any manner discriminate against any employee...," so that the discrimination prohibitions "are not limited to actions taken by employers against their employees."[178] Thus, the term "employee" must be literally construed and extended to applicants for employment as well as to traditional employees. Additionally, the extent of the business relationship "is to be based upon economic realities rather than upon common law doctrines and concepts" due to the "broad remedial nature" of the Act.[179] However, given the statutory definition and interpretations of "employer" and "employee" under the Act, public sector employees of states or other political subdivisions are excluded from the discriminatory protection provided under the Act.[180]

Protection under the OSH Act has been extended to labor organization representatives working within the confines of the employer's premises. In *Marshall v. Kennedy Tubular Products*,[181] the court extended protection against discrimination to a union business agent who was banned from the employer's facility after reporting safety violations to OSHA. The court ordered the employer to allow the business agent to return to the facility and participate in safety meetings. The court determined that the employer's discrimination against the employee's union representative was in effect discrimination against the represented employees.[182]

WHAT ACTIVITIES ARE PROTECTED?

The OSH Act prohibits discharging or otherwise discriminating against an employee who has filed a complaint, instituted or testified in any proceeding, or otherwise exercises any right afforded by the Act.[183] The Act also specifically gives employees the right to contact OSHA and request an inspection without retaliation from the employer if the employee believes a violation of a health or safety standard threatens physical harm or creates an imminent danger.[184] Employees exercising the right to contact OSHA with a complaint can also remain anonymous to the employer and public under the Act.[185]

Employees are also protected against discrimination under the Act when testifying in proceedings under or related to the Act, including inspections,[186] employee-contested abatement dates,[187] employee-initiated proceedings for promulgating new standards,[188] employee applications for modifying or revoking variances,[189] employee-based judicial challenges to OSHA standards,[190] or employee appeals from decisions by the OSHRC.[191] An employee "need not himself directly institute the proceedings" but may merely set "into motion activities of others which result in proceedings under or related to the Act."[192]

When testifying in any proceeding related to the Act, employees are protected against discrimination by employers. The protection is extended to proceedings instituted or caused to be instituted by the employee, as well as "any statement given in the course of judicial, quasi-judicial, and administrative proceedings, including inspections, investigations, and administrative rule making or adjudicative functions."[193]

The Act also provides protection against discrimination for employees who petition for hearings on variance requests,[194] request inspections,[195] challenge abatement dates,[196] accompany the OSHA inspector during the inspection,[197] participate in and challenge OSHRC decisions[198] and citation contests,[199] and bring actions for injunctive relief against the Secretary of Labor for imminent danger situations.[200]

There are few reported cases of discrimination and, although employee rights appear to be straightforward under the Act, determining when the protection attaches to the employee and the situation remains an unresolved area.

WAIVER OF RIGHTS

In *Marshall v. N.L. Industries*,[201] the court addressed the issue of when an employee waives discriminatory rights provided under the OSH Act. In this case, the Seventh Circuit Court of Appeals held that an employee's acceptance of an arbitration award did not preclude the Secretary of Labor from bringing an action against the employer based upon the same facts.[202] Specifically, the employee refused to load metal scraps into a melting kettle because the payloader did not have a windshield or enclosed cab to protect him from the molten metal. The employer discharged the employee, and the employee filed a complaint with OSHA and a grievance with his union. An arbitrator awarded the employee reinstatement without back pay, and the employee accepted the award. The lower court found that acceptance of the award constituted a voluntary waiver of the right to statutory relief under the Act.[203] The Seventh Circuit reversed, finding that "the OSHA legislation was intended to create a separate and general right of broad social importance existing beyond the parameters of an individual labor agreement and susceptible of full vindication only in a judicial forum."[204]

FILING A COMPLAINT AGAINST AN EMPLOYER

Specific administrative rules govern the nondiscrimination provisions of the OSH Act. An employee who believes he or she has been discriminated against may file a complaint with the Secretary within 30 days of the alleged violation which the Secretary will then will investigate.[205] The purpose of the 30 day limitation is "to allow the Secretary to decline to entertain complaints that have become stale."[206] This relatively short period can be tolled under special circumstances[207] and has no effect on other causes of action. When an employee has filed a complaint, the Secretary must notify him or her as to whether an action will be filed on his or her behalf in federal court. At least one court has ruled that OSHA may bring discrimination action against corporate officers as individuals[208] and against the corporation itself and the officers engaged in its official capacities.[209]

Regarding an employee's right to refuse unsafe or unhealthy work, the Supreme Court, in *Whirlpool Corp. v. Marshall*,[210] stated: "circumstances may exist in which the employee justifiably believes that the express statutory arrangement does not sufficiently protect him from death or serious injury. Such circumstances will probably not often occur, but such a circumstance may arise when (1) the employee is ordered by the employer to work under conditions that the employee reasonably believes pose an imminent risk of death or serious bodily injury, and (2) the employee has reason to believe that there is not sufficient time or opportunity either to seek effective redress from the employer or to apprise OSHA of the danger."[211]

In this case, two employees refused to perform routine maintenance tasks that required them to stand on a wire mesh guard approximately twenty feet above the work surface. The mesh screen was designed to catch appliance components that might fall from an overhead conveyor. While performing this activity in the past, several employees had punctured the screen, and one employee died after falling through the mesh guard. The employees refused to perform the task, and the employer reprimanded them. The district court denied relief but the Sixth Circuit reversed the decision.[212] The Supreme Court, in affirming the Sixth Circuit, found the Act's provisions were "designed to give employees full protection in most situations from the risk of injury or death resulting from an imminently dangerous condition at the worksite."[213]

PRIVATE LITIGATION UNDER THE OSH ACT

Although there is no common law basis for actions under the OSH Act, OSHA regulations are used in many tort actions, such as negligence and product liability suits, as evidence of the standard of care and conduct to which the party must comply. Additionally, documents generated in the course of business that are required under the OSH Act are usually discoverable under the Freedom of Information Act (FOIA) and can be used as evidence of a deviation from the required standard of care.

According to Section 653(b)(4) of the OSH Act:

> Nothing in this Act shall be construed to supersede or in any manner affect any workmen's compensation law or to enlarge or diminish or affect in any other manner the common law or statutory rights, duties, or liabilities of employers and employees under any law with respect to injuries, diseases, or death of employees arising out of, or in the course of, employment.[239]

This language prevents injured employees or families of employees killed in work-related accidents from directly using the OSH Act or OSHA standards as an independent basis for a cause of action (i.e., wrongful death actions).[240] However, many federal and state courts have found that Section 653(b)(4) does not bar application of the OSH Act or OSHA standards in workers' compensation litigation nor application of the doctrine of negligence or negligence per se to an OSHA violation.[241] These decisions do distinguish between use of an OSHA standard as the basis for a standard of care in a state or federal common law action and the OSH Act or OSHA standards creating a separate and independent cause of action.

NEGLIGENCE ACTIONS

OSHA standards are most widely used in negligence actions. The plaintiff in a negligence action must prove the four elements: duty, breach of duty, causation, and damages. *Black's Law Dictionary* defines negligence "per se" as:

> conduct, whether of action or omission, that may without any argument or proof as to the particular surrounding circumstances, either because it is in violation of a statute or valid municipal ordinance,

> or because it is so palpably opposed to the dictates of common pru-
> dence that it can be said without hesitation or doubt that no careful
> person would have been guilty of it.[242]

In simpler terms, if a plaintiff can show that an OSHA standard applied to the circumstances and the employer violated the OSHA standard, the court can eliminate the plaintiff's burden of proving the negligence elements of duty and breach through a finding of negligence per se.

The majority of courts have found that relevant OSHA standards and regulations are admissible as evidence of the standard of care,[243] and thus violation of OSHA standards can be used as evidence of an employer's negligence or negligence per se. It should be noted, however, that courts have prohibited use of OSHA standards and regulations, and evidence of their violation, if the proposed purpose of the OSHA standards use conflicts with the purposes of the OSH Act,[244] unfairly prejudices a party,[245] or is meant to enlarge a civil cause of action.[246] The Fifth Circuit, reflecting the general application, approves the admissibility of OSHA standards as evidence of negligence but permits the court to accept or reject the evidence as it sees fit.[247]

In using OSHA standards to prove negligence per se, HR professionals should be aware that numerous courts have recognized the OSHA standards as the reasonable standard of conduct in the workplace. With this recognition, a violation by the employer would constitute negligence per se to the employee.[248] A few other courts have held, however, that violations of OSHA standards can never constitute negligence per se because of Section 653(b)(4) of the Act.[249]

In *Walton v. Potlatch Corp.*,[250] the court set forth four criteria to determine whether OSHA standards and regulations could be used to establish negligence per se:

1. The statute or regulation must clearly define the required standard of conduct,

2. the standard or regulation must have been intended to prevent the type of harm the defendant's act or omission caused,

3. the plaintiff must be a member of the class of persons the statute or regulation was designed to protect, and

4. the violation must have been the proximate cause of the injury.[251]

If the court provides an instruction on negligence per se rather than an instruction on simple negligence, the effect is that the jury cannot consider the reasonableness of the employer's conduct. In essence the court has already established a violation that constituted unreasonable conduct on the part of the employer and that the conduct was prohibited or required under a specific OSHA standard. Thus, as a matter of law, the jury will not be permitted to address the reasonableness of the employer's actions.

OSHA STANDARDS AS DEFENSE

Under appropriate circumstances, EMS professionals may be able to use OSHA standards and regulations as a defense. Simple compliance with required OSHA standards is not in itself a defense, and the use of OSHA standards as a defense has received mixed treatment by the courts. However, at least one court has held that violation of a state OSHA plan by an employee could be considered in determining the employee's comparative negligence in a liability case.[252] Use of OSHA standards and regulations to demonstrate an appropriate standard of care in third-party product liability actions, workers' compensation litigation, and other actions may be permitted and should be explored by personnel managers in appropriate circumstances.

The use of OSHA citations and penalties in tort actions has also received mixed treatment by the courts. In *Industrial Tile v. Stewart*,[253] the Alabama Supreme Court stated:

> We hold that it was not error to admit the regulation if the regulations are admissible as going to show a standard of care, then it seems only reasonable that the evidence of violation of the standards would also be admissible as evidence that the defendant failed to meet the standards that it should have followed. Clearly, the fact that Industrial Tile had been cited by OSHA for violating the standards, and the fact that Industrial Tile paid the fine, are relevant to the conduct of whether it violated the standards of care applicable to its conduct. It was evidenced from a number of witnesses that the crane violated the 10-foot standards. It seems to us that evidence that Industrial Tile paid the fine without objection was properly admitted into evidence as a declaration against interest.[254]

Other courts have found that OSHA citations and fines are inadmissible under the hearsay rule of the Federal Rules of Evidence.[255] However, this can normally be easily overcome by offering a certified copy of the citations and penalties to the court, under the investigatory report exception to the Federal Rules of Evidence.[256]

Investigation records and other documents gathered in the course of an OSHA inspection are normally available under the FOIA. As noted previously, if particular citations are deemed inadmissible, a certified copy of the citations and penalties is normally considered admissible under Section 803(8)(c) of the Federal Rules of Evidence and 28 U.S.C. Section 1733 governing admissibility of certified copies of government records. Although the issue of whether OSHA citations and penalties are admissible is determined by the court under the Rules of Evidence, personnel managers should be prepared for all documents collected or produced during an OSHA inspection or investigation to be presented to the court. Given the nature of these government documents and the methods of presenting OSHA documents under the Federal Rules of Evidence, it is highly likely in any type of related litigation that the other party will obtain the documents from OSHA and that they will be submitted for use at trial. Other information and documents, such as photographs, recordings, and samples, may also be admissible under the same theory. EMS professionals should maintain as much control as possible over information gathered during an investigation or inspection (e.g., trade secrets and speculation by management team members, etc.) and be prepared for the information to become public through the FOIA and used by opponents in litigation or elsewhere.

Besides direct litigation with OSHA and negligence actions, OSHA standards used as evidence of the standard of care and citations used to show a breach of the duty of care have also been used in product liability cases,[257] construction site injury actions against general contractors,[258] and toxic tort actions.[259] Other actions where OSHA standards and citations have been found admissible include Federal Tort Claim Act actions,[260] against OSHA in the area of inspections, and actions under the Federal Employers' Liability Act.[261]

MEDIA RELATIONS

Often simultaneously with a governmental agency inspection (especially in circumstances involving a work-related fatality, multiple injury situation, environmental release, or other catastrophic event) will be the arrival of the media. In this age of instant news via such services as CNN, it can be expected that a media-worthy "story" will attract the roving media to the location of the incident. As an EMS professionals you must be aware of this situation and prepare beforehand to properly address the media in order to protect your company from potential efficacy losses.

When developing your plan to address the media, prepare for the worst and hope for the best. With the onset of "gorrilla journalism," EMS professionals must be prepared for the media to place your company in the worst possible light and prepare your plan to counteract, where possible, and minimize the possible damage to your company's image, good name, and so on. Remember, in most situations, your EMS organization has just incurred some traumatic situation whereby the stress level is extremely high and numerous abnormal activities, including governmental inspections, are taking place. Preparation beforehand minimizes the chances of a major blunder!

In many organizations, a written media plan addressing the various possible scenarios is prepared. These plans can list the following.

- Individual responsible for the information flow to the media and overall management of the media

- Centralized location for the media offering appropriate backround

- Identified spokesperson for the company with appropriate dress, and the like

- Approval procedure from management and legal department for all news releases

- Security and control of the media on site (i.e., keep them in one location)
- Availability of positive file footage

Management of the media during these extremely stressful situation is vital. For example, your company has incurred an accident in which there is a fatality. Do you want the fatally injured employee's family finding out that mom or dad is dead on the evening news? And additionally, the image sent via a thirty-second soundbite can have a direct impact on your company's image, the sales of your products, your ability to attract employees, and a number of other factors. The person who is acting as your spokesperson "is" your company to the viewing public. *It is vital that you properly manage the image of your EMS organization during these intense time periods!*

ALTERNATIVE STRATEGIES

With most governmental agencies, there are alternatives or nonroutine methods through which you can address specific needs or unique situations. However, these unique alternatives are seldom advertised and usually must be requested by your company. Several alternatives to consider in the area of safety and health include:

- **State Education and Training Programs.** In many states, specific education and training programs are provided, usually free of charge to employers, to assist the company in achieving and maintaining compliance with the requirements. These programs can include seminars, on-site consultation, on-site training, and on-site testing.
- **Variances.** A variance is a request to be exempt from the particular standard or regulation. Under the OSH Act, there are four basic types of variances, namely permanent variances, temporary variances, experimental variances, and National Defense variances. The most often utilized are the permanent or temporary variances, which apply to specific equipment, worksites, or situations, and are not blanket exemptions from the regulations. Experimental variances are available when participating in an OSHA or NIOSH approved project. National Defense variances are seldom utilized today.
- **Interim Orders.** OSHA regulations provide for interim orders that grant temporary relief from inspections or citations pending the outcome of a formal hearing regarding a variance application. Interim orders are normally included with variance petitions.

SUMMARY

Compliance with the numerous laws, standards, and requirements mandated by various governmental agencies has become an important part of some EMS professionals' job functions. Although we utilized the OSHA regulatory scheme as the template for this chapter, EMS professionals should be aware of the numerous regulatory requirements from other federal agencies including, but not limited to, the Environmental Protection Agency (EPA), Food and Drug Administration (FDA), U.S. Department of Agriculture (USDA), Equal Employment Opportunity Commission (EEOC), and various state and local agencies. Each of these agencies usually possesses written rules and administrative procedures that are required to be followed. Given the potential detrimental effects to your company or organization, as an EMS professional you must become proficient in the regulations applicable to your organization and/or acquire appropriate assistance. EMS professionals usually possess direct or indirect responsibility for this important area where achieving and maintaining compliance can be an enormous task. Proper management of this important function by the EMS professional will provide a multitude of benefits for the employees, the management team, and the organization. Failure to appropriately manage this important function is a recipe for disaster.

CHAPTER 11

Workplace Safety and Health

The market and this country were built on risk.
—Donald T. Regan

Behold the turtle. He makes progress only when he sticks his neck out.
—James Bryant Conant

In many operations, EMS professionals possess either direct or indirect responsibility for safety, health, and loss prevention. This very important function serves to create a safe and healthful work environment for all employees so that costly accidents involving monetary and human loss can be avoided. Safety, health, and loss prevention also possesses a legal component that requires that the employer achieve and maintain compliance with the myriad of safety and health-related regulations and standards promulgated by the Occupational Safety and Health Administration and by state programs.

EMS professionals will learn a proactive method through which to create, maintain, and efficiently manage a safety and loss prevention program encompassing the components essential to safeguarding their most precious asset, namely their employees, as well as complying with all governmental regulations. *The basic elements necessary to achieve and manage a successful safety, health, and loss prevention program include the following:*

- *Management commitment*

- *Accountability*

- *Proper planning and organization*

- *Proper direction and control*

- *Effective communications*

It is vitally important that EMS professionals identify their specific responsibilities within the organization in the areas of safety, health, and loss prevention. Although responsibilities vary depending on the size,

structure, hierarchy, and other factors in different organizations, personnel and human resource managers usually possess either direct day-to-
day responsibility or indirect oversight or supervisory responsibility for
the safety, health, and loss prevention function. For assistance in identifying your responsibilities in safety, health, and loss prevention, please
review the following queries and discuss them in detail with your
superiors:

- Who is responsible for writing safety policies and compliance programs?

- Who is responsible for inspecting the facility for hazards?

- Who is responsible for training employees in safety, health, and loss prevention?

- Who is responsible for dealing with OSHA or other governmental agencies?

- Who is responsible for coaching, counseling, or disciplining employees for
safety?

- Who possesses direct responsibility for safety in your management structure?

- Who is responsible for purchasing safety equipment? From your budget?

In most operations, the direct line of responsibility for safety, health,
and loss prevention is clear. However, in some organizations, safety, health,
and loss prevention has taken a "backseat" to other responsibilities. In either
situation, taking a planned proactive approach to effectively manage safety,
health, and loss prevention can pay substantial dividends to your organization in reduction of monetary costs and human losses, and in improved
morale and employee relations.

PLAN OF ACTION

In developing the appropriate mechanisms to manage OSHA compliance
in the workplace, a written plan of action is an initial step. A written plan
of action, not unlike a battle plan in military terms, sets forth the objective
of each activity, delineates the activity into smaller manageable elements,
names the responsible parties for each element of the activity, and provides
target dates at which time the responsible party will be held accountable for
the achievement of the particular element or activity. In order to manage
this planning phase, EMS professionals can use a planning document that
permits the safety and health professional to evaluate progress toward the
objective on a daily basis and to also hold the appropriate responsible party
accountable for the achievement of the particular element or activity. This
type of planning document can be computerized or simply completed in
written form.

MANAGEMENT TEAM MEMBERS

In developing a plan of action, all levels of the EMS organization team need to be involved in developing priorities and scheduling. This team involvement assists the management team members in "buying in" to the overall safety and health efforts of the organization. Additionally, it also permits input regarding potential obstacles and the development of a realistic targeted time schedule given the OSHA time requirements and workaday pressures. Ranking of the various mandated safety and health programs and other safety and loss prevention programs that are not required by OSHA should be given careful attention in order to give first preference to programs affording employees the maximum protection and meeting the OSHA target dates.

EMS team members should be advised that team members will be held accountable for the successful and timely completion of their assigned tasks and duties as set forth under the plan of action. With the required management commitment to the safety and health goals and objectives by top management and management team members' "buy in" during the development of the plan of action, management team members should be well aware of their specific duties and responsibilities within the framework of the overall safety and loss prevention effort of the organization. If necessary appropriate positive or negative reinforcement can be utilized to achieve this purpose in addition to appropriate disciplinary action.

COMPLIANCE PROGRAMS

EMS personnel should be cautious when developing written safety and health programs to meet compliance requirements. The methods used in the development and documentation of OSHA compliance programs are a direct reflection of the safety and health efforts of the organization. EMS personnel should always develop written safety and health compliance programs in a professional manner. Managers should be aware that the compliance officers' initial review when evaluating the written compliance programs may set the tone for the entire inspection or investigation.

Additionally, compliance programs should also be developed in a *defensive* manner. Every element of the OSHA standard should be addressed in written form and all training and education requirements should be documented. In the event of a work-related accident or incident that places the written safety and loss prevention programs "on trial," that program will be placed under a microscope and every detail scrutinized from every angle. Proper preparation, evaluation, and scrutiny when developing a written compliance program can avoid substantial embarrassment, cost, and other liabilities in the future.

TRAINING AND EDUCATION

In the area of required education and training elements mandated under a particular OSHA standard, documentation is vital. EMS professionals should closely evaluate the compliance program to ensure that all required training and education mandated under the standard are being completed in a timely manner. In addition, the training documentation should be clear so as to confirm, beyond a shadow of a doubt, that a particular employee attended the required training. This documentation should show that an individual employee not only attended but understood the information provided during the training and education session. To show employees' understanding and an adequate level of competency, a written examination may be helpful. If a required training and education element is not documented, then there is no proof to substantiate that employees underwent a certain type of training.

In the area of training and education elements with a compliance program, EMS managers are reminded of the educational maxim of "tell them, show them, and tell them again." Safety, health, and loss prevention training should be conducted, where feasible, in an atmosphere conducive to learning and at a time when employees are mentally alert. The individuals performing the training should be competent and enthusiastic. Hands-on training has been found to be the most effective method in providing the greatest understanding and the retention of information by employees. Audiovisual aids are an exceptional method of increasing the retention level but personnel and human resource managers should not rely solely on the audiovisual aid (i.e., especially videotape) for the total training experience.

Additionally, although safety, health, and loss prevention is a serious matter, training does not have to be a sober and boring endeavor that employees are required to endure on a periodic basis. Personnel managers should strive to make training an experience that attendees will remember. There is no reason why safety, health, and loss prevention training cannot be mentally stimulating or even fun. Remember, the information that is provided in a safety, health, and loss prevention training session may be the difference between an employee going home or not going home at the end of the day. Do everything possible to ensure that the employee is provided with, understands, and retains the information from the training session.

PERSONAL PROTECTIVE EQUIPMENT

Purchasing the appropriate personal protective equipment for the particular circumstance in order to achieve the objectives of the OSHA standard is vitally important. EMS managers should be actively involved in the selection, purchase, monitoring, inspection, and replacement of personal protective equipment. Although cost is always a factor, the safety parameters, comfort levels, approval or certifications, and other factors, need to be scrutinized in order to ensure that the personal protective equipment meets or exceeds the requirements mandated under the OSHA standard. The personal protective equipment must be of a type and quality that will not be difficult to use. Many EMS professionals initially evaluate and select broad types of personal protective equipment and permit the individuals who will be required to wear the personal protective equipment to make the final selection. This type of employee and management team-member involvement in the selection process often enhances employee participation in the program.

RECEIVING ASSISTANCE

If an EMS manager is unsure of the requirements of a particular standard, it is imperative that he or she acquire a definite answer or clarification. OSHA often provides clarification of a particular issue or problem without caller identification or OSHA may transfer the call to the state education and training division. In many state plan states and in federal states (usually through a state agency), a separate section of OSHA has been established to assist employers in achieving compliance. Upon request, the education and training section can assist employers with a wide variety of compliance issues ranging from program development to the acquisition of pertinent information at no cost. EMS managers should be aware that this section of OSHA is authorized to issue citations, but normally does not issue citations except in situations involving imminent harm or if the employers failure to follow prescribed advice.

AUDIT INSTRUMENT

Lastly, EMS managers should acquire a strategy to effectively manage a number of compliance programs simultaneously. The use of a safety, health, and loss prevention audit can be an effective tool in identifying deficiencies within a compliance program and permit immediate correction of the deficiencies. Although there are various types of safety, health, and loss prevention audit instruments, all audits possess the basic elements for identification of the required elements of a compliance program, that is to track the current level of performance, to identify deficiencies, and to identify potential corrective actions. A safety, health, and loss prevention audit mechanism can provide numerical scoring, letter or grade scoring, or another scoring method, so that the management team can ascertain their current level of performance and identify areas in need of improvement.

In achieving compliance with an OSHA standard, it is imperative to check and ensure that every area and requirement has been looked into and is in compliance. Each and every element of the specific OSHA standard must be in compliance and functioning effectively.

Example
Safety Audit Assessment

Quarterly Report for _____ Quarter of _____ Year

Facility Name _____

Total Points Available: XXXXX   Audit Performed by:_____

Total Points Scored: XXXXX   Signature:_____

Percentage Score: _____   Date:_____(Total points

scored divided by total points available)

Management Safety Responsibilities	Answer		Total Points	Score
1. Are the safety responsibilities of each management team member in writing?	YES	NO	10	
2. Are the safety responsibilities explained completely to each team member?	YES	NO	10	
3. Does each team member receive a copy of his/her safety responsibilities?	YES	NO	5	
4. Has each team member been provided the opportunity to discuss their safety responsibilities and add input into the methods of performing these responsible acts?	YES	NO	10	
SECTION TOTAL			35	

Safety Goals	Answer		Total Points	Score
1. Has each member of the management team been able to provide input into the development of the operations safety goals?	YES	NO	5	
2. Has each member of the management team been able to provide input into their department's goals?	YES	NO	10	
3. Are goals developed in more than one safety area?	YES	NO	10	

HOW ACCIDENTS HAPPEN

DOMINO THEORY

When your management team fully understands the cost factors involved in work-related accidents, EMS professionals should also be prepared to show the dividends, in both monetary and humanitarian terms, that can be acquired through a comprehensive and systematic management approach to safety, health, and loss prevention. To ensure that the management team fully understands the concepts involved in a proactive program, the management team should understand how accidents happen and how they can be prevented. Using the domino theory, EMS managers can easily explain the causal factors leading up to an accident and the negative impact following an accident. Additionally, the personnel and human resource managers can explain that through the use of a proactive safety, health, and loss prevention program, the causal factors that could lead to an accident can be identified and corrected before the risk factors ultimately leading to an accident, mount up.

In Figure 11.1 the first three dominos show the underlying factors that could lead to an accident. EMS managers should emphasize the fact that the underlying causes for workplace injuries and illnesses can be identified and corrected through the use of a practice safety, health, and loss prevention program. If the underlying factors leading to an accident are not identified and corrected, the dominos begin to fall and once the dominos begin to fall, it is almost impossible to prevent an accident from happening. The key is to ensure that the management group realizes that to prevent an accident, the underlying risk factors must be minimized or eliminated rather than reacting after an accident has already happened.

To amplify this point, EMS managers often use the following progressional model to drive home the point that near misses and other underlying factors, if not addressed, will ultimately lead to an accident. In this model, for every 300 equipment damage accidents or near misses an employer may experience, there will be 29 minor injuries. If the deficiencies and underlying risk factors are not identified and corrected, the 300 near misses will ultimately lead to one major injury or fatality. The key is to ensure complete understanding that the management team must take a practiced approach to the safety and loss prevention function rather than reacting when an incident or accident happens.

WHAT ACCIDENTS COST

DIRECT AND INDIRECT COSTS

In order for most management teams to embrace the concept of a practice safety, health, and loss prevention program, it is imperative that the management group be educated as to the cost-effectiveness of such an endeavor. EMS managers are often able to show the monetary, as well as the

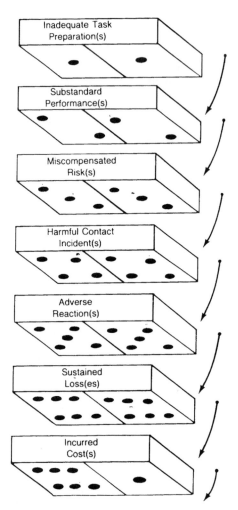

Figure 11.1: Domino   sequence   of   an   accident

humanitarian, benefits of a practice safety and health program through the use of a cost-benefit analysis.

Figure 11.2 is a diagram showing the iceberg effect of the potential cost of an accident.

This diagram is often used to exemplify the actual costs of accidents and the resultant injuries and illnesses in the workplace. When most individuals think of accident costs, the first thoughts that cross their minds are the direct costs. Direct costs include the cost of maintaining a medical facility at the workplace, the medical costs and time-loss benefits provided under workers'

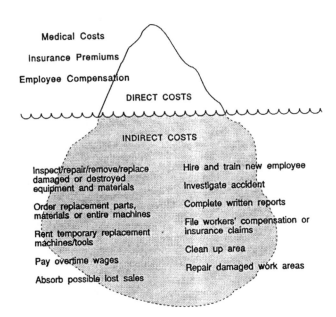

Medical Costs

Insurance Premiums

Employee Compensation

DIRECT COSTS

INDIRECT COSTS

Inspect/repair/remove/replace damaged or destroyed equipment and materials

Order replacement parts, materials or entire machines

Rent temporary replacement machines/tools

Pay overtime wages

Absorb possible lost sales

Hire and train new employee

Investigate accident

Complete written reports

File workers' compensation or insurance claims

Clean up area

Repair damaged work areas

Figure 11.2: Direct and indirect costs of an accident

compensation, and the premium costs of insurance. In most organizations, these cost figures are easily identified and illustrate for the management group the actual direct costs to their particular organization. These direct costs in most organizations are substantial and normally result in a percentage of the profits being utilized to pay for these costs (e.g., that 4 percent of the fiscal year 1993 profit was paid in workers' compensation benefits). When EMS management team members actually take the time to understand the amount of money (lost profits) that is being spent on the direct costs of accidents, they usually command the attention of the management group.

The ultimate goal for every EMS manager is to safeguard employees from harm in the workplace. A secondary goal, although vitally important, is the achievement and maintenance of compliance with the OSHA standards and requirements. To reach these important goals, the EMS management needs to develop a comprehensive approach to manage the safety and health function and an extensive, all-inclusive strategy to direct and control the completion of the required tasks.

A management philosophy should be incorporated to serve as the foundation and to provide the necessary style through which to manage the safety and health function. The selection of that management philosophy and style is an individual decision based upon the background and personality of the personnel and human resource manager, the type of industry, the employee population, and numerous other factors. The key to achieving compliance with the OSHA standards and regulations is to take control of the safety and health function rather than permitting the safety and health issues or problems to dictate to one's organization.

The management principles that management team members use in daily supervision of production, quality control, or any other operation are the same as those used in managing safety in the workplace. In production you *plan, organize, direct,* and *control* your operation to produce a product while in safety you *plan, organize, direct,* and *control*[1] the safety and health of the employees in the workplace.

1. Is the employer covered under the OSH Act?

2. Has the facility or workday been evaluated to ascertain which specific OSHA standards are applicable?

3. Has the management group been educated as to the requirements of the OSH Act and standards and acquired the necessary support and funding for the programs?

4. Is there a copy of the OSHA Standards (29 C.F.R. 1910 *et. seq.* and other standards) at the work site?

5. Is the *Federal Register* or are other appropriate sources for new standards or emergency standards being reviewed to see if they are applicable to the workday?

6. For new programs or new standards promulgated by OSHA, is the OSHA standard applicable to the workplace, situation, or industry?

7. Is there an OSHA Guideline for particular situations or hazards in the workplace?

8. If there is no applicable OSHA standard, will the situation qualify under the General Duty Clause as an unsafe or unhealthful situation or hazard?

9. If there is no applicable OSHA standard and the situation is deemed to qualify under the general duty clause, have NIOSH publications, American National Standards Institute (ANSI) standards, or other applicable journals and texts been reviewed to acquire guidance?

10. If there is no applicable OSHA standard or there is an OSHA standard that conflicts with other governmental agency regulations, are there other options such as to (1) contact the regional OSHA office and request consultation assistance; or (2) employ an outside consultant possessing the specific expertise to assist; or (3) pursue a variance action?

11. If there is an applicable OSHA standard, has *each and every* word of the standard been read so as to completely understand the requirement of the standard?

12. Is there a *written* program to ensure compliance with all requirements of the OSHA standard? Remember, if the program is not in writing, then there is no evidence to prove the existence of the program during an OSHA inspection or in litigation. Is the *original* of this *written* program in a secure location?

13. Is the program written in a defensive manner? Can the written program be scrutinized by OSHA or a court of law without identifying flaws in the program? Is the program written in a neutral and nondiscriminatory language?

14. Is the documentation of every purchase or equipment modification included in the program in order to ensure compliance with the OSHA standard? Is this documentation in the original copy of the written program or in a secure location?

15. Does the written program possess the *purpose* of this program? Is there a copy of the applicable OSHA standard for easy reference? Have the responsibilities been delineated and are they specific for each level of the management team and each position within the levels of management?

16. Have the OSHA standards and other applicable information been closely scrutinized and evaluated? Has each and every requirement in the standard been achieved and/or exceeded? Have any steps or elements that are required in the OSHA standard been omitted? If the standard is vague, make sure the program is clear, concise, and to the point.

17. Has all training been documented as required under the OSHA standard? (Remember, the OSHA standard is only a minimum requirement. Every program can be better than, but not less than, the OSHA standard requirements.)

18. Is there detailed documentation regarding each and every phase of the training? Is this documentation in the written program? Is documentation provided in the written program to prove the use of audiovisual aids, the instructor's qualifications, and other pertinent information?

19. Is there a schedule of the classroom and hands-on training sessions in the written program?

20. Have *all* employees who have completed the required training signed a document showing the exact training completed (in detail), the instructor's name, and the date of the training, etc.? Have auxiliary aids and other accommodations for individuals with disabilities been provided for in the training programs? (For employees who cannot read or write, a thumbprint can be used. Videotape documentation of the training is also an acceptable method of documentation. Remember to maintain the individual tapes on file, as with other documents, for future use as evidence of this training.)

21. Is the training offered in the languages used by the employees? Are the documents and the written program interpreted into the languages spoken by the employees and are the interpreted programs provided for use by these employees?

22. Is there a posting requirement under the applicable OSHA standard? Is the necessary poster from OSHA in the facility and has it been posted in an appropriated location by the required date? Have posters in the language of the employees been acquired and are they posted in an appropriated location by the required date?

23. Are there any other requirements? Labeling of containers? MSDS sheets? Does the OSHA standard require support or information from an outside vendor or agency? Have all requests to outside vendors or agencies requesting the necessary information (e.g., MSDS sheets) been documented and placed in the written program?

24. Is there a disciplinary procedure in the written program instructing employees of the potential disciplinary action for failure to follow the written program?

25. Has the written program been reviewed prior to publication? Does it meet or exceed each and every step required under the applicable OSHA standard?

26. Has the written program been reviewed by legal counsel or the upper management group prior to publication? Upon completion of the acquisition of necessary approvals of the written program, have copies of the program been made for distribution to strategic locations in the facility? Are translated copies available for use by the employees? Does the upper management group possess individual copies of the program?

27. Upon initiation of the program, is there a plan to review and critically evaluate the effectiveness of the program at least once per month for the first six months? When deficiencies are identified, are plans prepared to make the necessary changes and modifications while ensuring compliance with the OSHA standard?

28. Is there a developed safety and health audit assessment procedure and instrument? Is there a plan for auditing the programs on a periodic basis? Is the audit scheduled or to be scheduled?

The principles that managers use in their daily supervision of production, quality control, or any operation are the same principles that should be used when managing the safety, health, and loss prevention function in the workplace. In production, managers utilize the basic management principles of *planning, organizing, directing,* and *controlling*[2] the operation to produce a product. EMS managers should utilize the same basic management principles to *plan, organize, direct, and control* the safety and health function in the workplace.

For many years, the safety, health, and loss prevention function was a secondary job function, or in many cases, an afterthought. The safety, health, and loss prevention function was managed utilizing a "squeaky wheel" theory. That is, the only time the management team paid any attention to the safety, health, and loss prevention function was when the wheel squeaked after an accident had already occurred. Today, with the increasing costs of work-related injuries and illnesses, the increasing compliance requirements and liability, and other increasing costs in the area of safety, health, and loss prevention, a practice stance should be taken to ensure that a safe and healthful environment is created and maintained in the workplace.

In developing a regulatory compliance program, there is no substitute for knowledge of the OSHA standards, EPA regulations, or other applicable governmental regulations. Under the law, every organization covered under these regulations is bound to know the law. As stated by many courts throughout history, ignorance of the law is no defense.

So how can an EMS manager acquire a working knowledge of the OSHA regulations? The first step is to acquire a copy of the regulations by contacting the local OSHA office or purchasing the regulations through a book dealer. Second, the EMS manager must read through the regulations and become familiar with them. These OSHA standards are often used by managers as a quick reference and one can easily refer to the applicable standard through the index system located in the last section of 29 C.F.R. Section 1910.

Additionally, it is highly recommended that EMS managers attend continuing education conferences or seminars that provide current information regarding new and existing OSHA standards and regulations.

Another resource that should not be overlooked is the Consulting Division of OSHA, which is generally provided through the individual state's safety and health office.[3] This consultation program allows employers to bring OSHA or state plan consultants into the workplace to conduct audits, provide educational programs, and/or assist with compliance, usually at no cost to the employer. Under the terms of most consultation programs, an OSHA consultant cannot cite the employer for violations unless the situation involves imminent death. The state consultation services also have a library of safety resources available to the management team.

Another exceptional source for safety and health information is the National Institute of Occupational Safety and Health (NIOSH). This educational agency is predominately focused on research and possesses publications addressing virtually every area within the safety and health realm. NIOSH does not possess the same authority to issue citations for violations as OSHA. If an OSHA standard cannot be found that specifically addresses a particular situation in a facility, NIOSH is an excellent resource to direct the team on the right path.

When developing a regulatory compliance program, please keep in mind the source of the standard—a governmental agency. Therefore, when developing a compliance program, *if the program is not in writing, you do not have a program!* All compliance programs should be in writing and must meet the minimum requirements set forth in the applicable OSHA standard.

With most of the OSHA standards, the standard itself does not tell you how to develop the program but only what requirements must be achieved. Additionally, many of the OSHA standards reference other standards within 29 C.F.R. Section 1910 or other regulatory schemes such as those of ANSI. Safety and loss prevention professionals are required to know the standard and be able to acquire the reference information. The OSHA standards are usually the base level below which employers cannot go, but which they are encouraged to exceed to make their programs considerably better than the OSHA requirements. Additionally, OSHA does not normally tell employers how to develop their programs. OSHA normally provides the minimum requirements to meet the standard(s). The job of the personnel manager is to identify the needs of the operations, to identify the requirements of the standard, and to develop the compliance program that best serves your operation and achieves and maintains compliance with the applicable standard.

In addition to knowing the OSHA standards, EMS managers are encouraged to review the various professional safety and health publications and the *Federal Register* to identify new proposed standards that may affect their operations prior to the standard becoming law. When developing a new standard, OSHA is required to publish the proposed standard in the *Federal Register* and hold open hearings and accept comments from any source regarding the proposed standard. EMS managers are encouraged to voice any concerns they have regarding a particular proposed standard to OSHA at these hearings or in writing prior to the hearings. All Final Standards are published in the *Federal Register*. Employers are then normally given a period of time to achieve compliance by OSHA.

Basic and general guidelines to assist the EMS professional in developing a safety and health program for a particular standard are set forth below.

1. Read the OSHA Standard carefully and note all requirements.

2. Remember *all OSHA* compliance programs *must be in writing*.

3. Develop a plan of action. Acquire management commitment and funding for the program.

4. Purchase all necessary equipment. Acquire all necessary certifications, etc.

5. Remember to post any required notices.

6. Inform employees of the program. Acquire employee input in the developmental stages of the program. Inform labor organizations, if applicable.

7. At this point, you may want to contact OSHA for samples of acceptable programs (they sometimes have available a recommended format). You may also want to have them review your finished draft and provide comments.

8. Conduct all necessary training and education. *Remember to document all training!*

9. Conduct all required testing. *Remember to document all testing procedures, equipment, calibrations, etc.*

10. Implement the program.

11. Remember to ensure that all procedures are followed. Disciplinary action taken for noncompliance *must* be documented.

12. Audit the program on a regular periodic basis or as required under the standard.

Again, it is important to note that most OSHA standards do not provide any guidance as to how compliance is to be achieved. Most, if not all standards require only that the employer achieve and maintain compliance. In essence, the OSHA standard tells the EMS manager what has to be done but not how the compliance program is to be designed, managed, or evaluated. For example, an employer must have in place a facility evacuation plan. How the employer structures the plan and the specific details of the plan are left to the safety and health professional. Additionally, it is the responsibility of the EMS manager to determine what OSHA standards are applicable to the individual facility or workday to ensure that the facility and workday are in compliance with the applicable standards. An error or omission in not possessing a part or all of the required safety program necessary to achieve compliance with a specific standard is a violation, just as an inadequate or mismanaged program is a violation. Errors of omission and commission are both violations of the OSH Act.

EMS managers with responsibilities in the important areas of health, safety, and loss prevention can make a major impact on their organizations saving dollars as well as creating a safe, healthful, and enjoyable work environment for their employees. Safety, health, and loss prevention must be proactively managed with the same intensity as all other areas and must be one of the top priorities for your company.

You can do it—this is not rocket science. Apply your management skills and abilities to the safety, health, and loss prevention activities, and the results can be dramatic.

Basic Safety Program Elements

1. You must have management commitment for your safety effort.

2. Develop your safety plan—meet all compliance requirements. Acquire employee input in the development of your safety program.

3. All safety responsibilities must be in writing—communicate safety responsibilities to employees. Develop specific safety rules and policies.

4. Organize your safety efforts—put all safety programs in writing.

5. Train and direct your management team members and employees.

6. Discipline fairly and consistently when necessary.

7. Manage your safety programs.

8. Audit and evaluate your safety programs on a periodic basis.

9. Make all necessary modifications and adjustments.

10. Establish a safety committee to assist in your safety efforts.

CHAPTER 12

Workplace Violence Prevention and Liability

Violence is the last refuge of the incompetent.
—Isaac Asimov

Nothing good ever comes of violence.
—Martin Luther

POTENTIAL EMPLOYER LIABILITY

EMS personnel are at risk in their workplaces! Whether EMS personnel are responding to the scene, assisting in medical facilities, or even working at private sector workplaces, the potential of violence erupting is present. Any organization that is open to the public, has employees working in it, permits ex-employees into its workplace, or at any other time permits people for any reason in its workplace, has a potential risk of a workplace violence incident. Until a few years ago, most public and private sector employers did not even realize that potential risks existed until after an incident occurred. Without proper preparation after incidents of workplace violence occur, the only position an employer can take is to attempt to minimize the potential legal actions and correlating costs. With the emerging trend regarding the frequency and severity of workplace incidents as well as the substantial publicity being provided to the issue of workplace violence, employers are fast learning that new and novel theories of potential liability are evolving that can hold the employer ultimately liable for the injuries and damage incurred as a result of the violence.

In general, the potential for liability lies in three main areas of the law: (1) workers' compensation, (2) tort liability, and (3) governmental compliance.

In the area of workers' compensation, the employer is normally responsible for any work-related injury or illness that may occur in the workplace. Although every state has different laws in the area of workers' compensation, most states require the employer to pay all medical costs, a time-loss or temporary benefit that pays 60% to 70% of the employees average weekly wage, and a permanent or total disability benefit. For incidents where employees are killed in the workplace, most state workers' compensation laws provide for a death benefit as well as continuing benefits for the family. Although the potential monetary and legal risks from a workers' compensation claim as a result of a workplace violence incident are minimal in comparison to the other potential claims, the total cost of the medical care, time-loss benefits, and other benefits provided under the state workers' compensation laws can be substantial.

The second area of potential liability is within the tort area. The torts of negligent hiring, negligent retention, negligent security, and other potential tort theories are derived from the common law. These theories are based on the fellow servant rule, which operates to relieve the employer from liability when the employee was injured because of negligence, carelessness, or the intentional misconduct of a fellow employee when the risk on the job was usual and ordinary.[1] Under the Fellow Servant Rule, the employer would not be liable for incidents of workplace violence that were caused by other employees. However, over the years, courts have created exceptions to this especially harsh rule and have begun to recognize an employer's duty to create and maintain a safe and healthy workplace. In over twenty-eight states and the District of Columbia, the doctrine of negligent hiring has been recognized.[2] Additionally, courts have begun to recognize the theory of negligent retention (i.e., keeping an employee on the job with a recognized or known potential), and other negligent theories such as negligent training and negligent security.

In essence, the prima facie case of a negligent action requires four basic elements: (1) a duty by the employer, (2) a breach of that duty, (3) causation (i.e., a correlation between the breach of the duty and the injury), and (4) damages. A growing trend in the courts has been to create exceptions to the fellow servant rule to permit injured employees to recover damages for injuries or death caused by workplace violence incidents. An area that may come in conflict with this is the workers' compensation laws of the individual state, which normally are the sole remedy for workplace injuries and illnesses.

The third area of potential liability is the area of compliance with OSHA and/or state plan safety and health regulations. The Occupational Safety and Health Administration (OSHA) has recognized workplace violence as a problem in particular industries, such as the retail and healthcare industries. OSHA has promulgated guidelines targeting these particular industries as well as providing guidance to other industries in ways of preventing or addressing workplace violence incidents.[3] For employers, this creates another area of potential liability given the fact that OSHA may provide monetary penalties up to $70,000 per violation as well as the potential of criminal liability under the OSH Act. Although OSHA has provided these guidelines specifically to the retail and health care industry, employers should be aware that OSHA may cite incidents of workplace violence despite the fact that there is not a specific standard promulgated to address workplace violence incidents under the General Duty Clause.[4]

On the opposite side of this issue is the fact that employers may over-react and invade individual privacy areas or provide other areas of potential liability. The area of individual privacy laws has substantially expanded in the last twenty years in order to safeguard employee rights in the workplace. Additionally, the at-will doctrine has been quickly deteriorating with the courts providing a number of exceptions to this doctrine. Areas of potential liability that have readily been expanding include that of wrongful discharge or wrongful termination, defamation (libel and slander), and violation of a number of privacy-related laws such as the Privacy Act of 1974, the Freedom of Information Act, the Fair Credit Reporting Act, and the federal whistleblower statutes. Additionally, employers possess the potential of legal liabilities through the number of discrimination laws including Title VII of the Civil Rights Act of 1964 and 1991, the Rehabilitation Act, and the Americans with Disabilities Act.

Workplace violence is a fact of life today in the American workplace. We read about incidents of workplace violence in the newspaper on virtually a daily basis. But do workplace violence incidents only happen to large employers? Are EMS organizations immume from workplace violence? Are small EMS organizations less or more likely to incur workplace violence incidents? Are workplace violence incidents just a freak occurrence or is there a larger systemic problem? Just in 1993, companies in the United States spent more than 4.2 million dollars on medical bills, counseling, legal fees, and legal settlements stemming from workplace violence incidents. Smaller companies can be hit even harder by a workplace violence incident because their pockets are not as deep as larger companies. One workplace violence incident can cause the ruin of a smaller company or organization. And what about the effect on morale in the working environment at your organization? One bad apple can ruin the entire barrel with their compulsive or paranoid attitudes. What about the effect on the individuals? Remember, every year approximately twelve-thousand unhappy people commit suicide at work. So what can we do? Communicate with your workers, develop a plan, and be proactive!

The evasive area of violence in the workplace is fast becoming a part of everyday life and should be addressed by employers in a proactive fashion. There does not appear to be a "fast fix" or one answer that will fit all workplaces. Prudent employers should evaluate the potential risks within their workplace as well as the potential risk of any action or reaction to each workplace area in order to ascertain the best path to follow to safeguard and preserve the privacy rights of their employees. The potential risk will vary depending upon the employer, the management style, the types of activities, and various other factors. The type of industry or activity may increase risks from the outside, and the makeup of the work force itself may provide additional opportunities. Prudent employers should evaluate these risks rather than sticking their head in the sand and should take a proactive approach in order to address these potential safety, health, and legal risks.

WORKPLACE VIOLENCE PREVENTION PROGRAM

The Occupational Safety and Health Administration (OSHA) has stated in their regulations that "any employer in the business to provide goods and services that employs people shall provide a safe and healthful work environment." When we go to work we should not have to worry about someone bothering us or harassing us. But that is not the case today; there are disgruntled workers out there that misplace their anger and take it out on co-employees or the company they work for. The problem of workplace violence has escalated and is almost out of control; if companies do not take an initiative to stop it, there is no telling where it could lead.

We are accustomed to work being violence free. There is a civility and cooperation that is basic to the work environment; if there wasn't a business couldn't function. But now violence is not just on the streets, it has ventured into the office and we must all cope with it. In the past workers tried to leave their home life at home; we all remember the boss saying, "Don't bring your personal life to the office." Our world is becoming more violent and more people are bringing that violence to work with them and not leaving it at the door. What follows is a rude awakening: This can't happen to me or my company, it only happens on the news in another part of the country.

Many companies have already recognized this trend and are taking preventive measures to guard against it. Employee Assistance Programs (EAP), which were created during World War II to deal with alcoholism, are today being employed to cope with employees and their problems. EAPs deal with problems such as marital difficulties or substance abuse; the employee knows there is somewhere to go for assistance. Such assistance can sometimes mean more than a raise. It can lead to company loyalty, a more productive work force, and employee assurance that the company cares about them. Most EAPs are run by outside agencies because company staff are not trained to deal with these types of problems or to ensure employee confidentiality.

A preventive maintenence plan for violence should be in effect to deal with violence or even the threat of violence. The following is an outline of a preventive program for a company:

1. The creating of a management team to develop, review, and implement policies dealing with violence in the workplace. The creation of these policies should be included within the corporation policies and procedures.

Management backing is very important to any type of employment program. In creating the management team, responsibility should be assigned so that employees know the different portions of the team they are responsible for. Once the team has been created the first step should be an assessment of the possibility of a violent act occurring in their workplace. The team members should make themselves experts on the subject of workplace violence. They should contact all types of outside resources, so as to better equip themselves on the subject. Then the team should prepare for the possibility of a violent act occurring in their workplace. This should be an action plan to deal with a violent act. Then the team should educate the rest of the employees, supervisors, or team leaders.

2. Create a program where employees are able to detect early warning signals that could ultimately lead to a violent act.

The next step is to create a program so supervisors and/or mangers are able to detect early warning signals and deal with the situation head on before they become a potentially violent episode. This should be incorporated into an already existing training program or as a separate program. It has already been established that some of the early warning signals are:

1. Paranoid behavior. The employee acts like the world is out to get him.

2. Holding a grudge against the company or a specific employee. This attitude could lead to threats, harassment, intimidation of others, or prediction that a bad event will happen.

3. Being a loner. Employee does not associate with co-employees on a regular basis, and may be estranged from family.

4. Obsession with firearms. May own a collection of them and is always talking about them.

Managers, supervisors, or team leaders should be trained to spot these signs and report them to a member of the management team. During any type of company downsizing supervisors should be especially alert for any signs of the above behavior. When this type of behavior is spotted it should be immediately reported to a member of the management team. The appropriate member of the management team should then conduct an investigation.

3. Develop an investigation format for dealing with complaints or threats about a potentially violent employee.

The first rule of any threat is to take it seriously, because it could end up being a violent act. Investigating and recording incidents are a key to preventing a violent act in the workplace. In recording the investigation the four W's are an important key to start the investigation off.

- *Who*: Who made the actual complaint or threat? Who witnessed the actual threat?

- *When*: When did the threat take place? Were there any events leading up to the actual threat; if so, when did they take place?

- *What*: What exactly happened? Include all the facts that pertain to the actual threat and the investigators' assessment of what occurred.

- *Where*: Where did the threat take place? In an office or outside the company? This factor is important and is easily overlooked.

An incident report form, already prepared by the investigator, is the easiest way to handle the investigation. Some sample questions that may be included on the report form follow.

1. Who made the threat?

2. Who was the threat made against?

3. What were the actual words said in the threat?

4. Was there any threat of physical harm? If so what was it?

5. Where did the threat take place? (actual physical location)

6. What time did the threat take place? (be specific)

7. Who witnessed the actual threat?

8. What did the witnesses say occurred? (in their own words)

9. Ask the witnesses to write down their statements and attach to document?

10. Is there any other information that might pertain to the incident?

These questions are not inclusive and a company needs to create an incident form specific to the needs of their organization.

It is important when interviewing the person who made the threat to do so in a nonthreatening environment. Developing a strategy to deal with the person's anger is key. Focusing only on facts, not personal opinions or personality traits, will help the person deal with the situation in a calm rational manner and help to control emotional reactions.

In addition the interviewer can communicate signs of their interest in what is being said. Some of these signs are making eye contact; giving the person your full attention (do not work on notes or answer the phone, this can exacerbate the situation); ask open-ended questions; do not interrupt the person, let them finish what they are saying; speak in a calm rational voice; repeat what the person says in your own words to clarify their situation, so you understand fully.

4. Conduct any action necessary that would prevent an incident from occurring.

This may be disciplinary action, talking to a member of the management team in charge of workplace violence, or referral to the companies Employee Assistance Program for counseling. The investigator interviewing the person will come to a set of conclusions. The action that is taken should be based on the conclusions drawn from the interview. In some cases the person who made the threats may feel better immediately after talking to the interviewer. This may resolve the issue, but in some cases it won't and further action will be necessary. It is important to take a "zero tolerance" policy towards any threat. If the company takes the position that if Bob makes a threat, he will be suspended without pay for a day, and this progresses to escalated discipline of the next incident where Bob hits Joe, and then to suspension for three days the next time Bob threatens an employee, this progression may be an error. This type of action will not help the situation, but only make it worse. The idea is to help an adult solve a problem rather than treat him or her like a naughty child that needs to be disciplined.

5. Develop or improve upon security measures.

Technology has advanced security measures. Gone are the days of the security guard walking a solitary route around a building. Today, enhanced security cameras and laser beams are used to detect intruders. Electronic systems can provide or deny access to persons entering a workplace. Every employer needs to assess their needs and provide appropriate security measures. There are several security companies that will provide a review and recommend security measures. There are some that will handle every aspect of the security process. But providing security is key to protecting employees from the threat of a violent employee and from other types of incidents that could threaten a company. Immediate improvements that will provide a measure of safety include outdoor lighting, closed circuit television, an intercom system, and an alarm system. Aside from these few examples of what can be done, each company should survey its needs and provide appropriate security measures.

In addition to physical security measures policies concerning security measures need to be included within the corporate policies and procedures manual. When an employee would like to work late, what does the policy state about that? Does another employee need to stay also? Are they even allowed to stay after hours? The policy also needs to include statements regarding security when a threat has been made. Is security tightened? If it is, how so? These issues need to be addressed in the corporate policy statements and employees need to be aware of all of them.

In addition to the above measures the local law enforcement department needs to be contacted. It can provide valuable information regarding other companies' experiences— with threats, mistakes that were made, and lessons learned from these mistakes. A mistake learned from one company may save a life in another company. The local law enforcement can be a vital source of information.

6. Develop a crises plan in the event of an actual workplace violent act.

The chain of command in the management team needs to be detailed so that every person knows their individual responsibilities and there is no confusion when an incident occurs. When an incident occurs the responsibility will shift from the office manager or supervisor to a management team member.

When are other agencies notified? The local police should be the first agency notified, so they can provide protection. A person from the employee assistance program needs to be notified and available. Other agencies, such as the fire department and local police should be notified in an appropriate order.

In the crisis plan other resources should be made available, such as a trauma consultant (either a counselor or therapist to assist employees in dealing with the crisis), a security consultant, an in-house legal representative, and a medical physician.

What procedures should be immediately instituted to determine how safe the workplace is? Is there an internal security team that could isolate the area until the police department arrived? Include an immediate assessment to determine the effect of the incident on the workplace.

Conduct an immediate investigation of the incident. What are the facts of the case? Who were the witnesses? What is the relationship between the investigation that the employer is conducting and the investigation the police department will conduct.

What limits does the employer place on the release of information to other employees? Institute procedures regulating the release of information to the other employees, and establish regulations about what can be said during emergency situations.

What is the immediate public relations concern? How much information will be released to the public and who will release the information?

How does a company preserve control of the day-to-day running of the business while an incident is occurring?

These are just a few ideas that can be a part of a crises plan. Each company needs to develop a plan specific to its organization. After a plan has been written a hypothetical situation should be conducted to inform the employees of the plan and the company's intent in dealing with workplace violence.

7. Use the courts to deal with threats of violence.

The EMS organization must have a zero-tolerance policy towards threats of workplace violence or an actual incident of violence. When an employee has been discharged or is no longer employed by the company and continues to make threat towards the company or its representative, many organizations have found the courts to be an effective and acceptable method. The use of restraining orders prevents a person from obtaining access to the person or persons they have threatened. This is not a guarantee that an incident will be prevented, but it is a preventative measure that will minimize the chances of an attack occurring. When a state allows a restraining order the person making the threat has to stay a certain distance away from the person they made a threat against. When a court order is issued, the police department is authorized to arrest the person who made the threat.

In summation, EMS organizations are not immune from incidents of workplace violence. When EMS personnel respond to an accident scene and individuals shoot at the vehicle or threaten EMS personnel in hopes of acquiring drugs or equipment, this is workplace violence. Additionally, EMS personnel are under a substantial amount of work-related stress and stressors from outside the workplace. Prudent EMS organizations may want to take the appropriate proactive steps to safeguard their personnel on the job from the potential risks of workplace violence as well as the potential legal liabilities attached thereto.

Endnotes

Chapter 3

1. Americans with Disabilities Act § 305, 42 U.S.C. 12101 et. seq.

2. ADA § 101(5), 108, 42 U.S.C. 12111.

3. ADA § 204(a), 42 U.S.C. 12134.

4. *Id.*

5. ADA § 203(a), 306(a), 42 U.S.C. 12186.

6. ADA § 102(a), 42 U.S.C. 12112.

7. *Id.*

8. ADA § 101(8).

9. *EEOC Interpretive Rules*, 56 Fed. Reg. 35 (July 26, 1991).

10. 0 42 FR 22686 (May 4, 1977); S. Rep. 101–116; H. Rep. 101–485, Part 2, 51.

11. Subtitle A, § 3(2). The ADA departed from the Rehabilitation Act of 1973 and other legislation in using the term "disability" rather than "handicap."

12. 28 C.F.R. § 41.31. This provision is adopted by and reiterated in the Senate Report at page 22.

13. See *Jasany v. U.S. Postal Service*, 755 F2d 1244 (6th Cir. 1985).

14. S. Rep. 101–116, 23; H. Rep. 101–485, Part 2, 52–3.

15. 45 C.F.R. 84.3 (j)(2)(iv), quoted from H. Rep. 101–485, Part 3, 29; S. Rep. 101–116, 23:H. Rep. 101–485, Part 2, 53; also see *School Board of Nassau County, Florida v. Arline*, 107 S. Ct. 1123 (1987)(leading case).

16. *EEOC Interpretive Guidelines*, 56 Fed. Reg. 35, 742 (July 26, 1991).

17. S. Comm. on Lab. and Hum. Resources Rep. at 24; H. Comm. on Educ. and Lab. Rep. at 53; H. Comm. on Jud. Rep. at 30–31.

18. 29 C.F.R. § 1630.2(1).

19. ADA, Title I, § 101(8).

20. *EEOC Interpretive Rules, supra*, note 9.

21. *Id.*

22. ADA, § 103(b).

23. *EEOC Interpretive Guidelines.*

24. *Id.*

25. 56 Fed. Reg. 35,745 (July 26, 1991); also see *Davis v. Meese*, 692 F. Supp. 505 (E.D.Pa. 1988) (Rehabilitation Act decision).

26. ADA § 101(9).

27. *EEOC Interpretive Guidelines.*

28. *Id.*

29. See *Gruegging v. Burke*, 48 Fair Empl. Prac. Cas. (BNA) 140 (DDC 1987); *Bento v. ITO Corp.*, 599 F. Supp. 731 (DRI 1984).

30. *EEOC Interpretive Guidelines*, 56 Fed. Reg. 35,744 (July 26, 1991); also see Rehabilitation Act decisions including *Harrison v. March*, 46 Fair Empl. Prac. Cas. (BNA) 971 (W.D.Mo. 1988); *Wallace v. Veteran Admin.*, 683 F. Supp. 758 (D. Kan. 1988).

31. ADA § 101(10)(a).

32. S. Comm. on Lab. and Hum. Resources Rep. at 38; H. Comm. on Jud. Rep. at 42.

33. ADA, Title I, § 102(C)(2).

34. ADA § 102(c)(2)(A).

35. *EEOC Interpretive Guidelines*, 56 Fed. Reg. 35,751 (July 26, 1991). Federally mandated periodic examinations are covered by such laws as the Rehabilitation Act, Occupational Safety and Health Act, Federal Coal Mine Health Act, and numerous transportation laws.

36. ADA § 102(c).

37. ADA § 511(b).

38. ADA § 201(1).

39. S. Rep. 101–116, 21; H. Rep. 101–485, Part 2; Part 3, 26–27.

40. ADA § 302.

41. ADA § 302(b)(2)(A)(iv).

42. ADA § 301(9).

43. ADA § 3(1).

44. Report of the House Committee on Energy and Commerce on the Americans with Disabilities Act of 1990, H.R. Rep. No. 485, 101st Cong., 2d Sess. (1990)(hereinafter cited as H. Comm. on Energy and Comm. Rep.);

H. Comm. on Educ. and Lab. Rep., *supra*.; S. Comm. on Lab. and Hum. Resources Rep., *supra*.

45. ADA § 501.

46. ADA, § 511(a),(b); Section 508. There is some indication that many of the conditions excluded from the disability classification under the ADA may be considered a covered handicap under the Rehabilitation Act. See *Rezza v. US Dept. of Justice*, 46 Fair Empl. Prac. Cas. (BNA) 1336 (E.D. Pa. 1988) (compulsive gambling); *Fields v. Lyng*, 48 Fair Empl. Prac. Cas. (BNA) 1037 (D. Md. 1988) (kleptomania).

47. ADA §§ 102(b)(4) and 302(b)(1)(E).

48. H. Rep. 101–485, Part 2, 51.

49. ADA § 102(b)(4).

50. H. Rep. 101–485, Part 2, 61–62; Part 3, 38–39.

51. ADA § 105.

52. *EEOC Interpretive Guidelines*.

53. *Id*.

54. Civil Rights Act of 1991, § 102.

55. S. Rep. 101–116, 21; H. Rep. 101–485, Part 2, 51; Part 3, 28.

56. ADA §§ 505 and 513.

57. ADA § 101(2) and 42 U.S.C. 12111.

58. ADA §§ 509(a)(1), (b),(c)(2), and 42 U.S.C. 12209.

59. ADA § 101(5)(B) and 42 U.S.C. 12111.

60. H. Rep. 101–485, Part 2, p. 51.

61. *Technical Assistance Manual for the Americans with Disabilities Act*, EEOC at 1–3.

62. *EEOC Interpretive Guidelines*, 56 Fed. Reg. 35,740 (July 26, 1991); Report of the Senate Comm. on Labor and Human Resources on the Americans with Disabilities Act of 1989, S. Rep. No. 116, 101st Cong., 1st Sess. (1989).

63. S. Comm. on Lab. and Hum. Resources Rep. at 22.

64. *Technical Assistance Manual*, *supra*.

65. *Id*.

66. H. Comm. on Educ. and Lab. Rep. at 52; S. Comm. on Lab. and Hum. Resources Comm. at 22, 136 Cong. Rec. S9697 (July 13, 1990). See also *Technical Assistance Manual*, *supra*.

67. *Technical Assistance Manual, supra.*

68. *Id.*

69. *Id.*

70. *Id.*

71. *Id.*

72. *Id.*

73. Title I, Sec. 510 & 511.

74. EEOC Regs. at 29 C.F.R. § 1630.2(o)(1).

75. *EEOC Interpretive Guidelines,* 56 Fed. Reg. 35,744 (July 26, 1991).

76. Title I § 101(9)(B); EEOC Regs. at 29 C.F.R. § 1630.2(n)(2).

77. Title I § 101(10)(a); *EEOC Technical Assistance Manual, supra.*

78. *EEOC Technical Assistance Manual, supra.*

79. Title I § 101(10)(B); *EEOC Technical Assistance Manual, supra.*

80. Title I § 102(c)(1).

81. Title I § 103(b).

82. Title I § 101(c) and 29 CFR § 1530.2(r).

83. 480 US 273 (1987).

84. *Id.*

85. H. Comm. on Educ. and Lab. Rep. at 59, 137.

86. Title I § 102(b)(2); *EEOC Technical Assistance Manual, supra.*

87. 29 U.S.C. § 794.

88. Title II § 103(8).

89. H. Comm. on Educ. and Lab. Rep. at 84.; S. Comm. on Lab. and Hum. Resources Rep. at 44; H. Comm. on Energy and Comm. Rep. at 26.

90. HR (ELC) at 84–85.

91. *Id.*

92. HR (ELC) at 85.

93. H. Comm. on Educ. and Lab. Rep. at 98; S. Comm. on Lab. and Hum. Resources Rep. at 57–58.

94. 28 C.F.R. § 35.107.

95. Title III § 310(7).

96. Title III § 3(1).

97. 47 USC 201 *et. seq.*

98. H. Comm. on Energy and Com. Rep. at 28.

99. H. Comm. on Educ. and Lab. Rep. at 59.

100. *EEOC Interpretive Guidelines*, 56 Fed. Reg. 35,753 (July 26, 1991).

101. Title V § 513.

102. Note: It is recommended that all audit results be *documented.* Prudent organizations should evaluate their program on at least a quarterly basis for the first 2–3 years to ensure compliance.

103. *EEOC Revised Guidance on Employment Questions related to the ADA,* 10-10-95 (emphasis added).

Chapter 6

1. *Black's Law Dictionary*, West Publishing, 1983.

2. See Indiana Code § 9-4-1(d).

3. *See Helman v. County of Warren*, 111 A.D.2d 560, 67 N.Y.S. 799 (1986).

4. Restatement (Second) of Torts § 339.

5. *See*, for example, *Loney v. McPhillips*, 521 P.2d 340 (Or. 1974).

6. See *Jones v. Fisher*, 42 Wisc. 2d. 209, 166 N.W.2d. 175 (1969).

7. *Tabor v. Scobee*, 254 S.W.2d. 474 (Ky. 1953).

8. 243 N.C. 355, 90 S.E.2d. 754 (1956).

9. See *Lipman v. Atlantic Coastline Railroad Company*, 108 Sup. Ct. 151, 93 S.E.2d. 714 (1917); Restatement (Second) of Torts § 48.

10. See *Slocum v. Food Fair Stores, Florida*, 100 S.2d. 396 (FL. 1958).

11. Restatement (Second) of Torts § 46.

12. *Boston v. Muncy*, 204 Ok. 603, 233 P.2d. 300, 25 A.L.R. 1208 (1951).

13. *Katko v. Briney*, 183 N.W. 2d. 657 (Iowa 1971).

14. See *Totel v. May Department Store Company*, 348 Mo. 696, 155 S.W.2d. 74 (1941).

Chapter 7

1. *See*, for example, Kentucky Revised Statute 342.630, which states, "The following shall constitute employers mandatorily subject to, and required to comply with, the provisions of this chapter: (1) Any person, other than the one engaged solely in agriculture, that has in this state one or more

employees subject to this chapter; (2) The state, any agency thereof, and each county, city of any class, school district, sewer district, drainage district, tax district, public or quasi-public corporation, or any other political subdivision or political entity of the state that has one or more employees subject to this chapter."

2. See, e.g., Kentucky Revised Statute 342.990, which proscribes:

> (8) The following civil penalties shall be applicable for violations of particular provisions of this chapter; (a) Any employer subject to this chapter, who fails to make a report required by KRS 342.038, within fifteen (15) days from the date it was due, shall be fined not less than one hundred dollars ($100) not more than one thousand dollars ($1000) for each offense . . . .

3. See, e.g., Kentucky Revised Statute 342.990 (8)(c)(9), which states, "The commissioner shall initiate enforcement of a criminal penalty by causing a complaint to be filed with the appropriate local prosecutor . . . ." and Kentucky Revised Statute 342.990 (10), which states, "the following criminal penalties shall be applicable for violations of particular provisions of this chapter: (a) Any person violating KRS 342.040 (failure to maintain coverage), 342.335 (misrepresentation or fraud), 342.400 (notice of rejection of workers' compensation coverage), 342.420 (requiring employee to pay workers' compensation premium), or 342.630 (failure to acquire coverage), shall, for each offense, be fined not less than one hundred dollars ($100) or more than one thousand dollars ($1000), or imprisoned for less than thirty (30) days not more than one hundred and eighty (180) days, or both." (Definitions of KRS section added.)

4. See Kansas Workmen's Compensation Act, KSA § 44–501 *et. seq.*; Kentucky Revised Statute 342.165.

5. *Black's Law Dictionary, supra.*

Chapter 8

1. See "Report of the Committee on Employee Rights and Responsibilities," *The Labor Lawyer*, volume 10, No. 3, p. 615 (Summer 1994).

2. Restatement (Second) of Torts, §§ 652B, 652C, 652D, and 652E, respectively.

3. Restatement (Second) of Tort Section 652B (1977). In *Phillips v. Smalley Maintenance Servs., Inc.*, 711 F.2d 1524, 1532 (11th Circuit 1983), the Alabama Supreme Court, on certification, adopted the Second Restatement respecting privacy torts, and held that "acquisition of information from a plaintiff is not a requisite element of a § 652B cause of action."

4. *Johnson v. Corporate View Surv. Inc.*, 602 So.2d 385 (Ala. 1992); *Thomas v. General ELEC. Co.*, 207 F. Supp. 792 (W.D. Ky. 1962).

5. *Massey v. Victor L. Phillips Co.*, 827 F. Supp. 597 (W.D. Mo. 1993); *Brazinski v. Amoco Petroleum Additives Co.*, 6 F.3d 1176 (7th Circ. 1993).

6. *Id.*

7. Restatement (Second) of Torts § 652C.

8. Restatement (Second) of Torts § 652D.

9. *Anderson v. Low-Rent Housing Commission* 304 N.W.2d 239 (Iowa 1981) (False light theory, recovery permitted, public employer).

10. *Bratt v. International Business Machines Corp.*, 785 Fed.2d 352 (1st Cir. 1986).

11. *Id.* at 360.

12. *White v. Fraternal Order of Police*, 707 F. Supp. 579 (D.D.C. 1989).

13. *Parks v. City of Warner Robbins, GA*, 43 F.3d 609 (11th Cir. 1995), *Wright v. Metro Health Medical Ctr.*, 58 F.3d 1130 (6th Cir. 1995).

14. *Watkins v. United Parcel Service, Inc.*, 979 F.2d 1535 (5th Cir. 1992).

15. *Ferguson v. Freedom Forge Corp.*, 604 F. Supp. 1157 (W.D. Pa. 1985).

16. *Smythe v. Pillsbury Co.*, 914 F. Supp. 97 (E.D. Pa. 1996)

17. *Bourke v. Nissan Motor Corporation*, No. 91 Y. to C. 3979 (L.A. Cty. Superior Court).

18. *Shoars v. Epsom America*, Nos. 90 S.W.C. 112749, 90 B.C. 7036 (L.A. Cty Superior Court).

19. 18 USC § 2510 *et. seq.*

20. *Shahar v. Bowers*, 70 F.3d 1218 (11th Cir. 1995), *Petri v. Bank of New York Co.*, 582 N.Y.S.2d 608, 612 (Sup. Ct. 1992).

21. *Schowengerdt v. General Dynamics*, 823 F.2d 1328 (9th Cir. 1987) (cause of action available under U.S. Constitution against private sector employer providing security services to U.S. Navy under "Federal Act" theory).

22. *National Treasury Employees Union v. Von Raab*, 489 U.S. 656 (1989).

23. *Skinner v. Railway Labor Executives' Association*, 489 U.S. 602 (1989).

24. *Wilkinson v. Times Mirror Books*, 215 Cal. App. 3d 1034 (1989).

25. 49 U.S.C. § 1834 (App.), 45 U.S.C. § 431 (App.), 49 U.S.C. § 277 (App.), for aviation, railroads, and trucking, respectively. Testing is authorized for pre-employment, random, reasonable suspicion, periodic, return to work, and postaccident situations.

26. 41 U.S.C. § 5151–5160 (1990).

27. *O'Keefe Passiac Valley Water Com'n*, 624 A.2d 578, 582–584 (N.J. 1993).

28. *Baggs v. Eagle-Pitcher Industrial Inc.*, 957 F.2d 268 (6th Cir. 1992).

29. *McCall v. Courier-Journal & Louisville Times*, 623 S.W.2d 882, 884 (Ky. 1981).

30. *Colombia Sussex Corp. v. Hay*, 627 S.W.2d 270, 273 (Ky. Ct. App. 1982).

31. *Id.*

32. *Doe v. Cohn Nast Ampersand Graf*, 862 F. Supp. 1310 (E.D. Pa. 1994).

33. *O'Brien v. Papagino's of America*, 780 F.2d 1067 (1st Cir. 1986).

34. *Bell v. Courier-Journal & Louisville Times Co.*, 402 S.W.2d 84, 87 (Ky. 1966).

35. Peterson, Donald J. and Douglas Massengill, "The Negligent Hiring Doctrine—A Growing Dilemma for Employers," 15 *Employee Relations Law Journal*, p. 410, Note 1 (1989–1990).

36. *Western Stone Company v. Whalen*, 151 Ill. 472, 478, 38 N.E.241 (1894).

37. *Id.*

38. See, e.g., *Ballard's Administratrix v. Louisville and Nashville Railroad Co.*, 128 Ky. 826, 110 S.W.296 (1908).

39. See, *Missouri, Kansas, & Texas Railway Company v. Texas and Day*, 104 Tex. 237, 136 S.W.435 (1911).

40. See, *Mallory v. O'Neil*, 69 So.2d 313 (Fla. 1954).

41. See also *Argonne Apartment House Company v. Garrison*, 42 F.2d 605 (D.C. Cir. 1930).

42. See, e.g., *Geise v. Phoenix Company of Chicago, Inc.*, 246 Ill. App. 3d 441, 615 N.E.2d 1179 (2nd District 1993), reversed on other grounds, 159 Ill. 2d 507, 639 N.E.2d 1273 (1994).

43. *Id.*, 496 N.W.2d 422, citing *Semrad v. Edina Realty Inc.*, 493 N.W. 2d 528 at 534 (Minn. 1992).

44. *Id.*, 331 N.W.2d 911.

45. 496 N.W.2d 423, quoting *Ponticas v. K.M.S., Inc.*, 331 N.W.2d 907 (Minn. 1983).

46. *Id.*

47. *Yunker v. Honeywell, Inc.*, 496 N.W.2d 423.

48. 764 S.W.2d 601 (Ark. 1989).

49. Bensimon, Helen Frank, "Violence in the Workplace," *Training and Development*, 27 (January 1994).

50. *Id.*

51. *Census of Fatal Occupational Injuries*, Bureau of Labor Statistics, U.S. Department of Labor, August 1994.

52. Kurlan, Warren, M., "Workplace Violence," *Risk Management*, 76 (June 1993).

53. *Id.*

54. Physical Assault, from our research, has run the gamut from an employee shoving or punching another employee through the use of a weapon or explosive to kill that individual.

55. Workplace Violence: OSHA says guidelines will target the retail and health care sectors, 1995 DLR 16 (BNA, January 23, 1995).

Chapter 9

1. B. Lindemann and P. Grossman, *Employment Discrimination Law* (3rd ed.), American Bar Association, BNA Books, 1996.

Chapter 10

1. J. M. O'Brien, *Bitter Wages* (1973). (During the construction of a tunnel in 1930–1931, 476 workers died, and approximately 1,500 were disabled, primarily by silicosis.)

2. 29 C.F.R. § 651(b).

3. *Id.* § 1975.3(d).

4. *Id.* § 652(7).

5. See, e.g., Atomic Energy Act of 1954, 42 U.S.C. § 2021.

6. 29 C.F.R. § 1975(6).

7. 29 U.S.C.A. § 652(5) (no coverage under OSH Act, when U.S. government acts as employer).

8. *Id.*

9. See, e.g., *Navajo Forest Prods. Indus.*, 8 O.S.H. Cases 2694 (OSH Rev. Comm'n 1980), aff'd, 692 F.2d 709, 10 O.S.H. Cases 2159.

10. 29 U.S.C.A. § 654(a)(1).

11. In Section 18(b), the OSH Act provides that any state "which, at any time, desires to assume responsibility for development and the enforcement therein of occupational safety and health standards relating to any ... issue with respect to which a federal standard has been promulgated ... shall submit a state plan for the development of such standards and their enforcement."

12. 8 *Id.* § 667(c). After an initial evaluation period of a least three years during which OSHA retains concurrent authority, a state with an approved plan gains exclusive authority over standard setting, inspection procedures, and

enforcement of health and safety issues covered under the state plan. See also *Noonan v. Texaco*, 713 P.2d 160 (Wyo. 1986); Plans for the Development and Enforcement of State Standards, 29 C.F.R. § 667(f) (1982) and § 1902.42(c)(1986). Although the state plan is implemented by the individual state, OSHA continues to monitor the program and may revoke the state authority if the state does not fulfill the conditions and assurances contained within the proposed plan.

13. Some states incorporate federal OSHA standards into their plans and add only a few of their own standards as a supplement. Other states, such as Michigan and California, have added a substantial number of separate and independently promulgated standards. See generally *Employee Safety and Health Guide* (CCH) §§ 5000–5840 (1987)(compiling all state plans). Some states also add their own penalty structures. For example, under Arizona's plan, employers may be fined up to $150,000 and sentenced to one and one-half years in prison for knowing violations of state standards that cause death to an employee and may also have to pay $25,000 in compensation to the victim's family. If the employer is a corporation, the maximum fine is $1 million. See Ariz. Rev. Stat. Ann. §§ 13–701, 13–801, 23–4128, 23–418.01, 13–803 (Supp. 1986).

14. For example, under Kentucky's state plan regulations for controlling hazardous energy (i.e., lockout/tagout), locks would be required rather than locks or tags being optional as under the federal standard. Lockout/tagout is discussed in more detail in Chapter 2.

15. 29 U.S.C. § 667.

16. 29 U.S.C.A. § 667; 29 C.F.R. § 1902.

17. The states and territories operating their own OSHA programs are Alaska, Arizona, California, Hawaii, Indiana, Iowa, Kentucky, Maryland, Michigan, Minnesota, Nevada, New Mexico, North Carolina (partial federal OSHA enforcement), Oregon, Puerto Rico, South Carolina, Tennessee, Utah, Vermont, Virginia, Virgin Islands, Washington, and Wyoming.

18. Corn, M., *Policies, Objectives and Plans of OSHA*, 1976 ABA Nat'l Inst. on Occupational Safety & Health Law at 229.

19. See, e.g., *NLRB v. Fainblatt*, 306 U.S. 601, 604–05 (1939). See also *U.S. v. Ricciardi*, 357 F.2d 91 (2d Cir.), *cert. denied*, 384 U.S. 942, 385 U.S. 814 (1966).

20. *Secretary v. Ray Morin*, 2 O.S.H. Cases 3285 (1975).

21. *Whirlpool Corp. v. Marshall*, 445 U.S. 1, 8 O.S.H. Cases 1001 (1980).

22. 29 C.F.R. Section 1910 *et. seq.*

23. For example, consider a company with a corporate headquarters in Delaware and operations in Kentucky, Utah, California, and West Virginia. Facilities in Delaware and West Virginia are under federal OSHA jurisdiction,

whereas the operations in Kentucky, Utah, and California are under state plan jurisdiction.

24. 29 U.S.C. § 655(b).

25. 29 U.S.C.A. § 655(b)(5).

26. 29 U.S.C. 1910.

27. 29 C.F.R. § 1911.15. (By regulation, the Secretary of Labor has prescribed more detailed procedures than the OSH Act specifies to ensure participation in the process of setting new standards, 29 C.F.R. § 1911.15.)

28. 29 U.S.C. § 1910.

29. 29 U.S.C. § 655(b).

30. 5 U.S.C. § 553.

31. 29 C.F.R. § 1911.15.

32. *Taylor Diving & Salvage Co. v. Department of Labor*, 599 F.2d 622 7 O.S.H. Cases 1507 (5th Cir. 1979).

33. 29 U.S.C. § 655(c).

34. *Id.* at § 655(b)(1).

35. *Id.* at § 656(a)(1). NACOSH was created by the OSH Act to "advise, consult with, and make recommendations . . . on matters relating to the administration of the Act." Normally, for new standards, the Secretary has established continuing committees and ad hoc committees to provide advice regarding particular problems or proposed standards.

36. *OSHA Compliance Field Operations Manual (OSHA Manual)* at XI-C3c (Apr. 1977).

37. *Id.*

38. *Id.* at XI-C3c(2).

39. *Id.* at (3)(a).

40. 29 U.S.C. § 666.

41. *Id.* at § 666(b).

42. For example, if a company possesses 25 identical machines, and each of these machines is found to have the identical serious violation, this would theoretically constitute 25 violations rather than one violation on 25 machines, and a possible monetary fine of $175,000 rather than a maximum of $7,000.

43. *Occupational Safety & Health Reporter*, V. 23, No. 32, Jan. 12, 1994.

44. See *Infra* at § 1.140.

45. 29 U.S.C. §§ 658(a), 666(c).

46. *Id.* at § 666(j).

47. *Id.* at § 666(c).

48. *Id.* at (a).

49. *Id.*

50. *Id.* at (b).

51. *Id.* at (e).

52. *Id.* at § 658(a).

53. *Supra* note 62.

54. *Id.* at VII-B3a.

55. *Id.*

56. *Hood Sailmakers*, 6 O.S.H. Cases 1207 (1977).

57. *OSHA Manual supra* note 62, at VIII-B2a. The proper nomenclature for this type of violation is "other" or "other than serious." Many safety and health professionals classify this type of violation as nonserious for explanation and clarification purposes.

58. A nonserious penalty is usually less than $100 per violation.

59. *Crescent Wharf & Warehouse Co.*, 1 O.S.H. Cases 1219, 1222 (1973).

60. *OSHA Manual, supra* note 53, at VIII-B2a.

61. *Id.* at B2b(1).

62. *Id.* at (2).

63. See *Secretary v. Diamond In.*, 4 O.S.H. Cases 1821 (1976); *Secretary v. Northwest Paving*, 2 O.S.H. Cases 3241 (1974); *Secretary v. Sky-Hy Erectors & Equip.*, 4 O.S.H. Cases 1442 (1976). But see *Shaw Constr. v. OSHRC*, 534 F.2d 1183, 4 O.S.H. Cases 1427 (5th Cir. 1976) (holding that serious citation was proper whenever accident was merely possible).

64. 29 U.S.C. § 666(j).

65. *Id.*

66. *Id.* at § 666(i).

67. *OSHA Manual, supra* note 62, at IV-B-1(b)(3)(a),(c).

68. *Id.* at VIII-B1b(2)(c). In determining whether a violation constitutes a serious violation, the compliance officer is functionally describing the prima facie case that the Secretary would be required to prove, i.e., (1) the causal link between the violation of the safety or health standard and the hazard, (2) reasonably predictable injury or illness that could result, (3) potential of serious physical harm or death, and (4) the employer's ability to foresee such harm by using reasonable diligence.

69. *Id.* at VIII-B1c(3)a.

70. *Id.* at (4). See also, *Cam. Indus.*, 1 O.S.H. Cases 1564 (1974); *Secretary v. Sun Outdoor Advertising*, 5 O.S.H. Cases 1159 (1977).

71. *Cedar Constr. Co. v. OSHRC*, 587 F.2d 1303, 6 O.S.H. Cases 2010, 2011 (D.C. Cir. 1971). Moral turpitude or malicious intent are not necessary elements for a willful violation. *U.S. v. Dye Constr.*, 522 F.2d 777, 3 O.S.H. Cases 1337 (4th Cir. 1975); *Empire-Detroit Steel v. OSHRC*, 579 F.2d 378, 6 O.S.H. Cases 1693 (6th Cir. 1978).

72. *P.A.F. Equip. Co.*, 7 O.S.H. Cases 1209 (1979).

73. *OSHA Manual, supra* note 62, at VIII-B1c(4).

74. *Universal Auto Radiator Mfg. Co. v. Marshall*, 631 F.2d 20, 8 O.S.H. Cases 2026 (3d Cir. 1980).

75. *Haven Steel Co. v. OSHRC*, 738 F.2d 397, 11 O.S.H. Cases 2057 (10th Cir. 1984).

76. *Donovan v. Capital City Excavating Co.*, 712 F.2d 1008, 11 O.S.H. Cases 1581 (6th Cir. 1983).

77. *Ensign-Bickford Co. v. OSHRC*, 717 F.2d 1419, 11 O.S.H. Cases 1657 (D.C. Cir. 1983).

78. *OSHA Manual, supra* note 62, at VIII-B5c.

79. *Id.* at IV-B5(c)(1).

80. *Id.* at VIII-B5d.

81. *Id.*

82. *Id.* at XI-C5c.

83. 29 U.S.C. § 666(e)–(g). See also, *OSHA Manual, supra* note 62 at VI-B.

84. A repeat criminal conviction for a willful violation causing an employee death doubles the possible criminal penalties.

85. 29 C.F.R. § 5.01(6).

86. *U.S. v. Dye Const. Co.*, 510 F.2d 78, 2 O.S.H. Cases 1510 (10th Cir. 1975).

87. *U.S. v. Crosby & Overton*, No. CR-74-1832-F (S.D. Cal. Feb. 24, 1975).

88. 18 U.S.C. § 2.

89. These are uncharted waters. Employers may argue due process and double jeopardy, but OSHA may argue that it has authority to impose penalties in both contexts. There are currently no cases on this issue.

90. Jefferson, *Dying for Work*, A.B.A. #J. 46 (Jan. 1993).

91. See, e.g., Levin, *Crimes Against Employees: Substantive Criminal Sanctions Under the Occupational Safety and Health Act*, 14 Am. Crim. L. Rev., 98 (1977).

92. See Chapter 5.

93. See *L.A. Law: Prosecuting Workplace Killers*, A.B.A. #J. 48 (Los Angeles prosecutor's "roll out" program could serve as a model for OSHA).

94. See *infra*.

95. See *infra* §§ 1.10 and 1.12.

96. 29 C.F.R. § 1903.8.

97. 29 U.S.C. § 17(f). The penalty for providing advance notice, upon conviction, is a fine of not more than $1,000, imprisonment for not more than 6 months, or both.

98. *Occupational Safety and Health Law*, 208–09 (1988).

99. 29 C.F.R. § 1903.7(b) [revised by 47 Fed. Reg. 5548 (1982)].

100. See, e.g., 29 C.F.R. § 1903.9. (Under § 15 of the OSH Act, all information gathered or revealed during an inspection or proceeding that may reveal a trade secret as specified under 18 U.S.C. § 1905 must be considered confidential, and breach of that confidentiality is punishable by a fine of not more than $1,000, imprisonment of not more than one year, or both; and removal from office or employment with OSHA.)

101. It is highly recommended by the authors that a company representative accompany the OSHA inspection during the walk-through inspection.

102. *OSHA Manual*, *supra* note 62, at III-D8.

103. The OSHA 1 Inspection Report Form includes the following:

    • the establishment's name

    • inspection number

    • type of legal entity

    • type of business or plant

    • additional citations

    • names and addresses of all organized employee groups

    • the authorized representative of employees

    • the employee representative contacted

    • other persons contacted

    • coverage information (state of incorporation, type of goods or services in interstate commerce, etc.)

    • date and time of entry

    • date and time that the walk-through inspection began

    • date and time the closing conference began

- date and time of exit
- whether a follow-up inspection is recommended
- the compliance officer's signature and date
- the names of other compliance officers
- evaluation of safety and health programs (checklist)
- closing conference checklist and
- additional comments

104. 29 C.F.R. § 1903.7(e).

105. *OSHA Manual, supra* note 62, at III-D9.

106. 29 U.S.C. § 660(c)(1).

107. Id. at § 658.

108. *Fed. R. Civ. P.* 4(d)(3).

109. 29 U.S.C. § 659(a).

110. Schneid, T., *Preparing for an OSHA Inspection*, Kentucky Manufacturer, February, 1992.

111. 436 U.S. 307, 6 O.S.H. Cases 1571 (1978); see also, 29 C.F.R. § 1903.4 (objection to inspection).

112. 436 U.S. 307 (1078). (Court found violation of the Fourth Amendment of U.S. Constitution.)

113. *Id.*

114. 137 29 C.F.R. § 1903.11. The placement of limitations on the area is normally only applicable to complaint inspections.

115. 38 *Id.* § 1903.9. ("All information reported to or otherwise obtained by the Secretary or his representatives in connection with any inspection or proceeding under this Act which contains or which might reveal a trade secret ... shall be considered confidential. ...")

116. *Id.* ("the Secretary, the Commission, or the court shall issue such order as may be appropriate to protect the confidentiality of trade secrets ... ").

117. 29 C.F.R. §§ 1908.1–11.

118. 29 U.S.C. § 651 *et. seq.*, § 9(a) (1970).

119. *Id.* The statute of limitations contained in § 9(c) will not be vacated on reasonable promptness grounds unless the employer was prejudiced by the delay.

120. *Id.*

121. *Id.*

122. 29 U.S.C. § 651 *et. seq.*, § 10(a)(1970).

123. *B.J. Hughes*, 7 O.S.H. Cases 1471(1979).

124. 29 U.S.C. § 651 *et. seq.*, § 10(1970).

125. M. Rothstein, *Occupational Safety and Health Law* (2d ed., 1983), summarized and reprinted in Rothstein, Knapp, and Liebman, *Employment Law*, Foundation Press (1987), p. 509.

126. See, e.g., *Atlas Roofing Co. v. OSHRC*, 430 U.S. 442, 5 O.S.H. Cases 1105 (1977). The Supreme Court also held that there is no Seventh Amendment right to a jury trial in OSHA cases.

127. Rothstein, Knapp, and Liebman, *Employment Law*, Foundation Press (1987), p. 599.

128. 29 U.S.C. § 651 *et. seq.*, § 11(a)(1970).

129. 29 U.S.C. § 651 *et. seq.*, § 11(b)(1970).

130. *Gilles v. Cotting*, 3 O.S.H. Cases 2002, 1975–76, OSHD § 20,448 (1976).

131. 29 U.S.C. § 657(a).

132. 387 U.S. 523 (1967). (Court found Fourth Amendment protection against warrantless area-wide housing inspections.)

133. 387 U.S. 541 (1967). (Court found search warrant required for routine fire inspection of commercial warehouses.)

134. The name of this exception was taken from *Colannade Catering Corp. v. U.S.*, 397 U.S. 72 (1970) and *U.S. v. Biswell*, 406 U.S. 311 (1972).

135. *Stephenson Enters. v. Marshall*, 578 F.2d 1021, 6 O.S.H. Cases (5th Cir. 1978); *Stockwell Mfg. Co. v. Usery*, 536 F.2d 1309, 4 O.S.H. Cases 1332 (10th Cir. 1976); *Milliken & Co. v. OSHRC*, 7 O.S.H. Cases (4th Cir. 1979) (unpublished decision no precedential value under Fourth Circuit Rule 4).

136. *Johnson v. Zerbst*, 304 U.S. 458 (1938).

137. *U.S. v. Thriftmart*, 429 F.2d 1006 (9th. Cir.), *cert. denied*, 400 U.S. 926 (1970); *Horween Leather Co. v. OSHRC*, 1664 (ALJ final order 1979).

138. OSHA Memorandum, reported in 8 O.S.H. Rep. No. 1, at 3 (June 3, 1978).

139. *Stephenson Enterprises*, 578 F.2d 1021, 6 O.S.H. Cases 1860.

140. *Dorey Elec. Co. v. OSHRC*, 553 F.2d 357, 5 O.S.H. Cases 1285 (4th Cir. 1977).

141. *Western Waterproofing Co.*, 5 O.S.H. Cases 1496 (1977).

142. *Havens Steel Co.*, 6 O.S.H. Cases 1740 (1978).

143. *Accu-Namics*, 1 O.S.H. Cases 1751, *aff'd on other grounds*, 515 F.2d 828, 3 O.S.H. Cases 1299 (5th Cir. 1975), *cert. denied*, 425 U.S. 903 (1976). See also *Dan Scuillo & Co.*, 8 O.S.H. Cases 1585 (1980).

144. *Rakas v. Illinois*, 439 U.S. 128, *reh'g denied*, 439 U.S. 1122 (1978).

145. 397 U.S. 72 (1970).

146. 406 U.S. 311 (1972).

147. *Id.*

148. *Brennan v. Buckeye Indus.*, 374 F. Supp. 1350 (S.D. Ga. 1974).

149. *Brennan v. Gibson's Prods.*, 424 F. Supp. 154 (E.D. Tex. 1976), vacated and remanded with instructions to dismiss, 586 F.2d 668 (5th Cir. 1978).

150. see *supra* 118.

151. see *supra* nn. 121 and 122.

152. Note: An *ex parte* search warrant can be issued without notice to the employer on the basis of OSHA's presentation of probable cause to a magistrate prior to the inspection. Safety and health professionals should note that it is more difficult to challenge a compliance officer's right to inspect or investigate once an *ex parte* warrant is issued.

153. *Id.*

154. *Id.*

155. *Marshall v. North Am. Car Co.*, 8 O.S.H. Cases 1722 (3d. Cir. 1979); *Burkart Randall Div. of Textron v. Marshall*, 8 O.S.H. Cases 1467 (7th Cir. 1979).

156. Two percent of all inspections required a warrant in 1978; in 1979 the figure was 2.4%.

157. M. Rothstein, *OSHA Inspections After Marshall v. Barlow's, Inc.*, 1979 Duke L.J. 63, 99 n.219.

158. Although not discussed in this text, employers may consider alternatives to the search warrant requirement such as protective orders modifying the scope or timing of the inspection or assuring confidentiality of trade secrets.

159. Given the legal nature of this search warrant requirement, employers may want to have legal counsel present or available via telephone to assist the management team during this preinspection or inspection period.

160. Employers may use a combination of these routes depending on the circumstances. Challenges that have taken place *after* the inspection has taken place have been least successful.

161. *Cerro Metal Prods. v. Marshall*, 467 F. Supp. 869 (E.D. Pa. 1979). (The facts of this case are unique. The employer knew that the compliance officer was seeking an ex parte warrant because the compliance officer told the employer of his intention when denied entry to the facility.)

162. 29 C.F.R. § 1903.4(d); 45 Fed. Reg. 65,916 (Oct. 3, 1980).

163. 29 C.F.R. § 1903.4(b)(1).

164. 436 U.S. 307, 6 O.S.H. Cases 1571 (1978).

165. *Id.* (The Supreme Court affirmed the injunctive relief sought by the employer but also affirmed the district court's declaratory judgment.)

166. 610 F.2d 1128 (3d Cir. 1979).

167. *Donovan v. Hackney*, 769 F.2d 650 (10th Cir.), *cert. denied*, 106 S.Ct. 1458 (1986); *In re Establishment Inspection of Trinity Industries*, 13 O.S.H. Cases 1343 (W.D. Okla. 1987).

168. *Marshall v. Multicast Corp.*, 6 O.S.H. Cases 1486 (D.Ohio 1978); *In re Gilbert & Bennett Mfg. Co.*, 589 F.2d 1335 (7th Cir. 1979), *cert. denied*, 444 U.S. 884 (1980); *In re Blocksom & Co.*, 582 F.2d 1122 (7th Cir. 1978).

169. *Chromalloy American Corp.*, 7 O.S.H. Cases 1547 (1979).

170. 592 F.2d 611 (1st Cir. 1979).

171. *Id.*; see also *Babcock & Wilson Co. v. Marshall*, 610 F.2d 1128 (3rd Cir. 1979); *Whittaker Corp. v. Marshall*, 610 F.2d 1141 (3rd Cir. 1979); *In re Central Mine Equipment*, 608 F.2d 719 (8th Cir.1979); *Marshall v. Burlington Northern*, 595 F.2d 373 (7th Cir.1979).

172. The Seventh Circuit did find jurisdiction for enjoining enforcement of citations after an inspection occurred under a protested ex parte warrant. However, this decision may be limited since the warrant was found facially invalid. *Weyerhaeuser Co. v. Marshall*, 592 F.2d 373 (7th Cir. 1979).

173. *Electrocast Steelcast Foundry*, 6 O.S.H. Cases 1562 (1978); *Milton Morris Mfg. Co.*, 6 O.S.H. Cases 2019 (ALJ, 1979).

174. *Babcock & Wilcox Co. v. Marshall*, 7 O.S.H. Cases 1052 (10th Cir. 1979); *Marshall v. Chromalloy American Corp.*, 589 F.2d 1335 (7th Cir. 1979).

175. I.e., a complaint inspection normally only required the compliance officer to view the area of the facility where the complaint originated versus a wall-to-wall inspection. Keeping in mind that a compliance officer is required to cite any visible hazard, the employer may select routes to and from the area of the complaint that would provide to the compliance officer the least likely chance of viewing a potential hazard.

176. The regional director usually possesses the authority to modify the inspection to protect trade secrets, disruption of work, undue influence from labor disputes, and other problem areas.

177. 29 C.F.R. § 652(4).

178. 29 C.F.R. § 1977.4.

179. 29 C.F.R. § 1977.5.

180. 29 C.F.R. § 1977.5(c).

181. 5 O.S.H. Cases 1467 (W.D. Pa. 1977).

182. *Id.*

183. 29 C.F.R. § 1977.5.

184. OSH Act § 8(f)(1); 29 U.S.C. § 657(f)(1).

185. *See generally*, 29 C.F.R. Part 1977.

186. OSH Act § 8; 29 U.S.C. § 657.

187. OSH Act § 10(c); 29 U.S.C. § 659(c).

188. OSH Act § 6(b); 29 U.S.C. § 655(b).

189. OSH Act § 6(b); 29 U.S.C. § 655(d).

190. OSH Act § 6(d); 29 U.S.C. § 655(f).

191. OSH Act § 11(a); 29 U.S.C. § 660(a).

192. 29 C.F.R. § 1977.10(b).

193. 29 C.F.R. § 1977.11.

194. OSH Act § 6(f); 29 U.S.C. § 655(f).

195. OSH Act § 6(f); 29 U.S.C. § 657(f). See also 29 C.F.R. § 1903.10 and 1903.11.

196. OSH Act § 10(a); 29 U.S.C. § 569(a).

197. OSH Act § 8(e); 29 U.S.C. § 657(e).

198. OSH Act § 11(a); 29 U.S.C. § 660(a).

199. OSH Act § 10(c); 29 U.S.C. § 659(c).

200. OSH Act § 13(d); 29 U.S.C. § 662(d).

201. 618 F.2d 1220 (7th Cir. 1980).

202. *Id.*

203. *Id.*

204. *Id.*

205. *Taylor v. Brighton Corp.*, 616 F.2d 256 (6th Cir. 1980).

206. 29 C.F.R. § 1977.15(d)(2).

207. 29 C.F.R. § 1977.15(d)(3).

208. *Donovan v. RCR Communications*, 12 O.S.H. Cases 1427 (M.D. Fla. 1985).

209. *Moore v. OSHRC*, 591 F.2d 991 (4th Cir. 1979).

210. 445 U.S. 1, 100 S. Ct. 883, 63 L.Ed. 2d 154 (1980).

211. *Id.*

212. *Id.*

213. *Id.*

214. 29 U.S.C. § 653 (b)(4).

215. *Byrd v. Fieldcrest Mills*, 496 F.2d 1323, 1 O.S.H. Cases 1743 (4th Cir. 1974).

216. *Pratico v. Portland Terminal Co.*, 783 F.2d 255, 12 O.S.H. Cases 1567 (1st. Cir. 1985). ("Our review of the legislative history of OSHA suggests that it is highly unlikely that Congress considered the interaction of OSHA regulations with other common law and statutory schemes other than workers' compensation. The provision is satisfactorily explained as intended to protect worker's compensation acts from competition by a new private right of action and to keep OSHA regulations from having any affect on the operation of the worker's compensation scheme itself."); *Frohlick Crane Serv. v. OSHR Cases*, 521 F.2d 628 (10th Cir. 1975); *Dixon v. International Harvester Co.*, 754 F.2d 573 (5th Cir. 1985); *Radon v. Automatic Fasteners*, 672 F.2d 1231 (5th Cir. 1982); *Melerine v. Avondale Shipyards*, 659 F.2d 706, 10 O.S.H. Cases 1075 (5th Cir. 1981).

217. *Black's Law Dictionary*, Fifth Edition, West Publishing Co. (1983).

218. *Id.* See also *Teal v. E.I. Dupont de Nemours & Co.*, 728 F.2d 799, 11 O.S.H. Cases 1857 (6th Cir. 1984); *Johnson v. Niagara Machine & Works*, 666 F.2d 1223 (8th cir. 1981); *Knight v. Burns, Kirkley & Williams Construction Co.*, 331 So.2d 651, 4 O.S.H. Cases 1271 (Ala. 1976).

219. *Cochran v. Intern. Harvester Co.*, 408 F. Supp. 598, 4 O.S.H. Cases 1385 (W.D. Ky. 1975)(OSHA standards not applicable where plaintiff worker was independent contractor); *Trowell v. Brunswick Pulp & Paper Co.*, 522 F. Supp. 782, 10 O.S.H. Cases 1028 (D.S.C. 1981) (Motion in Limine prevented use of OSHA regulations as evidence).

220. *Spankle v. Bower Ammonia & Chem. Co.*, 824 F.2d 409, 13 O.S.H. Cases 1382 (5th Cir. 1987). (Trial Judge did not err in prohibiting OSHA regulations to be admitted, which he thought were unfairly prejudicial under Fed. R. Evid. 403.)

221. *Supra* at n. 240.

222. *Melerine v. Avondale Shipyards, supra* at n. 237.

223. *Supra* at n. 237.

224. *Wendland v. Ridgefield Construction Service*, 184 Conn. 173, 439 A.2d 954 (1981); *Hebel v. Conrail*, 273 N.E.2d 652 (Ind. 1985); *Cowan v. Laughridge Construction Co.*, 57 N.C. App. 321, 291 S.E.2d 287 (1982).

225. *Walton v. Potlatch Corp.*, 781 P.2d 229, 14 O.S.H. Cases 1189 (Idaho 1989).

226. 741 P.2d at 232.

227. *Zalut v. Andersen & Ass.*, 463 N.W.2d 236 (Mich. Ct. App., 1990).

228. 388 So.2d 171 (Ala. 1980).

229. *Id. at Lowe v. General Motors*, 624 F.2d 1373 (5th Cir. 1980) (applied to National Traffic & Motor Vehicle Safety Act standards).

230. Fed. R. Evid., 28 U.S.C.A. § 803.

231. *Id.*

232. *Spangler v. Kranco*, 481 F.2d 373 (4th Cir. 1973); *Bunn v. Caterpillar Tractor Co.*, 415 F. Supp. 286 (W.D. Pa. 1976); *Scott v. Dreis & Krump Mfg. Co.*, 26 Ill. App. 3d 971, 326 N.E.2d 74 (1975); *Bell v. Buddies Super-Market*, 516 S.W.2d 447 (Tex. Civ. App. 1974); *Brogley v. Chambersburg Engineering Co.*, 452 A.2d 743 (Pa. Super. Ct. 1982). (Note: OSHA standards are usually used as evidence of acceptable standards of machine design, industrial standard of care, or of reasonable conduct by employer or industry.)

233. *Secretary v. Grossman Steel & Aluminum Corp.* "The general contractor normally has responsibility to assure that the other contractors fulfill their obligations with respect to employee safety which affects the entire site. The general contractor is well situated to obtain abatement of hazards, either through its own resources or through its supervisory role with respect to other contractors. It is therefore reasonable to expect the general contractor to assure compliance with the standards in-so-far as all employees on the site are affected. Thus, we will hold the general contractor responsible for violations it could reasonably have been expected to prevent or abate by reason of its broad supervisory capacity." *Secretary v. Grossman Steel & Aluminum Corp.*, 4 O.S.H. Cases 1185 (1976).

234. See, e.g., *Hebel v. Conrail*, 475 N.E.2d 652 (Ind. 1985); *Sprankle v. Bower Ammonia & Chemical Co.*, 824 F.2d 409, 13 O.S.H. Cases 1382 (5th Cir. 1987). (Note: Toxic tort cases can utilize various theories ranging from failure to warn under a strict liability or negligence theory to wanton misconduct.)

235. See, e.g., *Blessing v. U.S.*, 447 F. Supp. 1160 (E.D. Pa. 1978) (Allegations of negligent OSHA inspections states a viable Federal Tort Claim Act claim under Pennsylvania law.); *Mandel v. U.S.*, 793 F.2d 964 (8th Cir. 1986).

236. 20 U.S.C. § 2671 *et. seq.* See also *Blessing*.

Chapter 11

1. *Managing Employee Safety and Health Manual*, Tel-A-Train, Inc.

2. *Id.*

3. For example, the Education and Training Division of the Kentucky Labor Cabinet in the Commonwealth of Kentucky.

Chapter 12

1. Comment, "The Creation of a Common Law Rule: The Fellow Servant Rule, 1837–1860," at 132 *U. Pa. L. Rev.* 579 (1984). Also see "Workplace Violence Generates Two Kinds of Torts," *National Law Journal* (April 17, 1995).

2. Petersen, Donald J. and Douglas, Masengill, "The Negligent Hiring Doctrine—A Growing Dilemma for Employers," 15 *Employee Relations Law Journal*, p. 419, note 1 (1989–90).

3. "Workplace Violence: OSHA says guidelines will target night retail, health care sectors," 1995 DLR 16 (BNA), January 25, 1995.

4. 29 C.F.R. 1910.5(A)(1).

Index